MASS MEDIA: MARCONI TO MTV

A Select Bibliography of
New York Times
Sunday Magazine Articles on
COMMUNICATION

1900–
1988

Compiled by
Gerald V. Flannery, Ph.D.
Professor of Communication

UNIVERSITY
PRESS OF
AMERICA

Lanham • New York • London

Copyright © 1989 by

University Press of America,® Inc.

4720 Boston Way
Lanham, MD 20706

3 Henrietta Street
London WC2E 8LU England

All rights reserved

Printed in the United States of America

British Cataloging in Publication Information Available

Library of Congress Cataloging-in-Publication Data

Flannery, Gerald V.
Mass media : Marconi to MTV : a select bibliography of New York
Times Sunday magazine articles on communication, 1900–1988 /
compiled by Gerald V. Flannery.
p. cm.
Bibliography: p.
Includes index.
1. Mass media—Bibliography. 2. Communication—Bibliography.
I. Title.
Z5630.F56   1989
[P90]
016.00151—dc19   89–5592 CIP

ISBN 0–8191–7421–1 (alk. paper)

All University Press of America books are produced on acid-free paper.
The paper used in this publication meets the minimum requirements of American
National Standard for Information Sciences—Permanence of Paper for Printed Library
Materials, ANSI Z39.48–1984.   ∞

This Book is Dedicated to

My Father
Michael Joseph Flannery

My Mother
Mamie Harty Flannery

My Wife
Laura Chaipel Flannery

Table of Contents

Decades by Page v
    1901-1910 1
    1911-1920 21
    1921-1930 35
    1931-1940 54
    1941-1950 77
    1951-1960 111
    1961-1970 168
    1971-1980 197
    1981-1988 240

Years by Page vii

Preface ix

Headings By Page 319

Authors By Page 323

Years by Page

1901.......................1	1922........................36
1902.......................1	1923........................37
1903.......................3	1924........................39
1904.......................5	1925........................41
1905.......................7	1926........................44
1906......................11	1927........................46
1907......................12	1928........................47
1908......................14	1929........................49
1909......................15	1930........................51
1910......................18	1931........................54
1911......................21	1932........................55
1912......................22	1933........................56
1913......................23	1934........................59
1914......................24	1935........................60
1915......................25	1936........................63
1916......................27	1937........................65
1917......................29	1938........................68
1918......................30	1939........................69
1919......................31	1940........................74
1920......................32	1941........................77
1921......................35	1942........................78

Year	Page	Year	Page
1943	79	1966	183
1944	82	1967	186
1945	85	1968	188
1946	90	1969	192
1947	93	1970	194
1948	98	1971	197
1949	102	1972	198
1950	105	1973	202
1951	111	1974	204
1952	115	1975	208
1953	119	1976	211
1954	124	1977	215
1955	126	1978	220
1956	133	1979	228
1957	142	1980	235
1958	146	1981	240
1959	157	1982	251
1960	165	1983	259
1961	168	1984	268
1962	170	1985	277
1963	173	1986	287
1964	175	1987	297
1965	177	1988	307

Preface

The New York Times Sunday Magazine section contains articles that are a good blend of scholarly research and popular writing; generally they are written by experienced journalists or experts in the area under scrutiny. It has been my experience that students eagerly research topics in the Sunday Magazine section but reluctantly undertake reports or presentations that involve our scholarly journals or abstracts.

The New York Times is available on microfilm in most libraries in America, making it readily accessible to high school students, college students and serious scholars. One problem, however, was that the New York Times Index did not isolate those articles from its general listings, making it difficult to locate the longer, "think" pieces from the shorter news articles under general listings.

I began this work as a labor of love, focusing first on listings in broadcasting, then being led to widen the scope to its present nature. Professors, teachers, researchers and students can develop a wide range of assignments, reports, papers and presentations using this work. Just reading four or five pages of titles gets one interested in reading some of the articles.

The work does not replace the detailed, infinite listing in the Times Index, nor is it meant to. It is my selection of the articles most likely to engage those with an interest in some aspect of communication.

Please notify me if you discover any mistakes or omissions. Good reading!

Year 1901

Newspaper: _____; "A Pioneer Newspaper Woman", Section 3, July 14, 1901, p. 24.

Telephone: _____; "C. O. D. Telephones in Chicago", Section 3, December 8, 1901, p. 9.

Year 1902

Theatre: Henderson, W. J.; "Twentieth Century Musical Taste", Section 3, January 5, 1902, p. 8.

Theatre: _____; "As Seen From The Wings", Section 3, January 5, 1902, p. 7.

Newspaper: _____; "Newspaper Scoops Under Difficulties", Subtitle: Seeking Information. Section 3, January 5, 1902, p. 14.

Theatre: Klauber, Adolph; "Some Theatrical Experiments and Their Results", Section 3, January 12, 1902, p. 9.

Theatre: _____; "Heredity on the American Stage", Section 3, January 12, 1902, p. 10.

Theatre: _____; "Notes of the Foreign Stage", Section 3, January 12, 1902, p. 9.

Theatre: Klauber, Adolph; "Stage Themes in Miniature", Section 3, January 19, 1902, p. 8.

Newspaper: _____; "How Wall Street Gets the News", Section 3, January 19, 1902, p. 12.

Theatre:	_____; "In Foreign Theatres", Section 3, January 19, 1902, p. 8.
Theatre:	Klauber, Adolph; "Ins and Outs of Theatre", Section 3, January 26, 1902, p. 3.
Newspaper:	_____; "Quaint Contents of Rare Old Newspapers", Section 3, January 26, 1902, p. 4.
Wireless:	_____; "Cable Men Do Not Fear Marconi", Section 3, February 16, 1902, p. 4.
Theatre:	Corbin, John; "The Leading American Playwright and Others", Section 3, March 2, 1902, p. 11.
Wireless:	_____; "From the Current Magazine", Subtitle: How Marconi Tunes. Section 3, March 9, 1902, p. 15.
Theatre:	_____; "Plays on Many Stages", Section 3, March 30, 1902, p. 9.
Theatre:	_____; "The Speculation of Plays", Section 3, March 30, 1902, p. 10.
Theatre:	Corbin, John; "Adapted and Imported Plays", Section 3, April 6, 1902, p. 8.
Theatre:	_____; "Lights and Shadows of the Stage", Section 3, April 6, 1902, p. 7.
Theatre:	Corbin, John; "The Impossible Play of 'King Lear'", Section 3, April 13, 1902, p. 7.
Theatre:	Corbin, John; "The Dramatic Mirror and Human Fear", Section 3, April 20, 1902, p. 9.

Theatre:	Corbin, John; "Shakespeare and the Sentimentalists", Section 3, April 27, 1902, p. 8.
Newspaper:	C. E. S.; "When Victoria Was Crowned", Subtitle: Description of the Coronation of 1838, by an Eye-Witness of the Imposing Ceremonial. Section 3, May 11, 1902, p. 14.
Theatre:	Klauber, Adolph; "Heard Where Actors Meet?", Section 3, June 22, 1902, p. 7.
Theatre:	Klauber, Adolph; "Playgoers Who Pose", Section 3, November 6, 1902, p. 7.
Theatre:	_____; "Theatrical ODDS and ENDS", Section 3, November 16, 1902, p. 7.

Year 1903

Newspaper:	_____; "Six Publications Run by Columbia Undergraduates", Subtitle: The Most Important Is the Daily Spectator, Which Employs Twenty Young Men to Get Out Equivalent of Three Columns of An Ordinary Newspaper. Section 3, January 4, 1903, p. 1.
Newspaper:	Klauber, Adolph; "Some Current Fiction of Press Agents", Section 3, January 11, 1903, p. 3.
Theatre:	Klauber, Adolph; "Side Lights on Vaudeville", Section 3, January 18, 1903, p. 5.
Newspaper:	_____; "Fun in the 'Ad' Columns", Section 3, March 22, 1903, p. 4.

4 — *Mass Media: Marconi to MTV*

Theatre: McKenna, W. E.; "The Endowed Theatre", Section 3, April 5, 1903, p. 4.

Wireless: _____; "Wireless Telegraph Outdone", Section 3, April 5, 1903, p. 5.

Newspaper: _____; "The Press Club Woman Who Wrote", Section 3, April 19, 1903, p. 15.

Photography: _____; "The Value of a Picture", Section 3, June 7, 1903, p. 13.

Newspaper: Smith, Victor; "His Big News 'Beat'", Section 3, November 1, 1903, p. 12.

Newspaper: Lampton, William J.; "Poetry for the Paper", Section 3, November 8, 1903, p. 12.

Newspaper: _____; "College Boys and the News", Section 3, November 8, 1903, p. 12.

Theatre: Klauber, Adolph; "Stage Life for Women", Section 3, December 6, 1903, p. 11.

Newspaper: _____; "A Little of Everything", Subtitle: Devotion of the Press. Section 3, December 6, 1903, p. 13.

Theatre: _____; "Stories of the Stage", Section 3, December 6, 1903, p. 11.

Theatre: _____; "The Gentle Passion on the Stage", Section 3, December 20, 1903, p. 3.

Theatre: _____; "A Little of Everything", Subtitle: One Actor's Downfall. Section 3, December 27, 1903, p. 11.

Theatre: _____; "A Little of Everything", Subtitle: Those Gentle Critics. Section 3, December 27, 1903, p. 11.

Theatre: _____; "Odd Ways of a Writer", Section 3, December 27, 1903, p. 16.

Year 1904

Photography: _____; "Lightning As A Photographer", Section 3, March 13, 1904, p. 8.

Film: _____; "The Great Train Robbery, As Rehearsed in New Jersey", Section 3, March 13, 1904, p. 3.

Telephone: _____; "Telephones to Reach a Million Farmers", Subtitle: The Country No Loger Isolated — Stock Quotations Get There Fast, and There is Hope of Winter Evening Concerts by Wire. Section 3, March 27, 1904, p. 8.

Newspaper: _____; "Electronic Marvels in Uncle Sam's Printing Office", Subtitle: Government Equipment Complete in Every Detail and Staff Capable of Meeting Any Emergency. Section 3, April 10, 1904, p. 4.

Theatre: Corbin, John; "Drama and Propaganda", Subtitle: W. B. Yeats and His Second Volume of "Plays for An Irish Theatre". Section 3, April 17, 1904, p. 4.

Television: Collins, A. Frederick; "Common Sense Applied to Radium", Subtitle: Some of the Extravagant

Wireless: _____; Stories Told About the Metal and the Real Basis for Them. Section 3, May 8, 1904, p. 4.

_____; "Story of the Inception and Growth of the DeForest Wireless System", Subtitle: The Inventor Chose His Field Deliberately, and What He Has Accomplished All the World Knows. Section 3, May 8, 1904, p. 4.

Advertising:
Wireless: _____; "Advertisement for the DeForest Wireless Telegraph", Section 3, May 15, 1904, p. 16.

Photography: _____; "Photographing Birds and Insects", Subtitle: An Interesting Pastime That Requires Great Perseverance And Patience. Section 3, May 29, 1904, p. 4.

Telephone: _____; "The Ear Is A Wonder", Section 3, July 17, 1904, p. 8.

Telephone: _____; "Great Obstacles Overcome in Building Telephone Lines", Subtitle: Mountain Range and River No Barriers to Modern Progress. Section 3, July 24, 1904, p. 5.

Telephone: _____; "British View of American Telephone", Subtitle: Herbert Louis Webb Contrasts Service in Two Countries. Section 3, August 7, 1904, p. 8.

Newspaper: _____; "Unique Mission of Galiguoue's Messenger Has Ended", Subtitle: Passing of the Oldest Newspaper in English Language Printed on the Continent — Thackery Was One of Its Editors. Section 3, August 21, 1904, p. 8.

Wireless: _____; "Employing the Wireless to Detect Smugglers", Subtitle: Successful Efforts At Barring Out Chinese and Opium From Puget Sound Ports — The New Alaskan Cable. Section 3, September 4, 1904, p. 7.

Telephone: _____; "Seeing By Telephone: Oregon Man's Remarkable Invention", Subtitle: Can See Your Friend Who is Talking To You Miles Away ... J. B. Fowler Hopes to Be Able to Reproduce on A Screen in a Hall a Horse Race or Baseball Game in Progress At Any Distance Over Which Telephonic Communications is Practicable. Section 3, October 2, 1904, p. 4.

Photography: _____; "Says He Has Discovered Secret of Color Photography", Section 3, October 9, 1904, p. 2.

Telephone: _____; "Telephonograph Storehouse for Telephone Messages", Section 3, December 4, 1904, p. 4.

Year 1905

Theatre: _____; "Amusements of the Week", Subtitle: Plays That Hold. Section 4, January 1, 1905, p. 3.

Theatre: _____; "Some Impressions of Current Plays", Subtitle: Miss Viola Allen's Hermione and Perdita Considered as Expressions of the Actor's Art — Entitled to Attention When Her Ambition Leads Her to Attempt Such Types of Shakespeare's Women — Stars and Their Support. Section 4, January 1, 1905, p. 2.

8 — *Mass Media: Marconi to MTV*

Theatre: Klauber, Adolph; "Simple Womanliness and the Drama", Subtitle: Types Revealed in a Study of the Current Plays — Why Some Actresses Are Successful — A Disappointing Playwright — Notes of the Theatres. Section 4, January 8, 1905, p. 2.

Theatre: _____; "On the London Stage — Odds and Ends of News and Gossip", January 8, 1905, p. 2.

Theatre: _____; "Theatre Features of the Current Week", Subtitle: Plays That Hold. Section 4, January 8, 1905, p. 2.

Theatre: Klauber, Adolph; "About Plays, Players, and Playwrights", Subtitle: Receptivity of the Auditor and Its Bearing on the Player's Work — What Mrs. Leslie Carter Has Achieved in 'Adrea' — Arnold Daly's Rescue. Section 4, January 15, 1905, p. 2.

Theatre: _____; "Amusements of the Current Week", Subtitle: Plays That Hold. Section 4, January 15, 1905, p. 3.

Theatre: Klauber, Adolph; "A Survey of the Current Theatre", Subtitle: Promises for To-morrow in the Drama of To-day — Readjusting the Manager's Point of view — Light That Follows From the Waning of the Stars — Arts and Musical Comedy. Section 4, January 22, 1905, p. 2.

Theatre: _____; "Notes of the Foreign Stage — Arnold Daly on English and American Actors

— In the World of Art", Section 4, January 29, 1905, p. 2.

Theatre: Klauber, Adolph; "American Plays For American Playgoers", Subtitle: The Outlook for a Native Drama as Reflected in the Works of One Week — What DeMille, Fitch and Broadhurst Have Achieved — Criticising the Critics. Section 2, February 5, 1905, p. 2.

Theatre: Klauber, Adolph; "French Plays and the American Public", Subtitle: Why Paris Successes Do Not Always Interest New York Theatre-goers — The Actor's Share in a General Result — Ada Rehan's Revival. Section 4, February 12, 1905, p. 2.

Theatre: Klauber, Adolph; "Maxim Gorki's Work as Acted Drama", Subtitle: The 'Night Refuge' Reveals Contrasting Types of Degenerate Humanity in Photographic Impressions Rather Than Dramatic Action — Effect of Such Exhibitions in the Theatre — Brilliant Acting of Irving Place Company. Section 4, February 19, 1905, p. 1.

Theatre: _____; "Esmond's Newest Play: Forbes Robertson's Offering", Subtitle: 'Love and the Man' in Its Relation to the Drama of the Past, the Present, and the Future — A View of Life Limited by the Theatrical Nose — Tradition in the Playhouse. Section 4, February 26, 1905, p. 4.

Rhetoric: _____; "Latter-Day Congressional Orators and Oratory", Subtitle: Why Senator Bailey's Burst of Eloquence Almost Paralyzed His Confrères — The Chill of the Upper Chamber

10 — *Mass Media: Marconi to MTV*

— Qualities of the Men Who Command Attention in the House. Section 3, March 5, 1905, p. 4.

Theatre: _____; "Columbia's Thespians Will Elevate the Stage", Subtitle: Dramatic Society of the University Will Present a Home-Made Comic Opera, 'The Khan of Kathan,' At Carnegie Lyceum To-morrow Night — Expects to Give Broadway Managers More Than One New Wrinkle in the Business of Play Production. Section 3, March 12, 1905, p. 4.

Theatre: _____; "Fad and Folly in the Theatre", Subtitle: A Papier-Maché Snake and the Garden of Eden — Feminine Frenzied Finance in the Spotlight's Glare — Pale Pink Heroines Versus Healthy Personality. Section 4, March 12, 1905, p. 4.

Magazine: Pendennis; "H. M. Alden — Veteran Among Magazine Editors", Subtitle: Impressions Made By A Visit to the Editorial Sanctum of 'Harpers' — Mr. Alden's Views of Missions and Scope of the High-Class Monthly — The Magazine and Art. Section 3, July 2, 1905, p. 5.

Magazine: _____; "Making a Magazine: How Frank Leslie Set the Pace", Section 3, July 23, 1905, p. 6.

Telegraph: _____; "Railway Block Signaling By Means of Wireless Telegraph", Section 3, July 23, 1905, p. 2.

Theatre: Pendennis; "When New York's Rialto Is In Ferment", Subtitle: Busy or Anxious Days for the Stars and Lesser Lights of the Stage. Section 3, August 13, 1905, pp. 1-2.

Photography: _____; "Dogs at the Photographers", Section 3, August 27, 1905, p. 2.

Wireless: Turney, Walter S.; "Prof. Braun's Experiment in Directing Wireless Messages", Section 3, September 3, 1905, p. 4.

Film: W. De W.; "Thomas A. Edison At Work in His World of Magic", Section 3, September 17, 1905, p. 2.

Telephone: _____; "The Telephone As A Revealer of Character", Section 3, November 12, 1905, p. 5.

Rhetoric: _____; "Some Observations on After-Dinner Speaking and Speakers", Section 3, December 31, 1905, p. 2.

Year 1906

Newspaper: _____; "New York City Literally Run By Newspaper Reporters", Subtitle: Scores of Important Offices From the Mayorality Down Now Filled By Graduates From Journalism. Section 3, January 7, 1906, p. 3.

Newspaper: _____; "Sir Francis Burand's Twenty-Three Years As Editor of Punch", Section 3, February 19, 1906, p. 5.

Books: _____; "A Novel That Satirizes Socialism", Subtitle: 'The Scarlet Empire' written by a Self-

Made Millionaire Manufacturer — A Story that Reduces Socialists Theories to an Absurdity — Amusing Picture of Life Where the Theories of Social Democracy Are Supposed to Prevail — A Forthcoming Book That is Likely to Provoke Discussion. Section 3, March 18, 1906, pp. 1-2.

Newspaper: _____; "Interesting Sidelights on Foreign News", Subtitle: Another Romance of the British Peerage — Sultan of Turkey Finds An Apologist — Alfred de Masset's Memory — An Advocate of Patriotic Socialism. Section 3, March 18, 1906, p. 7.

Telegraph: _____; "Giant of Modern Times Rounds Half-Century Mark", Section 3, April 1, 1906, p. 5.

Wireless: _____; "New Wireless Invention", Section 3, August 5, 1906, p. 2.

Wireless: Chalmer, Stephen; "Running a Newspaper Aboard Ship With the Aid of the Wireless", Section 3, August 26, 1906, p. 4.

Year 1907

Telephone: _____; "What's The Matter With The Telephone Service?", Section 3, January 13, 1907, p. 3.

Wireless:
Telephone: _____; "The Wireless Telephone of Louis Maiche, French Savant", Subtitle: Aerial Message Projected Only in the Desired Direction — Words Are Inaudible Elsewhere — A

Years 1901-1910 — 13

                    Demonstration in Paris. Section 3, January 27, 1907, p. 5.

Wireless: _____; "Sending Photographs By Telegraph", Subtitle: Professor Korn Has Triumphantly Succeeded in Transmitting Portraits Over Long Distances By Wire — Experiments in France and Germany Conclusive — Description of the Marvelous Instrument. Section 3, February 24, 1907, p. 7.

Wireless: _____; "Edison, At Sixty, Outlines Wonders of the Future", Subtitle: The Wizard of the North Announces He Is No Longer An Inventor — Plans New Career. Section 5, May 19, 1907, p. 7.

Telephone: _____; "Startling Possibilities for the Navy in Wireless Telephone", Subtitle: Accidents That Have Happened Under Existing Flag System Will Be Impossible When One Ship Can 'Speak' to Another Through a Fog. Section 5, October 13, 1907, p. 1.

Wireless: _____; "New Wonders With 'Wireless'", Subtitle: Twenty-Year-Old Inventor Has Perfected Wireless So That His Messages Will Be Sent And Received Without Interference or Detection by Any Present System. Section 5, November 3, 1907, p. 1.

Television:
Wireless:
Telegraph:
Photography: _____; "Photographs By Telegraph: Television Next?", Subtitle: Successful Test of Professor Korn's Remarkable Invention Indicates the Possibility of Another Field for the

Scientific Discoverer. Section 5, November 24, 1907, p. 7.

Year 1908

Rhetoric: Hale, William Bayard; "The Bryan of Twelve Years Ago and of To-day", Subtitle: His Audacity of Twelve Years Ago Has Been Superceded by Poise and Maturer Confidence — An Analogy By Which He Is Portrayed As Essentially a Preacher or Pulpit Orator. Section 5, February 9, 1908, p. 3.

Theatre: _____; "Is the Good Old-Fashioned Melodrama Really Doomed?", Subtitle: Villains Have Been Too Villainous and Heroines Have Been Too Rudely Annoyed — A New School of Writers Supplies Polite and Courteous Scoundrels. Section 5, March 15, 1908, p. 4.

Newspaper: W. B. B.; "Americans as Seen in British Papers", Subtitle: English Journalists Are Not Very Flattering, But They Like Our Millionaires. Section 5, April 5, 1908, p. 9.

Newspaper: _____; "An Interview That Failed", Subtitle: Why the Gorilla Refused to Confide in the Reporter. Section 5, April 5, 1908, p. 2.

Wireless: _____; "Wireless Marvels of Present and Future", Section 5, May 17, 1908, p. 9.

Newspaper:
Theatre: _____; "Paris Newspapers Handled Severely on the Stage", Section 5, December 6, 1908, p. 10.

Wireless: _____; "Trials of a Telegrapher", Section 5, December 6, 1908, p. 6.

Year 1909

Theatre: Anderson, Mary; "Art Declining", Subtitle: Famous American Actress, After Twenty Years' Absence from the Stage, Talks of the Past and Present of the Stage. Section 5, January 3, 1909, p. 6.

Film: _____; "The Nation-Wide Wave of Moving Pictures", Subtitle: How It Has Swept Over the Country Until It Represents an Investment of Forty Millions of Dollars and the Employment of 100,000 Persons. Section 5, January 3, 1909, p. 10.

Theatre: _____; "The Spread of the War on the Sunday Show", Subtitle: King Edward in London, Mayor McClellan in New York, a Similar Campaign Is Just Now Being Waged By Both. Section 5, January 10, 1909, p. 2.

Theatre: _____; "Melodrama and Metaphysics", Subtitle: How the Combination Has Resulted in Several Instances, the Latests of Which Is Mrs. Burnett's Cheerful Little Play "The Dawn of a To-morrow" — G. P. Huntley, a Comedian Worth Seeing. Section 5, January 31, 1909, p. 14.

Theatre: _____; "Mrs. Frances Hodgson Burnett on the New Drama", Subtitle: The Author of "The Dawn of a To-morrow" Traces Through Various Fields of Art — An Awakened Ideal Which Is Reflected on the Stage To-day. Section 5, January 31, 1909, p. 9.

Theatre: Clarke, Joseph I. C.; "Conditions On the Stage and Their Causes", Subtitle: Archbishop Farley's Denunciation of Present Tendencies Directs Attention to Some Recent Stage History — Future American Drama. Section 5, February 14, 1909, p. 8.

Public Relations:
Advertising: _____; "Cities That Advertise — And How They Do It", Subtitle: Art of Publicity Men Has Full Swing in Booming New Towns. Section 5, April 11, 1909, p. 9.

Rhetoric: _____; "Oratory As It Is Practiced in the Senate", Subtitle: Men Who hold Audiences In Spite of Adverse Rules. Section 5, June 27, 1909, p. 2.

Wireless: _____; "Wireless Control of the Ships of the Navy", Subtitle: With Completion of Government's Plans in Two Years, Experts Predict Revolution in Naval Warfare. Section 5, June 30, 1909, p. 3.

Telephone: _____; "Testing Telephone Human Nature", Subtitle: Radical and Philosopher Have a Few Illuminating Experiences With the Company's New "Book of Suggestions". Section 5, August 1, 1909, p. 11.

Theatre:	_____; "How the Actor Fares When 'On The Road'", Subtitle: "One Night Stands" and the Like Made a Part of His Season the Opposite of a Bed of Roses. Section 5, September 12, 1909, p. 15.
Theatre:	_____; "The Dramatic Censor Under Fire", Subtitle: England's Venerable Institution, Just Now the Target for Attack By Such Men as Shaw, Archer, James, and others, in Danger of Downfall. Section 5, September 12, 1909, p. 7.
Newspaper:	Fayant, Frank; "'Inside News' — And What It Means to Wall Street", Subtitle: Elaborate Mechanism By Which Events That Might Influence Great Financial Movements Are Flashed From All Parts of the World — What Happens When Machinery Breaks Down?. Section 6, September 19, 1909, p. 5.
Theatre:	_____; "Does Crime on the Stage Inspire It in Life?", Subtitle: Experts Take Issue With Actors in Vital Psychological Problem. Section 5, September 19, 1909, p. 7.
Books:	_____; "The 'Best Sellers' — With Stories of Their Careers", Subtitle: Books That Live and Books That Die, Their Fate Is Almost Human in Its Obscurity, Say Experts. Section 5, October 24, 1909, p. 4.
Film:	_____; "The New Moving Pictures — Their Recent Developments and Services to Commerce", Subtitle: Some Interesting Experiments With the Camera That Open Up Suggestive Fields of Usefulness in Science of Photography. December 12, 1909, p. 3.

18 — *Mass Media: Marconi to MTV*

Telephone: _____; "Prof. Bell's Telephone Vision and How It Came True", Subtitle: Complete Fulfillment of the Inventor's Estimate of the Telephone's Possibilities Made Over Thirty years Ago and Ridiculed As A Utopian Dream. December 19, 1909, p. 4.

Books: _____; "The State of the 'Short Story' Industry", Subtitle: What Winners in Fiction Make Rise of the Literary Millionaire. December 26, 1909, p. 7.

Year 1910

Photography: _____; "A Glimpse of the Future", Subtitle: The First Aeroplane Hour; Photo by Brown Bros., New York. January 23, 1910, (last page).

Newspaper: _____; "A Latter-Day Industry and Its Rewards", Subtitle: How a Group of Illustrators Is Making Fortunes by Drawing Pictures of the "Modern Girl". February 6, 1910, p. 9.

Newspaper: _____; "Fresh News Published Every Minute", Subtitle: Some of the Marvelous "Beats" That Come From the Ticker. February 13, 1910, p. 10.

Wireless: _____; "S. O. S.' — The Ambulance Call of the Sea", Subtitle: How Famous Wireless Distress Signal Originated — Science in Role of Life Saver at Sea. February 13, 1910, p. 7.

Broadcasting: _____; "Should We Have Amusement on Sunday?", Subtitle: Noted Theatrical People

Years 1901-1910 — 19

Discuss Question of Sabbath Entertainment. February 13, 1910, p. 3.

Film: _____; "Moving Pictures Sound Melodrama's Knell", Subtitle: Tricks of Films Explained and Methods of Making Told By Those on the Inside. March 20, 1910, p. 6.

Wireless: _____; "Wireless Wonder Aged 14 Amazes Senate Committee", Subtitle: Young W. E. D. Stokes, Jr. Glibly Discussed Radio-Activity and Modern Electricity in a Way That Made Staid Solons Wonder. May 1, 1910, p. 5.

Wireless: _____; "Torpedo Airship Controlled by Wireless Is the Latest Invention", Subtitle: Thomas R. Phillips, Who Made It, Claims to Control a Dirigible Balloon Loaded With Bombs Without Leaving His Office. May 27, 1910, p. 5.

Newspaper: _____; "The Frank Confessions of a Publisher", Subtitle: John Adams Thayer Writes His Life Story in a Book and Tells Many Interesting Incidents in a Very Active Career. July 3, 1910, p. 3.

Photography: _____; "Unusual Snapshots Taken At Thrilling Moments", Subtitle: Work of Camera Men With Presence of Mind To Press the Button at Critical Times. August 14, 1910, p. 7.

Film: _____; "How Those Amusing Freak Moving Pictures Are Made", Subtitle: Ingenious Devices Make It Easy for a Man Apparently to Walk on the Ceiling, Climb Up the Side of a House and Work Other Impossibilities. August 21, 1910, p. 11.

Broadcasting:

Radio: _____; "How A Man With An Idea Made Millions In Twelve Years", Subtitle: A Little One Room Shop Earning Ten Dollars a Week Becomes Fifteen Acres of Industry Earning $30,000,000 a Year. August 28, 1910, p. 9.

Film: _____; "X Ray Moving Picture Machine Shows Brain At Work", Subtitle: Dr. Max Boff of Clark University Tells of the Remarkable Invention of a Scientist of Buenos Aires Which May Pry Into the Soul's Secrets. September 4, 1910, p. 4.

Music: _____; "How Popular Song Factories Manufacture a Hit", Subtitle: The Original Score Is Sometimes Hardly Recognizable After the Tinkering Is Completed — Such a Big Factor in the Business. September 18, 1910, p. 12.

Rhetoric: _____; "The Spellbinder's Voice That Gets the Vote", Subtitle: Secret of Success in Campaigning Lies Largely in the Control of Organs of Speech — Speakers Who Were Experts at the Tricks of the Trade. November 6, 1910, p. 4.

Year 1911

Newspaper: _____; "Centeniary of Horace Greely, The Great Editor", Subtitle: The "Tramp" Printer Who Became a Power in Politics, a Maker of History, and America's Foremost Journalist. Section 5, January 29, 1911, p. 10.

Telephone: _____; "Gives Up Royalties on Great Telephone Invention", Subtitle: Major G. O. Squire of the Army Turns Over His Patent to the Government — His Multiplex Telephone May Revolutionize Long Distance Talking. Section 5, March 5, 1911, p. 11.

Film: _____; "Wind in the Moving Pictures", March 5, 1911, p. 11.

Photography: Proctor, Mary; "A Great Sixty-Inch Reflector Which Photographs the Stars", Subtitle: Wonderful Instrument Erected By the Carnegie Institution At Mount Wilson, California. Section 5, May 21, 1911, p. 6.

Film: _____; "The Campaign to Curb the Moving Picture Evil in New york", Subtitle: Organized Efforts to Censor Exhibitions Which Under Existing Conditions Are Harmful. Section 5, July 2, 1911, p. 15.

Books: Kelly, Fred C.; "Must the Nickel Novel Die Out?", Subtitle: It Calls for Ability to Write One, Though You Might Not Think So, And the Supply of Authors Is Decreasing — Less Than Fifteen of Them to Supply the Demand. Section 5, July 30, 1911, p. 13.

Film: _____; "Moving Pictures Suggested To End the Tramp Evil", Subtitle: James Forbes, Hobo Expert Proposes Also the Equipment of Every Village Police Department and Railroad Stations With a Mendicant "Rogues Gallery" to Help Stam Out the Nuisance. Section 5, August 13, 1911, p. 7.

Film: _____; "Is the Moving Picture To Be the Play of the Future?", Subtitle: Inventions Which Will Vastly Increase Its Capabilities — How These Dramas Are Obtained and Why Actors Give Uo the Stage to Enter This New Profession. Section 5, August 20, 1911, pp. 8, 11.

Newspaper: Townsend, James B.; "The Many-Sided Pulitzer, By One Who Knew Him", Section 5, November 5, 1911, p. 3.

Year 1912

Wireless: _____; "Marconi Plans New Inventions As Useful As Wireless", Subtitle: Wants to Establish the Basic Theories Before He Tells What They Are — Believes Practical Wireless Telephone Will Be In Use Soon, That Passenger Traffic Will Be Carried by Aeroplane in Near Future. Section 5, March 24, 1912, p. 3.

Wireless: _____; "Wireless Crowns a Remarkable Record As Life-Saver", Subtitle: Wireless at Cape Race Where All Messages About the Titanic Were Received. Section 5, April 21, 1912, p. 2.

Wireless: Bride, Harold; "Thrilling Tale By Titanic's Surviving Wireless Man", Section 5, April 28, 1912, p. 7.

Wireless: Cottam, Harold Thomas; "Titanic's 'C.Q.D.' Was Caught By a Lucky Fluke", Section 6, April 28, 1912, p. 3.

Wireless: _____; "New Discoveries Will Help Wireless To Defy Weather", Subtitle: When Powerful High-Frequency Electrical Generators Replace the Spark-Gap Method of Sending Oscillations A Big Forward Step Will Be Marked Says Professor Pipen. Section 6, October 6, 1912, p. 4.

Wireless: _____; "Government Wireless Control Ends Anarchy of Air", Subtitle: Every Amateur As Well As Professional Will Hereafter Be Compelled to Undergo An Examination for a Certificate Before Being Allowed to Operate An Instrument for Pleasure. Section 5, December 15, 1912, p. 3.

Year 1913

Film: _____; "Wants City To Run Movies And Dance Halls For Poor", Subtitle: This Is Only Part of a Comprehensive Plan Suggested by John Collier of the People's Institute to Solve the Big Problem of Recreation for Children . Section 5, April 27, 1913, p. 7.

Theatre: _____; "This Woman Built A Theatre to Prove Her Theories", Subtitle: Mrs. Beulah E. Jay Put Up Playhouse in Philadelphia to Produce

Plays That Go Begging Because They Don't Promise Big Profits. Section 5, June 22, 1913, p. 13.

Film:
Propaganda: _____; "'Movies' To Solve Problem of Getting Army Recruits", Subtitle: The Familiar Flaming Poster Has Lost Its Magic in Persuading Men to Enlist, So Moving Pictures May Be Used to Fill Up the Gaps In the Ranks. Section 5, July 13, 1913, p. 11.

Film: _____; "Writing the Movies: A New and Well-Paid Business", Subtitle: The Latest Professions Assuming Great Proportions and Making Fortunes For Those Who Can Make a Success of It — Some of the Men and Women Who Have Hit the Right Note — Why Most of Those Who Attempt It Are Unsuccessful. Section 5, August 3, 1913, p. 4.

Newspaper: _____; "Earliest Newspaper in English Found After 300 Years", Subtitle: It Antedates by Eight Months the "First" Newspaper Treasured in the British Museum — Accidentally Found by a New York Collector of Hungarian MSS — Known to Experts, But No Copy Was Thought To Exist. August 13, 1913, p. 7.

Year 1914

Magazine: Grierson, Walter; "Magazines Suffering From Muckraking and Sex Stories", Subtitle: So Says Walter Grierson of George Newnes', London. He Believes the Public Is Now Yearning For

	Something Fresh and Wholesome. Section 5, February 22, 1914, p. 9.
Film:	Barry, Richard; "Five Dollar Movies Prophesized", Subtitle: D. W. Griffith Says They Are Sure to Come With the Remarkable Advance in Film Productions. Section 5, March 28, 1914, p. 16.
Film:	Goodman, Daniel Carson; "'Movies' Now Attracting Well-known Authors", Subtitle: It Is Prophesized That the Majority of Prominent Novelists and Short Story Writers Will Soon Be Having Their Creations Thrown Upon the Screen. Section 6, April 19, 1914, p. 6.
Telegraph:	Marshall, Edward; "'Stimulated Luck' Often the Key to Great Successes", Subtitle: An Interesting Exposition of the Psychology Which Wins in Business Made by Newcomb Carlton. Newly Elected President of the Western Union — Needs to Pedigree Its Forces. Section 5, June 21, 1914, p. 8.

Year 1915

Wireless:	_____; "Wireless Around the World in Three Minutes", Subtitle: When All the Links are Complete Messages Can Be Sent and Received at the Same Time at the Rate of 100 Words a Minute. Section 5, January 24, 1915, p. 7.
Film:	_____; "How Our Moving Picture Plays Are Censored", Subtitle: Plenty of Changes Must Often Be Made Before Films Are Ready

For Audiences. Section 5, February 21, 1915, p. 20.

Film: Kilmer, Joyce; "Pantomime Revived By John Bunny", Subtitle: Art of Silent Comedy After a Lapse of Centuries, Appears in Moving Pictures of Famous Actor Who Died Last Week. Section 5, May 2, 1915, p. 15.

Newspaper: _____; "French Newspaper Issued By Soldiers", Subtitle: "L'Indiscret" Has All Sorts of Intimate Items of Everyday Life Among French Troops. Section 5, May 23, 1915, p. 4.

Film: Kilmer, Joyce; "'Movies' Improve Our Fiction", Subtitle: Rex Beach Says They Have Made Authors More Careful Regarding Actuality and Vividness. Section 4, July 1, 1915, p. 9.

Wireless: Marshall, Edward; "Telsa Visions Wireless Wonders", Subtitle: Declares They May Simplify National Defense and Solve Some of World's Greatest Problems. Section 4, August 1, 1915, p. 11.

Wireless: Marshall, Edward; "What Transcontinental Wireless Phone Means", Subtitle: Theodore W. Vail Discusses Significance of Recent Development in Communication When Human Voice Was Heard For First Time Across Continent. Section 4, October 17, 1915, pp. 9-10.

Film: _____; "Prison Moving Pictures Taken By a Girl", Subtitle: Miss Katherine R. Bleecker Tells Her Experience While Making Films in Three Big Penal Institutions of This State —

Years 1911-1920 — 27

	Now Believes in Prison Reform. Section 4, November 21, 1915, p. 19.
Film:	Kilmer, Joyce; "Movies and the Way Have Not Hurt the Drama", Subtitle: Haddon Chambers Discusses Difference Between Writing for the Stage and Writing for the Screen — English Audiences Still Fill Their Theatres. Section 4, December 26, 1915, p. 8.

Year 1916

Newspaper:	Ade, George; "George Ade Is Reminiscent About Celebrities", Subtitle: Relates the Story of a Group of Western Newspaper Migrants, Who Tarried in Chicago a While and Then Moved on to More Fertile Fields. Section 4, January 2, 1916, p. 14.
Film:	_____; "At Least $500,000,000 Invested in 'Movies'", Subtitle: They Now Rank Fifth in List of Country's Big Businesses — Moving Picture Shows Attract 10,000,000 Paying Spectators Every Week. Section 4, January 2, 1916, p. 20.
Books:	Kilmer, Joyce; "Too Many Books Spoil the Modern Child", Subtitle: Says Tudor Jenks, Who Deplores Heavy Flood of Informing Juvenile Fiction, and Believes New System of Education "Is Not Worth a Snap". Section 5, February 6, 1916, pp. 17-18.
Magazine:	Kilmer, Joyce; "Our Rich Authors Made Cheap Literature", Subtitle: Ida M. Tarbell Laments Tendency of Some of Our Modern Writers to

Sacrifce Their Independence and Self-respect for the Sake of High Prices. Section 5, February 13, 1916, pp. 15-16.

Books: Kilmer, Joyce; "The War Is Making England a Nation of Readers", Subtitle: George E. Doran Tells of the Extraordinary Changes That Have Come Over the London Authors, Booksellers and Reading Public. Section 6, February 27, 1916, p. 6.

Photography: _____; "New Color Photograpy Process Perfected", Subtitle: Two Young Inventors Make Pictures in Natural Hues and Take as Many Prints as They Desire From One Exposure. Section 6, March 26, 1916, pp. 12-13.

Magazine: Kilmer, Joyce; "Harper's to Move After Nearly 100 Years", Subtitle: Publishing Firm Will Leave Its Quaint Old Franklin Square Building With the Memories of Many Famous Authors. Section 6, April 23, 1916, pp. 6-7.

Books: Braendle, Fred J.; "Rare Book Find May Solve Old Controversy", Subtitle: Twelfth Century Volume Discovered in Washington Contains Impressions of the Dance of Death, Which Has Been Long a Subject of Debate. Section 5, August 6, 1916, pp. 8-9.

Film: Kilmer, Joyce; "Moving Pictures Have Commercialized Writers", Subtitle: Says Clark Hanson, Owner, Poet and Editor, Who No Longer Finds Magazine Editing an Adventure, as It Was Years Ago. Section 5, September 24, 1916, p. 17.

Magazine: Kilmer, Joyce; "Shackled Magazine Editors Harm Literature", Subtitle: Says Tom Masson, Who Deplores the Ownership of Magazines By Brokers and Soap-Makers Who Make "Hired Men" Editors. Section 5, October 1, 1916, p. 14.

Year 1917

Film: Blashfield, Edwin H.; "'Movies' Bridge Ages from Cave Man to Us", Subtitle: Visual Appeal Always the Same, Says Noted Artist, Who Discusses the Educational and Artistic Future of Motion Pictures. Section 5, March 4, 1917, p. 14.

Film: _____; "Three Film Stars Get $1,000,000 a Year Each", Subtitle: Motion Picture Business, At Pinnacle of Success, Sees No Sign of Waning Popularity — Tax Talk Stops Boasting of Profits. Section 6, May 27, 1917, p. 11.

Film: _____; "Canada's Safety First 'Movie' Car", Section 6, June 3, 1917, p. 9.

Radio: _____; "Marconi on the War Needs and Ideals of Italy", Subtitle: Wireless Telegraph Inventor Tells How America Can Help His Country — He Thinks Submarine Problem Still Unsolved. Section 6, June 3, 1917, p. 5.

Books: _____; "Soldier Artist Who Looks At War's Comic Side", Subtitle: In Spite of Terrors Surrounding Him, Captain Bairnsfather Has Managed to Write a Book As Well As to Make Sketches. Section 6, June 17, 1917, p. 5.

Newspaper: _____; "How Patriotic Is the German-American Press?", Subtitle: Recent Excerpts From Local Newspapers Which Before We Entered the War Were Openly Ranged on the Kaiser's Side. Section 6, June 24, 1917, p. 15.

Radio: Mapes, Harold T.; "Wireless Man Tells of Solver Shell's Fight", Subtitle: First Complete Story of Authenticated Battle in Which American Can Ship Sank Submarine — No Chance to Save Enemy Crew. Section 6, July 8, 1917, p. 7.

Radio: _____; "Progress in Wireless Equipment on Submarines", Subtitle: Balloons and Other Devices Have Enormously Increased Distance Over Which U-Boats Can Send Messages — Allies Discovering German Secrets. Section 6, December 23, 1917, p. 15.

Year 1918

Newspaper: _____; "Thirty-Two Camps Have Newspaper in Common", Subtitle: Four Pages of Each Issue Printed Here for All, Four More Pages of Local Interest in Nearby Cities for Each Cantonment. Section 7, January 6, 1918, pp. 5-6.

Photography: _____; "Using the Camera to Illustrate Fiction", Subtitle: Models Pose for Photographs Showing Scenes in the Story — How Two Artists Originated the Plan. Section 7, January 6, 1918, p. 15.

Propaganda: Smith, Henry Louis; "Propaganda to German People By Balloon Routes", Subtitle: Scientists Novel Idea of Using Air Currents to Flood the Enemy's Land With Educational Messages on Inumerable Small Carriers. Section 7, February 24, 1918, p. 4.

Censorship: Green, Francis Vinton; "Uses and Misuses of Censorship", Subtitle: Modern War Function Has Developed Until Many of Its Rules Serve Only to Annoy People at Home Without Concealing News From the Enemy. Section 7, April 28, 1918, pp. 4-5.

Film: _____; "Millions of Feet of Movie Films for Soldiers", Subtitle: How a Woman Directs the Complex Task of Selecting Subjects, Censoring, and Shipping Motion-Picture Equipment to All American Camps. Section 7, May 5, 1918, p. 5.

Film: _____; "Showing Movies Under Shellfire in France", Section 6, August 18, 1918, p. 9.

Year 1919

Photography: _____; "Columbia's Unique War Photograpy School", Subtitle: With Armed Guards at Doors to Keep Proceedings Secret, Hundreds of Cameramen Were Trained There for the Army. Section 7, February 16, 1919, p. 6.

Film: _____; "Lo, The Movies Have Achieved 'Revivals'!", Section 7, March 9, 1919, p. 9.

Propaganda: _____; "How Paper Bullets From Air Helped Win the War", Subtitle: D'Amnuzio's "Three Ounces of Eloquence" Credited With Lowering German Morale More than Shell — Propaganda From Planes for Victory Loan. Section 7, April 20, 1919, p. 4.

Film: _____; "Arch of Marcus Aurelius as a Movie Theatre", Section 7, June 1, 1919, p. 14.

Film: Croy, Homer; "How Doughboy Critics Make for Better Movies", Section 7, July 6, 1919, p. 2.

Film: Forman, Margaret; "Uncensored German Movies", Section 7, August 24, 1919, p. 2.

Telephone: Harrington, John Walker; "Business Before Pleasure on the Wire", Subtitle: Effect of Phone Philandering on the Call Frequency Curve of the City and Some Suggested Mitigations. Section 7, September 28, 1919, pp. 6, 11.

Press:
Propaganda:
Public Relations: _____; "Against Bolshevist Propaganda Among Workmen", Subtitle: Hundreds of Employers Are Issuing Their Own Magazines and Newspapers to Counteract the Influence of the I.W.W. in the Plants. Section 4, October 26, 1919, pp. 3, 14.

Year 1920

Film: Chenery, William L.; "Maeterlinck Thinks Movie An Epochal Art", Section 4, January 18, 1920, p. 9.

Years 1911-1920 — 33

Film:	_____; "Survivors of a Vanishing Race in the Movie World", Subtitle: "Lecturers on the Lower East Side — Five of 'Em — Still Explain Eloquently What Is Happening on the Screen, and Regard Their Work as Art. Section 4, January 18, 1920, p. 4.
Film:	_____; "Motion Pictures Notes", Section 4, February 22, 1920, p. 8.
Film:	_____; "Movies As Evidence", Section 4, February 22, 1920, p. 8.
Film:	_____; "In the Film Firmament", Section 6, May 16, 1920, p. 4.
Film:	_____; "Motion Pictures in Japan", Section 6, May 16, 1920, p. 4.
Film:	_____; "The International Cinema", Section 6, May 16, 1920, p. 4.
Film:	_____; "Educational Pictures", Section 6, June 6, 1920, p. 2.
Film:	_____; "Motion Picture Notes", Section 6, June 6, 1920, p. 2.
Film:	Lowery, Helen Bullitt; "Brand of the Movies on Babies' Names", Section 3, August 22, 1920, p. 17.
Magazine:	_____; "Current Magazine", Section 3, September 12, 1920, p. 30.
Magazine:	_____; "Current Magazine", Section 3, October 3, 1920, p. 28.

Film:	_____; "Nursery Movie Galleries", Subtitle: East Side Practice That Led to Loss of Life in Theatre. Section 6, November 21, 1920, p. 8.
Photography:	_____; "Photographing Thought", Section 6, November 21, 1920, p. 2.
Newspaper:	Bartholow, Dr. Paul; "Crime and the Newspapers", Section 6, December 19, 1920, p. 12.
Magazine:	_____; "Current Magazines", Section 3, December 19, 1920, p. 27.
Wireless:	_____; "Germany's Wireless", Subtitle: Increase in Stations Indicates Plans For Extensive Trade System for Basis. Section 6, December 19, 1920, p. 11.

Year 1921

Film: Yearra, T. R.; "Blasco Ibanez, Movie Fan", Section 3, January 23, 1921, pp. 16, 22.

Film: _____; "Behind the Screen in the Movies", Section 3, May 15, 1921, p. 14.

Film: Lowery, Helen Bullitt; "Mortal Actors and Immortal Film Faces", Section 3, May 22, 1921, p. 6.

Film: DeCasseres, Benjamin; "Film Censorship as a Sport", Section 3, June 5, 1921, p. 11.

Advertising: Collins, James E.; "The Bear Market in Grub Street", Section 3, June 26, 1921, p. 6.

Film: DeCasseres, Benjamin; "Seven Months in the Movies", Section 3, June 26, 1921, p. 17.

Advertising: Freeman, William C.; "Advertising As An Art", Section 3, June 26, 1921, p. 18.

Film: Lowery, Helen Bullitt; "Wall Street's Heel on the Prodigal Movies", Section 3, July 24, 1921, pp. 6, 22.

Advertising: DeCasseres, Benjamin; "The New High Art of 'Ad Writing'", Section 3, August 7, 1921, p. 11.

Film: Lowery, Helen Bullitt; "Sophisticating the Movies", Section 3, August 7, 1921, pp. 1, 14.

Rhetoric: Matthews, Brander; "The Whole Art of Speechmaking", Subtitle: (A Book Review). Section 3, August 21, 1921, p. 5.

Film: Jones, Henry Arthur; "Silent Sirens of the Magic Film", Section 3, August 28, 1921, pp. 7, 26.

Film: Cushing, Charles P.; "Old and New Faces on the Screen", Section 3, December 25, 1921, pp. 15, 29.

Film: _____; "Studio Atmosphere", Section 6, December 25, 1921, p. 2.

Year 1922

Film: MacMahon, Henry; "Thomas Carlyle in Movies", Section 3, January 1, 1922, p. 14.

Film: DeCasseres, Benjamin; "Our Romantic Movies and the Germans", Section 3, March 26, 1922, pp. 10, 31.

Books: _____; "Novel of Tomorrow", Section 3, April 16, 1922, p. 21.

Film: Emperle, A. M.; "Movie Unmasking of Fridericus Rex", Section 3, June 25, 1922, p. 13.

Radio: Harrington, John Walker; "Risks of Radio Literature", Section 3, August 6, 1922, p. 12.

Censorship: Walton, Theodocia; "Tarkington Looks At the Censor", Section 3, August 20, 1922, p. 3.

Theatre: Rice, Diana; "Augustus Thomas, Play Censor, Speaks", Section 3, August 27, 1922, pp. 22, 24.

Censorship:	Talley, Truman H.; "Censorship Curb", Section 3, August 27, 1922, pp. 1, 22.
Film:	DeCasseres, Benjamin; "Movies That the People Want", Section 3, September 3, 1922, p. 7.
Press:	Galliene, Richard Le; "Outpouring of the Newspaper Muse", Section 3, September 3, 1922, pp. 6, 9.
Photography:	Dukes, Paul; "Self-Portrait of the Soviet Camera", Section 3, September 10, 1922, pp. 1, 16.
Censorship:	Bigelow, Poultney; "Practical Shirtsleeve Censorship", Section 4, October 29, 1922, pp. 7, 13.
Theatre:	Bourbon, Diana; "Odd Remarks on Brains and Acting", Section 4, November 19, 1922, p. 8.
Newspaper:	_____; "Lament for the Country Editor", Section 4, November 19, 1922, p. 2.
Theatre:	Bourbon, Diana; "On That Necessary Evil, the Audience", Section 4, December 17, 1922, p. 11.

Year 1923

Rhetoric:	Wilstach, Frank J.; "The Art of After-Dinner Oratory", Section 4, January 7, 1923, p. 11.
Film:	_____; "'Ben-Hur' Passes Over to the Movies", Section 4, January 7, 1923, p. 3.

Theatre: _____; "The Chinese Stage and the Dark Lady of Its Sonnets", Section 4, January 21, 1923, p. 11.

Books: Masson, Thomas L.; "Read With Speed", Section 4, February 18, 1923, pp. 5, 13.

Propaganda: _____; "Safety First From Propaganda", Section 4, March 18, 1923, pp. 8, 11.

Film: Seton, Grace Thompson; "The Movies Japanned", Section 4, March 25, 1923, pp. 12, 14.

Photography: Siren, Oswald; "A Chinese Emperor Plays Photographer's Assistant", Section 4, April 22, 1923, pp. 5, 15.

Public Relations: _____; "Booking Agent of Musical Magicians", Section 4, April 22, 1923, p. 7.

Newspaper: _____; "Your Morning Paper in Soviet Russia", Subtitle: What's In It and What's Not That You Are Used to Getting With your Breakfast At Home. Section 4, May 13, 1923, p. 5.

Advertising: DeCasseres, Benjamin; "Ads That Are Writ In Air", Section 4, June 17, 1923, p. 2.

Film: _____; "Use of Motion Picture in Eduction", Subtitle: (A Book Review). Section 4, July 15, 1923, p. 22.

Newspaper: _____; "Sixteenth Century Newspapers", Subtitle: "Fugger-Zictunger," the Earliest Regular Periodicals Preserved Intact in Series. Section 4, September 9, 1923, pp. 4, 15.

Theatre: Brock, H. I.; "Grand Street Art Theatre", Subtitle: The Neighborhood Playhouse Imports the Russian Method for Irish Plays. Section 4, October 28, 1923, p. 9.

Propaganda: Levick, M. B.; "History in Slogans", Subtitle: Phrases That Have Overshadowed Issues and Won and Lost Elections. Section 4, November 11, 1923, pp. 2, 12.

Theatre: Eaton, Walter Prichard; "Curbing Drama to History", Subtitle: Difficulty to Training the Characters to the Facts. Section 4, November 25, 1923, p. 6.

Year 1924

Radio: _____; "Crystal Sets in England Hear Pittsburgh", Section 7, January 6, 1924, p. 14.

Newspaper: _____; "America's Most Important Newspaper", Subtitle: Extracts From an Article by Jason Rogers in First Issue of the Advertiser's Weekly. Section 9, January 13, 1924, p. 10.

Books: Golsmith, Margaret O.; "Selling Books Off Wall Street", Section 4, January 20, 1924, p. 11.

Film: Hall, Mordaunt; "Satan's Tor in the Pictures", Subtitle: Henry M. Flagler's Sea-Encompassed Estate on the Sound Has Become the Setting of a Movie Studio. Section 4, February 10, 1924, p. 10.

Radio: Thompson, Charles Willis; "The Radio Takes the Stump", Subtitle: And This Will Be a Campaign of Inescapable Speeches, Speeches Poured in Every Ear. Section 4, March 19, 1924, p. 9.

Wireless: _____; "Madness is to Wireless Near Allied", Subtitle: Some Observations Upon the Radio Nut Who Would Be a Nut By Any Other Name. Section 4, April 13, 1924, p. 2.

Radio: Freed, ClarenceI.; "Lord Kelvin's Centenary", Subtitle: The Man Who Discovered the Basic Law of Modern Radio. Section 4, June 22, 1924, p. 7.

Radio: Lowery, Helen Bullitt; "Political Revolution By Radio", Subtitle: Old Tricks of the Trade Must Be Scrapped Now The Millions Can Hear the Actual Wheels Go Round. Section 4, July 20, 1924, pp. 1, 14.

Wireless: Riddeliot, Renfield; "Along the Northern Telegraph Trail", Subtitle: A Lineman's Story of Adventure on the Lonesome Wild White Way to Dawson City. Section 4, October 19, 1924, pp. 4, 13.

Communication: Cesare, Oscar; "Across America With the Air Mail", Subtitle: The Story of a Flight Over the Route of the Pilots Who Span the Continent — A Tale of Battles With Storms and Soaring Climbs Over the Mountain Ridges. Section 4, December 14, 1924, pp. 1, 2, 13.

Year 1925

Radio:	Thompson, Charles Willis; "Silent Men Are Finding Their Voices", Subtitle: Morgan and Baker Illustrate Change in Relations Between Big Business and Public. Section 4, February 15, 1925, pp. 14, 21.
Rhetoric:	Irving, Carter; "A Fourth of July for the American Language", Subtitle: Dictionary of Our Speech Will Be Completed Under Supervision of Professor Craigie of Oxford. Section 4, March 8, 1925, p. 9.
Film:	Hall, Mordaunt; "How Charlie Chaplin Got His Waddle", Subtitle: Law Suit to Protect It Brings Out The Story of a Derelict of the London Streets. Section 4, March 15, 1925, p. 11.
Radio:	Wilson, P. W.; "When Parliamentarians Go On the Air", Subtitle: Premier's Proposal to Broadcast the British Debates Has a World-Wide Significance. Section 4, April 12, 1925, pp. 3, 22.
Public Relations:	White, Owen P.; "El Paso Finds New York Almost Angelic", Subtitle: Press Agents All Wrong, Says a Stranger, When They Talk of a Wicked Metropolis. Section 4, April 19, 1925, pp. 7, 19.
Radio:	Bent, Silas; "Many Minds Aided in Capturing Radio", Subtitle: Of the Magical Consequences Not the Least is the Prodigious Business That It Set Going. Section 4, May 10, 1925, pp. 6, 16.

Film:	Wilson, P. W.; "Hollywood Subdues The Proud Briton", Subtitle: His Film Industry Brought to a Standstill by American Competition, Not One British Celluloid Drama Is Now in the Course of Preparation. Section 4, May 24, 1925, pp. 3, 18.
Magazine:	Clark, Evans; "College Youth In a Flippant Revolt", Subtitle: Suppressed Student Publications Mark Ferment of the Academic Year That is Now Closing. Section 4, June 7, 1925, pp. 3, 22.
Film:	Watts, Claude S.; "Uncle Same Is Now a 'Movie' Producer", Subtitle: Films of Department of Agriculture Adapt Romantic Tales for Campaign of Education. Section 4, June 7, 1925, p. 11.
Public Relations:	Tinckom-Fernandez, W.; "British Schools of Politics Begin", Subtitle: Each Party Gives Summer Lecture Courses in Appealing to Youth — Labor Inroads Lead to Study of Socialism. Section 4, July 12, 1925, p. 20.
Film:	Hall, Mordaunt; "Shy Charlie Chaplin Opens His Heart", Subtitle: Famous Comedian Tells How He Builds His Pictures — A Glimpse, Too, of Early Struggles. Section 4, August 9, 1925, p. 5.
Film:	White, Owen P.; "Frontier Children Needed No Movies", Subtitle: Even When Very Young They Became Actors in Thrilling Episodes Now Monopolized by the Movies. Section 4, August 9, 1925, pp. 20, 22.
Radio:	Beard, Miriam; "Waves of the Air Lure Boys to New Adventure", Subtitle: Their Brotherhood, the American Radio Relay League, Has

Comrades Scattered Over the World. Section 4, August 16, 1925, p. 6.

Rhetoric: Thompson, Charles Willis; "Oratory Changes, But It Still Lives", Subtitle: Bryan Has Recently Been Called the Last of the Great Political Orators, and So Were Many in the Past — Oratory Antedated Demosthenes, and In Every Age Survived Its Exponents. Section 4, August 23, 1925, p. 22.

Rhetoric: Phillips, R. Le Clerc; "First Aid for Tied Tongues: A Course In Small Talk", Subtitle: Designed to Cure the Socially Timid, It Might Have Found Pupils in Many Famous Men of Older Days. Section 4, August 30, 1925, p. 13.

Telephone: Bent, Silas; "Telephone Approaches Its Fiftieth Birthday", Subtitle: It Has Become a Confirmed American Habit, and We Use It Nine Times As Often As Our British Cousins. Section 2, September 6, 1925, p. 2.

Recording: Scherffauer, Herman George; "Sounds of Today Will Echo 10,000 Years", Subtitle: Berlin Professor Preserves Speech, Songs of Men and Current Noises on Masty Records of Brass. Section 4, September 13, 1925, pp. 7, 13.

Film: Nichols, Robert; "A Poet Dissects Our Movies", Subtitle: Well-Known English Writer, After Visiting Holywood, Makes an Unsparing Report of What He Found — He Says That "Hick" Public Dictates, But Also Blames Writers and Producers. Section 4, September 27, 1925, pp. 1, 18.

Radio: Hayward, Walter B.; "Ardent Radio 'Ham' Must Pass a Mystic Portal", Subtitle: In Room 603 at the Customs House Uncle Sam's Examiners Judge the Boys Who Explore the Ether. Section 4, October 25, 1925, p. 2.

Film: _____; "Zita, Royal Pauper, Turns to the Films", Subtitle: Ex-Empress of Austria, Now Living in Lequieto, Spiritedly Determines to Support Her Children. Section 4, October 25, 1925, p. 4.

Newspaper: Shaw, Allanson; "City Press Attains Its 200th Birthday", Subtitle: William Bradford Printed The Gazette First New York Newspaper on November 8, 1725. Section 4, November 8, 1925, p. 6.

Radio: Beard, Miriam; "More and More We Listen", Subtitle: Radio Extends the Painless and Popular Method of Instruction Fostered for Many years by Lyceum and Chautaugua. Section 4, November 13, 1925, p. 2.

Press: Young, James C.; "Tramp Printer Returns in a Flivver", Subtitle: Though the Journeyman's Method of Travel Has Changed, He Carries the Same Fund of Cheer and Wisdom. Section 4, December 13, 1925, p. 10.

Year 1926

Radio: Hayward, Walter B.; "Listening in On the New Air Language", Section 4, March 14, 1926, p. 20.

Years 1921-1930 — 45

Advertising:	_____; "Advertising Show is Artistic Triumph", Subtitle: Fifth Annual Exhibition at Art Center Displays Increasing Ability of Artists, Working in Harmony With the Demands of Business, to Produce Pictures of Intrinsic Beauty and Merit. Section 4, May 16, 1926, pp. 10-11.
Radio:	Brock, H. I.; "Gilbert and Sullivan Go On the Air", Subtitle: Radio Carries Their Melodies Far and Wide and Helps to Create a New Demand for Genuine Comic Opera. Section 4, June 27, 1926, pp. 8-20.
Film:	Scheffauer, Herman G.; "New Shadow Film Enriches the Screen", Subtitle: Arabian Nights' Story Lives Again in a Striking Two Dimensional Picture. Section 4, July 18, 1926, pp. 6-7.
Newspaper:	_____; "Our Paper in China", Section 4, July 18, 1926, p. 23.
Film:	_____; "Clergy on the Screen", Section 4, September 19, 1926, p. 18.
Newspaper:	McCormick, Anne O'Hare; "Il Duce Pictures The New State", Subtitle: Mussolini Explains the Working of the Cooperative Fascist-State Which is Planned to Direct All Italian Activities and to Remove "The Last Vestige" of a Discarded Liberal System. Section 4, October 24, 1926, pp. 1-22.
Radio:	Harbord, Major Gen. J. G.; "The Radio 'Broadcatcher' Is Revealed", Subtitle: He Discloses His Likes and Dislikes to the Man

46 — *Mass Media: Marconi to MTV*

Behind the Microphone and His Wishes are Duly Heeded. Section 4, November 14, 1926, p. 5.

Year 1927

Newspaper: _____; "Court Pictures Barred", Section 4, January 23, 1927, p. 19.

Radio: Thompson, Herbert C.; "The Radio Man Mends American Voices", Subtitle: The Tones and the Pronunciation of the Broadcaster Are Caught in Our Speech. Section 4, February 6, 1927, pp. 14, 19.

Wireless:
Radio:
Film:
Television: Minnigerode, F. L.; "Marconi Takes a Look Into the Future", Subtitle: Famous Inventor Shuns Prophecy But Believes In Wireless Transmission of Power, Radio, Movies and Television. Section 4, February 13, 1927, p. 3.

Radio: _____; "From Static Room to Sea", Subtitle: "Here Today and Gone Tomorrow" is the Slogan of the Brotherhood of Radio Operators. Section 4, February 13, 1927, p. 16.

Radio:
Television: Price, Clair; "A Saga of the Radio Age — And Its Hero", Subtitle: Baird, Who Led in Race to Achieve Television, Was Once Too Poor to Buy Any But Crudest Material. Section 4, March 27, 1927, pp. 6, 18.

Radio: Wells, H. G.; "Mr. Wells Bombards the Broadcaster", Subtitle: Having Weighed the Radio As He Encounters It Abroad, He Finds It

Wanting and Foresees Its Speedy Decline. Section 4, April 3, 1927, pp. 3, 16.

Film: Wells, H. G.; "Mr. Wells Reviews a Current Film", Subtitle: He Takes Issue With This German Conception of What the City of One Hundred Years Hence Will Be Like. Section 4, April 17, 1927, p. 6.

Newspaper:
Film: Deri, Emery; "Germany Has an 'Emperor' of Publicity", Subtitle: Hugenberg, Who Leans Toward the Monarchists, Adds the UFA Film Company to His Newspaper Orchestra. Section 4, May 29, 1927, p. 6.

Radio: Dyott, G. M.; "Through Perils to the River of Doubt", Subtitle: How the Radio Was Used to Outwit Jungle Bandits — Headwriters of the Stream Placid and Narrow. Section 4, June 19, 1927, pp. 8, 19, 21.

Film: D. E. W., ; "Only the Politest Apollos Need Apply", Subtitle: Our Movie Theatre Ushers, Who Have Youth, Elegance, and Physique, Would Surprise Dickens and Mrs. Trollope. Section 4, September 11, 1927, p. 14.

Newspaper: _____; "From Your Own Home Town", Subtitle: Newspapers and Magazines From All Over the World Sell Briskly in New York. Section 4, October 9, 1927, p. 14.

Year 1928

Rhetoric: Williamson, S. T.; "'Copy' Has Sharpened Many Dull Pens", Subtitle: The Retiring Boylston

| | Professor of Rhetoric at Harvard Had Ways of His Own to Inflame Literary Lights. Section 5, February 19, 1928, pp. 9, 20. |

Radio: E. A. J., ; "In New York's Radio Tower", Subtitle: There Music Fills the Air and Shops Fairly With Devices For Fans of the Ether. Section 5, March 11, 1928, p. 23.

Television: Kaempffert, Waldemar; "Wizard Science Is Annihilating Space", Subtitle: Airplane, Television and Radiophone Are Signs of Wonders Yet to Come. Section 5, April 13, 1928, pp. 4-5, 21.

Radio: Shelby, Gertrude W.; "The Capitol of the Vast Radio Empire", Subtitle: Broad Street Here Is the Chief Nerve Center of Earth's Wireless. Section 5, June 10, 1928, pp. 13, 21.

Film: Brock, H. I.; "With Ellen Terry a Stage Era Closes", Subtitle: The Last of Four Famous Actresses Who Were Greater as Women Than as Artists. Section 4, August 5, 1928, pp. 8-9.

Film: Spearing, James; "Now the Movies Go Back to Their School Days", Subtitle: As the "Talking" Film Is Developed Our Idols in the Silent Drama of the Screen Must Study Voice Culture and Learn a More Difficult Technique. Section 4, August 19, 1928, pp. 12-13.

Radio: Reeves, Earl; "Enter Now the Radio Political Managers", Subtitle: Their Task Is to Develop the Technique of a New Art in Which the Soft Voice Conquers. Section 5, September 30, 1928, pp. 4, 22.

Radio:	McCormick, Anne O'Hare; "The Candidate Is Everywhere at Once", Subtitle: His Radio Voice Reaches a National Audience and the Old Psychology Goes Down Before the Microphone. Section 5, October 28, 1928, pp. 3, 20.
Communication:	Pope, Virginia; "Christmas Cards Mirror Their Times", Subtitle: With the Old We Now Have the Sophisticated Modern Design Which Reflects the Spirit of This Generation. Section 5, December 16, 1928, p. 10.

Year 1929

Radio:	Woolf, S. J.; "The Newsboy Who Became a Radio Chief", Subtitle: David Sarnoff, Operating Head of the R.C.A., Got Into Communications Field Through an Accident of Fate. Section 5, January 6, 1929, pp. 3, 21.
Film:	Losser, David; "The New Art of the Talking Picture", Subtitle: It Demands a Technique of Its Own and a Studio That Bars Sound. Section 5, January 13, 1929, pp. 10-11, 23.
Newspaper:	Woolf, S. J.; "Two Rulers of Fleet Street Opinion", Subtitle: Rathermere and Beaverbrook, Lords of the British Press, Who Were Recent Visitors in New york, Present Strong Contrasts in Personality in Their Attitudes Toward Public Questions. Section 5, March 17, 1929, pp. 3, 20.
Film:	Ross, Betty; "Russian Movies Use Untrained Actors", Subtitle: Soviet Director Casts His

50 — *Mass Media: Marconi to MTV*

Characters From Persons Who Live Their Parts Daily. Section 5, March 24, 1929, pp. 8, 18.

Film: _____; "Picture Theatres Made to Fit Our Day", Subtitle: Interiors in the Modernistic Manner Are Replacing the Decorations of Another Generation. Section 5, June 9, 1929, pp. 14-15.

Film: Pirandello, Luigi; "Pirandello Views the 'Talkies'", Subtitle: The Cinema, Says the Noted Italian Playwright, Will Never Take the Place of the Theatre; Its Proper Field, He Believes, Lies in the Realm of Music Rather Than the Spoken Word. Section 5, July 28, 1929, pp. 1-2.

Theatre: Aikman, Duncan; "Broadway Finds a Home in Hollywood", Subtitle: There the Stage Folk Who Make Talkies Follow a New Ritual of Life. Section 5, September 6, 1929, pp. 6-18.

Newspaper: Adams, Mildred; "A Small Town Editor Airs His Mind", Subtitle: Sherwood Anderson, Famous Author, Talks of His Experience as Director of Two Newspapers in Virginia, Where He Reports He Has Found "A Working Compromise With the Machine Age". Section 5, September 22, 1929, pp. 3, 20.

Film: Nichols, Lewis; "Our Country Club Life — In the Movies and Out", Subtitle: Its Fitful Fevers Register Best in the Films Because the Thing in Itself is Largely Composed of Golf. Section 5, September 22, 1929, pp. 6, 21.

Rhetoric: Wilson, P. W.; "Orators Still Sway a Modern World", Subtitle: Briand, MacDonald and Mussolini Stand Out Among Those Who Work

Magic With Words. Section 5, October 20, 1929, pp. 8-9.

Rhetoric:
Communication: Free, E. E.; "Man's Webb of Speech Links All People", Subtitle: Growing Channels of Communications May Be the Answer to the Need for Racial Cooperation. Section 5, November 17, 1929, pp. 10-11, 17.

Film: Nichols, Lewis; "Every Little Movie Has a Theme Song All Its Own", Subtitle: In the French Scene It Is Called the Chansonette and Wars (In Celluloid) Are Stopped While It Is Sung. Section 5, December 1, 1929, p. 12.

Year 1930

Advertising: _____; "Window Shows That Catch the Eye", Section 5, January 12, 1930, pp. 22, 4.

Radio: Feld, Rose; "Seeking the Radio God's Favor", Subtitle: Many Storm the Studio But Few Are Chosen In Tests Before the Microphone. Section 5, February 2, 1930, pp. 12, 22.

Radio:
Music: Woolf, S. J.; "Damrosch Waves a Baton Over America", Subtitle: Radio, Says the Conductor, Has Erected a Concert Hall in Every Hamlet and Broadcast Treasures of Music. Section 5, March 2, 1930, p. 7.

Radio: Reinity, Bertram; "When Doom Clutches the Radio Villain", Subtitle: A Flick of a Cardboard Shoots Him and a Bit of Insinglass Adds

	Crackling Flames in the New Drama of the Air. Section 5, March 16, 1930, pp. 10, 23.
Wireless:	Duffus, R. L.; "The Great Moments of the Machine Age", Subtitle: Epochal Inventions, From Watt to Edison, Make Up the Industrial Picture That Has Changed the World. Section 5, March 30, 1930, pp. 6, 7.
Radio:	Storey, Walter Rendell; "Radio Cabinets in Decorative Schemes", Subtitle: They Are Designed to Serve Both the Spirit and the Economy of the Rooms in Which They Appear. Section 5, May 25, 1930, pp. 14, 17.
Radio:	Martyn, T. J. C.; "Science Gives New Miracles", Subtitle: A Picture of Changes to be Wrought on Air Travel and War by Strange Devices From the Laboratory. Section 5, June 22, 1930, pp. 6, 22.
Communication:	Layman, Lauren D.; "A Night Flight East With the Air Mail", Subtitle: As the Great Plane Soars Along From the Coast to Chicago, Mountains and Valleys Combine in Strange Panorama. Section 5, July 20, 1930, pp. 4-5.
Film:	MacWilliams, Walter E.; "When the Battleship Is a Movie Theatre", Subtitle: The Big Guns, Turrets and Winches Form the Seats, the Sea and Starry Sky the Background, and "S.R.O." Is the Rule. Section 5, July 27, 1930, p. 20:2.
Advertising:	Rutter, Eldon; "Things That Lure the Crowd", Section 5, September 7, 1930, p. 18:3.
Film:	_____; "Crowds That Attend Morning Movies", Section 5, October 19, 1930, p. 20:3.

Advertising:	Storey, Walter; "Advertisers Now Aid Phonetic Spelling", Section 5, October 26, 1930, p. 18:2.
Radio:	Thompson, Charles Willis; "Radio Takes the Bunk Out of Campaigns", Subtitle: Under Its Cruel Test, It Changes the Ways of Candidates and Makes Them More Subtle. Section 5, October 26, 1930, pp. 10, 21.
Newspaper:	_____; "Heirs To Subway Newspapers", Section 5, October 26, 1930, p. 18:3.
Radio:	Price, Clair; "The Poet Laureate Talks of Poetry", Subtitle: John Masefield Visions a Day When Bards, Using the Radio, Will Relate Their Narratives to the People Just as the Ancient Poets Sang the Homeric Poems in the Market Place. Section 5, November 16, 1930, pp. 6, 23.
Newspaper:	_____; "A Tale of Two Cities — By a Cartoonist", Subtitle: He Contrasts Types of New York With the More Stolid Londoners. Section 5, November 16, 1930, pp. 10-11.

Year 1931

Newspaper: _____; "Long Lost Newspaper Found", Subtitle: A Genuine Ulster County Gazette Telling of Washington's Death Comes to Light. Section 5, May 17, 1931, p. 16.

Film: Hanley, Parke F.; "Ghosts in the Cradle of the Movies", Subtitle: Fort Lee, Once the Center of Film Works, Is Now a Ruined Shell, Thanks to Hollywood and Herbert Hoover. Section 5, May 31, 1931, pp. 15, 23.

Radio: Martyn, T. J. C.; "Royalty Speaks on the Air", Subtitle: The Radio is Helping to Breakdown the Traditional Isolation of the Monarch. Section 5, July 19, 1931, p. 18.

Film: Young, James C.; "Headlines Who Meet the Screens Rigid Test", Subtitle: Before the Cameras and the Microphone, They Present Those Qualities, Varied and Mysterious, That Make for Popularity Among World Audiences. Section 5, July 19, 1931, pp. 12-13.

Radio: Hood, Raymond M.; "Hanging Gardens of New York", Subtitle: The Babylonian Dream to Be Made Reality in Radio City is Seen by the Architects as a Huge Experiment Holding the Possibility of a Completely Transformed Metropolis. Section 5, August 23, 1931, pp. 1-2.

Radio: Kaempffert, Waldemar; "Three Clicks That Made Radio History", Subtitle: Marconi's Experiment of 30 Years Ago Opened the Way for the Still Expanding Miracles of the Ether Waves. Section 5, December 6, 1931, pp. 8-9.

Film: McCormick, Anne O'Hare; "Hollywood: Mob Art Factory", Subtitle: Here is a New Kind of Mass Production, Synthesizing Science and Business. Section 5, December 6, 1931, pp. 4-5.

Year 1932

Wireless: Brockway, Jean; "The Artist Who Gave Us the Telegraph", Subtitle: A Hundred Years Ago Samuel F. B. Morse Evolved the Idea That Was to Turn Him From a Painter's Career. Section 5, February 14, 1932, pp. 11, 22.

Radio: Banfield, A. W.; "Savage Drums That Can Broadcast News", Subtitle: In the Wilds of Africa They Speed Complicated Messages From One Village to Another and They Also Sing of Joy or Danger. Section 5, March 20, 1932, p. 14.

Radio: McCormick, Anne O'Hare; "Radio: A Great Unknown Force", Subtitle: With the Air Full of Far-Flung Utterance, of Music and Entertainment, This Marvel of Science Represents a Power, in Shaping the World of the Future, Which is Still to Be Determined. Section 5, March 27, 1932, pp. 1, 2, 14.

Radio: McCormick, Anne O'Hare; "Radio's Audience: Huge, Unprecedented", Subtitle: With Its Listening Posts Set Thousands of Miles Apart, It is a Phenomenon as Strange as the Radio Itself. Section 5, April 3, 1932, pp. 4, 5, 17.

Radio: McCormick, Anne O'Hare; "The Mind Behind the Radio Broadcast", Subtitle: Young and Essentially American, It Has Developed with Characteristic Zest An Oracle We Begin to Question. Section 5, April 10, 1932, pp. 3, 22.

Advertising: Nichols, Lewis; "Changing Arts of Ballyhoo", Subtitle: With the Decline of Barkers Have Come More Sandwich Men and Window Demonstrators. Section 5, April 10, 1932, p. 11.

Film: Pope, Virginia; "The Changing Cycle of Entertainment", Subtitle: After a Long Era of Shadows and Voices Comes a New Call for the Actor. Section 6, October 16, 1932, pp. 7, 19.

Radio: Dunlap, Orrin E.; "'Mike Fright': The Nightmare of Radio", Subtitle: Fear of the Unseen Millions Grips the Veteran Platform Orator As Well As the Novice. Section 6, December 11, 1932, pp. 8, 15.

Year 1933

Rhetoric: Owen, Russell; "Huey Long Keeps Washington Guessing", Subtitle: As He Struts Across the Stage the Senate Wonders If He Is Demagogue or New Apostle of Strange Doctrines. Section 6, January 29, 1933, pp. 3, 14.

Rhetoric: Lengyel, Emil; "Hitler At the Top of His Dizzy Path", Subtitle: At Last He Achieves the Chancellorship, But Not Without Compromise. Section 6, February 5, 1933, pp. 3, 16.

Years 1931-1940 — 57

Rhetoric:	Hager, Alice Rogers; "Glamorous Pageant of Our Inaugurals", Section 6, February 26, 1933, pp. 8, 9, 18.
Rhetoric:	Lengyel, Emil; "Hitler As a Mussolini — An Appraisal", Subtitle: The Dictators Present Striking Contrasts Both in Character and in Methods. Section 6, April 2, 1933, pp. 4-5.
Press: Propaganda:	Callender, Harold; "Europe's Propaganda Mills Keep Busy", Subtitle: The Boom in Nationalism Finds Them Influencing Opinion, Often in Opposite Directions, At Home and Abroad. Section 6, April 9, 1933, pp. 9, 14.
Film:	Robbins, L. H.; "The Magical Pageant of the Films", Subtitle: One May Follow In An Exhibition at the Public Library the Fantastic Progress of the Cinema Since the First Drama Flickered for a Nickel Thirty Years Ago. Section 6, May 7, 1933, pp. 10-11, 17.
Rhetoric:	Dunlap, Orrin N.; "When Roosevelt Goes on the Air", Subtitle: In His Chats With Americans He Reveals a Mastery of Radio Tactics. Section 6, June 18, 1933, p. 17.
Theatre:	Brook, H. I.; "Away From Broadway The Drama Lives", Subtitle: in Town Halls and Barns, With a Notable Array of Talent, The Theatre Wins New Support. Section 6, July 16, 1933, pp. 9, 18.
Rhetoric:	Duffus, R. L.; "Ingersoll's Thunder Barely Heard Now", Subtitle: The Centenary of the Agnostic Orator Finds Few Echoes From a

Career That Stirred the World of Yesterday. Section 6, August 6, 1933, pp. 8, 19.

Communication: Kaempffert, Waldemar; "Electric Fingers That Span the World", Subtitle: The Vast Change in International Communication in the Seventy-Five Years Since the First Cable Was Laid. Section 6, August 6, 1933, pp. 6, 7, 16.

Radio:
Propaganda: Price, Clair; "Europe Wages a War of Electric Words", Subtitle: As the Race for Radio Armaments Grows, Projectiles of Propaganda Speed Across the National Borders. Section 6, September 10, 1933, pp. 6, 14.

Radio: _____; "London Police Use Maps and Radio", Section 6, September 17, 1933, p. 13.

Radio: Dunlap, Orrin E.; "Marconi Visions A New Wireless Era", Subtitle: The Inventor Talks of the Micro-Waves and the Possibilities They Hold out. Section 6, October 15, 1933, pp. 5, 14.

Press: Duffus, R. L.; "For a Free Press: A Momentous Battle", Subtitle: Two Centuries Ago Was Won a Victory That Still Resounds in Our Press. Section 6, October 22, 1933, pp. 10-11.

Rhetoric: Woolf, S. J.; "On the Stump With Three Contenders", Subtitle: A Picture of O'Brien, McKee, and LaGuardia in the Heat of the Campaign, With Statements of Their Views. Section 6, October 22, 1933, pp. 6-7, 19.

Radio: Carlisle, John M.; "Priest of a Parish of the Air Waves", Subtitle: Father Coughlin's Radio Sermons Bring Him a Flood of Letters Telling

What People Are Thinking About. Section 6, October 29, 1933, pp. 8, 19.

Propaganda: Stone, Shepard; "Hitler's Showmen Weave a Magic Spell", Subtitle: By a Vast Propaganda Aimed at Emotions, Germany's Trance is Maintained. Section 6, December 3, 1933, pp. 8-9.

Year 1934

Theatre: Skinner, Otis; "An Actor Discourses on the Audience", Subtitle: Otis Skinner Says the Player Must Attune Himself to Its Mood and Capture It If He Is to Achieve Success. Section 6, January 21, 1934, pp. 8, 15.

Film: Eaton, Walter Prichard; "From Stage to Screen and Back", Section 6, January 28, 1934, pp. 10, 16.

Advertising: Brenner, Anita; "Paris and London War On the Garish Sign", Section 6, April 15, 1934, p. 22.

Film: Churchill, Douglas W.; "Now Mickey Mouse Enters Art's Temple", Subtitle: He and Minnie Are Acclaimed as Classics by the Learned, but Walt Disney Creates Them With the Aid of Careful Mathematical Calculations, And Is Intent Chiefly on Earning a Living. Section 6, June 3, 1934, pp. 12, 21.

Film: Churchill, Douglas W.; "Hollywood Heeds the Thunder", Subtitle: Bewildered by the Widespread Crusade for Cleaner Pictures, the Film Center Now Listens to Main Street and,

Contrite as Never Before, Accepts the Verdict of Its New Censor. Section 6, July 22, 1934, pp. 1, 2, 11.

Radio: Dunlap, Orrin E.; "Furiously Proceeds Radio's Gag Hunt", Subtitle: It Goes On Without Intermission, For the Show is Fleeting and After One Broadcast A Joke Is Stale and Useless. Section 6, August 26, 1934, pp. 12, 15.

Newspaper: Wilson, P. W.; "When Newspapers Were Handwritten", Subtitle: To This Country Have Come Newsletters 250 Years Old Revealing A Taste For News Like That Of Our Own Day. Section 6, August 26, 1934, pp. 9, 13.

Radio: Dunlap, Orrin E.; "Tracking the Likes of the Radio Fan", Subtitle: The Will of the Listener Is Hard to Determine, So Broadcasters Provide a Bit of Everything. Section 6, November 25, 1934, pp. 7, 19.

Radio: _____; "Radio Doctoring in Australia", Section 6, December 16, 1934, p. 16.

Year 1935

Film: Churchill, Douglas W.; "Hollywood Discovers That Virtue Pays", Subtitle: Self-Censorship Imposed Under Pressure Six Months Ago, Has Brought an Increase in the Box-Office Receipts. Section 6, January 20, 1935, pp. 4, 15.

Rhetoric: Mackenzie, Catherine; "The Lecture Business is Picking Up, Too", Subtitle: Prices Are Down, But Bookings Rise — Foreigners Are Few, But

	Our Celebrities Satisfy an Old American Craving. Section 6, January 20, 1935, pp. 9, 17.
Telephone:	Robbins, L. H.; "Long Distance Rings, The World Heeds", Subtitle: Since New York Called San Francisco Twenty Years Ago the Telephone Has Outstripped the Inventor's Dreams. Section 6, January 27, 1935, pp. 7, 23.
Newspaper:	Mallon, Paul; "Has the New Deal Colored the News?", Subtitle: An Observer at the Capital Says Facts Reach the Public in the Long Run. Section 6, February 17, 1935, pp. 6, 22.
Communication:	Robbins, L. H.; "Mickey Mouse Emerges as Economist", Subtitle: Citizens of the World, Unexplained Phenomenon, He Wins Victories in the Field of Business Man and Banker. Section 6, March 10, 1935, pp. 8, 22.
Theatre:	Cohan, George M.; "Cohan Rediscovers the Theatre Public", Subtitle: It is Still With Us, Says the Veteran Actor, Home From the Road, and Can Be Won Back for the Playhouse. Section 7, May 26, 1935, pp. 8, 20.
Censorship:	Duranty, Walter; "Censors in Europe Extend Their Sway", Subtitle: A Close View of the Men Who Wield the Blue Pencil and Their Methods. Section 7, June 2, 1935, pp. 8, 20.
Press:	Hurd, Charles W. B.; "President and Press: A Unique Forum", Subtitle: Mr. Roosevelt Develops His News Conference on Striking Lines. Section 7, June 9, 1935, pp. 3, 19.
Radio:	Dunlap, Orrin E.; "Amateur Night: Radio's Door to Fame", Subtitle: With Ethereal

Listeners as a Jury, the Novices of America Gayly Seek a Place Among the Stars. Section 7, June 23, 1935, pp. 8, 21.

Rhetoric: Adams, Mildred; "'We the People' Speak", Subtitle: America Is More Articulate Than Ever, If One Judges by the Letters and Telegrams Reaching Washington. Section 7, June 30, 1935, pp. 9, 18.

Film:
Theatre: Eaton, Walter Prichard; "The Stage Eyes the Screen's Domain", Subtitle: An Observer Considers FERA's Plan to Aid Drama and Concludes That Hollywood Should Also Help. Section 6, July 14, 1935, pp. 11, 18.

Press:
Propaganda: Tolischus, Otto D.; "A Muzzled Press Serves the Nazi State", Subtitle: German Newspapers Always Docile, Are Only Organs of Propaganda. Section 6, July 14, 1935, pp. 8-9.

Radio: Clark, Delbert; "The President's Listening-In Machine", Subtitle: What the People Think About Him is Conveyed to His Ear by an Efficient Organization. Section 7, September 1, 1935, pp. 3, 14.

Rhetoric: Robbins, L. H.; "American Humorists ", Subtitle: Will Rogers, The Latest, Came of a Long Line Who Have Commented Upon the Passing Show. Section 7, September 8, 1935, pp. 8-9, 14.

Communication: Hill, Frank E.; "Back to 'Town Meetings'", Subtitle: Studebaker, Commissioners of Education, Calls Forums That He Hopes Will

	Revive Neighborhood Discussions. Section 7, September 15, 1935, pp. 9, 17.
Newspaper:	Crawford, Bruce; "A New Type of Country Editor Emerges", Subtitle: Less Picturesque Than the Old, He Still Plays a Part in the Drama of His World, and Finds it Satisfying. Section 7, September 22, 1935, pp. 12, 17.
Photography:	Brock, H. I.; "Broadening Art of the Camera", Subtitle: The Modern Photographer Uses His Equipment of Light to Achieve the Results at Which the Brush and the Pencil of an Older Tradition Arrived. Section 7, September 29, 1935, pp. 12-13.
Film:	Wilson, P. W.; "Hollywood Tries Out Mr. Shakespeare", Subtitle: The Bard Has Crossed the Vasty Deep to Go Into the Pictures and His Talent is Received With Favor. Section 7, October 13, 1935, pp. 9, 19.
Radio:	Dunlap, Orrin E.; "Sarnoff Scans the Radio World", Subtitle: He Contrasts Its Freedom in America With the Control That is Exercised in Europe. Section 7, October 27, 1935, pp. 5, 17.

Year 1936

Radio:	Nichols, Lewis; "Tin Pan Alley Stirred to Civic Song", Subtitle: But While It Seeks to Turn Out an Anthem for New York, It Has Other Troubles in Which Radio Figures. Section 7, January 5, 1936, pp. 8, 21.

Film:	Nugent, Frank S.; "Celluloid Pageant", Subtitle: The March of "Arts" is Vividly Portrayed in a New Museum Devoted to the Film. Section 7, January 19, 1936, pp. 8-9, 17.

Radio:
Communication:	Brock, H. I.; "From Post Rider to the Radio", Subtitle: Progress of Communications Made Vivid by a Drama in Seven Scenes. Section 7, March 1, 1936, pp. 12, 19.

Rhetoric:	Clark, Delbert; "National Drama — Producer: Roosevelt", Subtitle: The President, a Born Showman, Has Developed His Talent Into a Rare Political Asset. Section 7, March 1, 1936, pp. 3, 23.

Theatre:	Price, Clair; "Broadway Tides Swirl in Piccadilly", Subtitle: The American Invasion Includes Fashions, Books and Plays. Section 7, June 7, 1936, pp. 10, 22.

Music:	Taubman, H. Howard; "Stokowski Finds Us Turning to Music", Subtitle: On His Tour of the Country He Feels Our Appreciation Growing. Section 7, June 14, 1936, pp. 7, 19.

Film:
Censorship:	Churchill, Douglas W.; "Hollywood Walks Warily", Subtitle: The Movie Capital Still Listens to the Prompting of the Censor, Though It Believes That It Has Moved Toward a Cleaner Screen Stage of Film Production. Section 7, August 23, 1936, pp. 8, 18.

Rhetoric:	Huston, Lester A.; "The Voters Still Sing, Though Faintly", Subtitle: They Have a Rival in the Blaring Sound Track Which Carries Its Own

Musical Messages. Section 7, September 27, 1936, pp. 13, 21.

Film: Fuller, Eunice Barnard; "Children of Hollywood's Gold Rush", Subtitle: A New Get Rich Quick Scheme Dazzles Their Parents But Prizes are Won by the Few. Section 7, October 4, 1936, pp. 10-11, 23.

Film: Goldway, Samuel; "What's the Matter With the Movies", Section 8, November 29, 1936, pp. 6-7, 27.

Year 1937

Press: Robbins, L. H.; "Mr. Dooley Remains a Much-Quoted Oracle", Subtitle: His Well-Known Words About the Supreme Court Were One of Many Commentaries on Our Life. Section 8, January 24, 1937, pp. 9, 23.

Music: Taubman, H. Howard; "Music's Young Hopefuls Storm the City Gates", Subtitle: A Debut in New York is the Start They Seek. Section 8, January 24, 1937, pp. 12, 27.

Communication: Low, David; "Streamlining the Cartoon", Subtitle: Uncle Sam and Uncle Bull Presenting New Symbols. Section 8, February 7, 1937, pp. 10-11, 26.

Communication: _____; "As the Cartoonists Say Lincoln", Section 8, February 7, 1937, p. 7.

Propaganda: Ross, Albion; "Goebbels Edits the Popular Mind in Germany", Subtitle: Thought Control Now

	Achieved in the Reich. Section 8, February 14, 1937, pp. 3, 27.
Newspaper:	Layman, Edward A.; "To the Editor: Sir ____", Subtitle: The Reader Who Takes Pen in Hand Has Lately Had a Field Day in the Supreme Court Debate. Section 8, February 28, 1937, pp. 8, 26.
Film:	Zukor, Adolph; "From the Nickelodeon to the Picture Palace", Subtitle: Zukor Tells the Story of Twenty-Five Years. Section 8, February 28, 1937, pp. 14-15, 25.
Telephone:	Robbins, L. H.; "Telephone Era Honors Him Who Made It", Subtitle: Ninety years After Alexander Bell's Birth, Sound Communication Has Transformed Life. Section 8, March 7, 1937, pp. 10-11, 20.
Communication:	Aikman, Duncan; "An Epic War of Public Opinion Pages", Subtitle: On the Supreme Court Question of Democracy Mobilizes Two Vociferous Armies of Citizens. Section 8, March 14, 1937, pp. 1-2, 18.
Photography:	H. I. B., ; "The Camera's 100 Years", Section 8, March 14, 1937, pp. 14-15.
Press: Censorship:	Byas, Hugh; "Japan's Censors Aspire to 'Thought Control'", Subtitle: Their Task It Is to Keep an Empire Free From Ideas That Might Disturb The State. Section 8, April 18, 1937, pp. 4, 27.

Film:
Censorship: Nugent, Frank S.; "New Censorial Swords Hanging Over Hollywood", Section 8, May 9, 1937, pp. 16-17, 22.

Press: Robbins, L. H.; "'Deadeye Dick' Has Become a Collector's Item", Subtitle: The Dime Novel Grandfather Used to Read Is a Literary Antique and It's Bringing Prices According to Rarity. Section 8, September 19, 1937, pp. 10-11, 25.

Communication: Kieran, James; "The President Listens In On the Nation", Subtitle: Roosevelt, Completing His Tour, Has Faith In His Ability To Gauge Public Sentiment. Section 8, October 3, 1937, pp. 1-2, 17.

Radio: Berger, Meyer; "A Brazen Blockhead Revives an Art", Subtitle: His Name is Charlie McCarthy and He Has Made Ventriloquism Again All the Rage. Section 8, November 7, 1937, pp. 11, 17.

Radio: Dunlap, Orrin E.; "Down the Field and Over the Air Waves", Subtitle: The Football Hero Is Dramatized by Radio for the Benefit of the Old Grad at Home. Section 8, November 7, 1937, pp. 10, 20.

Film: Russell, Herbert; "L'Affaire Mickey Mouse", Subtitle: An Inquiry Into a Plot of World-Wide Scope. Section 8, December 26, 1937, pp. 4, 17.

Year 1938

Film: Churchill, Douglas W.; "The Million-Dollar Mania Grips", Subtitle: The Budget of the Ambitious Film is Spread Over Expensive People and Costly Production. Section 8, January 23, 1938, pp. 8-9, 22.

Newspaper: Palmer, Colonel Frederick; "Re-Enter the War Correspondent", Subtitle: In Stricken Spain and China, He Carries on in Direct Line of His Glamorous Tradition. Section 8, January 30, 1938, pp. 10-11, 25.

Film: Churchill, Douglas W.; "Disney's Philosophy", Subtitle: His Creatures of the Screen, He Says, Are Simply Laughing at Our Human Weaknesses. Section 8, March 6, 1938, pp. 9, 23.

Film: Churchill, Douglas W.; "Gold-Rush Days are Fading Out in Hollywood", Subtitle: While the Big People Are Still in Pay Dirt, Lesser Ones Find That the Vein is Running Thin. Section 8, May 8, 1938, pp. 4, 26.

Film: Churchill, Douglas W.; "Life of the Child Star: A Hollywood Fairy Tale", Section 8, May 22, 1938, pp. 6, 22.

Television: Kaempffert, Waldemar; "Big 'If's' Cloud the Television Screen", Subtitle: A Review of Progress and of the Obstacles. Section 7, June 5, 1938, pp. 6, 21.

Film: Woolf, S. J.; "Walt Disney Tells Us What Makes Him Happy", Subtitle: He's Doing the Thing He

Most Wants to Do. Section 7, July 10, 1938, pp. 5, 18-19.

Radio: Storey, Walter Rendell; "Radio Cabinets Harmonizing with Antiques", Section 7, September 11, 1938, p. 16.

Photography: Kaempffert, Waldemar; "Photograph Triumphs Over Space", Subtitle: By Wire and Wireless It Keeps Up With News. Section 8, October 23, 1938, pp. 12-13.

Rhetoric: Catledge, Turner; "Why Do Voters Vote As They Do?", Subtitle: Self-Interest Is With Them Always, But There Are Many Motives Influencing Their Choice. Section 8, October 30, 1938, pp. 7, 15.

Advertising: Wharton, Hazel K.; "The Skywriters Art", Section 8, November 6, 1938, p. 17.

Press: Robbins, L. H.; "To People Never 'In the News'", Subtitle: Why Not, On this Day, Give Them the Spotlight?. Section 8, December 25, 1938, pp. 2, 11.

Radio: _____; "A Saturday Night in the Arctic", Section 7, December 25, 1938, p. 15.

Year 1939

Film: Pryor, Thomas M.; "An Adventurous Life For the Newsreel Man", Subtitle: Events Recorded on Film Scanned by Governments — Big Public Now Expects Quick Camera Reporting. Section 7, January 1, 1939, pp. 10, 12.

Press: Wood, Julius B.; "Channeling the News for Nazis", Subtitle: How the Government, Through the Press, Influences Thought in a Common Direction. Section 7, January 15, 1939, pp. 4, 23.

Press: Brook, H. I.; "Currier and Ives, Printmakers to America", Section 7, January 22, 1939, pp. 12, 13, 14.

Communication: Tebbutt, Geoffrey; "Exploring America's Jungle", Subtitle: A Foreigner Looks at Us and Finds We Fit the Pattern Hollywood Sets. Section 7, February 5, 1939, pp. 8, 16.

Magazine: Price, Clair; "Is Punch Funny? Yes, Says Punch", Subtitle: Its Humor in Principle is Like American Humor, the Editor Holds, Though its Audience and Subject Differ. Section 7, February 19, 1939, pp. 12-13, 20.

Rhetoric: Leacoch, Stephen; "Our 'Living' Language: A Defense", Section 7, February 26, 1939, pp. 9, 14.

Rhetoric: Markham, S. F.; "American Speech: An Indictment", Section 7, February 26, 1939, pp. 8, 22.

Film: Nugent, Frank S.; "Disney Is Now Art — But He Wonders", Subtitle: That Picture in the Mseum Is Not All His, He Reveals. Section 7, February 26, 1939, pp. 4-5.

Theatre: Lang, Daniel; "From Tryout to Hit (Perhaps)", Subtitle: First the Dog Town, and Then

Broadway. Section 8, March 19, 1939, pp. 10, 23.

Music: Gilbert, Gama; "From 'Hearts and Flowers' to 'Jeepers Creepers'", Section 8, March 26, 1939, pp. 12-13, 17.

Press: Robbins, L. H.; "The Book of a Thousand Tongues", Section 8, April 2, 1939, pp. 10, 15.

Film: Churchill, Douglas W.; "We'll Head 'Em Off at Eagle Pass", Subtitle: The Cow Woddies Are Riding Again and Hollywood Is Turning Out a Block of Grand-Scale Horse Operas. Section 8, April 23, 1939, pp. 12-13, 14.

Telephone: Bracker, Milton; "Hello — And Behold", Subtitle: The Wonders of the Phone. Section 8, May 14, 1939, pp. 5, 19.

Film: Nugent, Frank S.; "The Movie Finger Writes", Section 8, May 21, 1939, pp. 14-15.

Telephone: Borland, Hal; "America Speaking", Subtitle: We Reveal ourselves in the Long-Distance Calls at the World's Fair. Section 7, June 11, 1939, pp. 8, 18.

Rhetoric: Bracker, Milton; "Leather-Lungs of Our Midways", Subtitle: The Barkers are a Raucous Tribe of Showmen in Trade — They Admit They Mislead But Deny They Deceive. Section 7, June 18, 1939, pp. 11, 16.

Film: Nugent, Frank S.; "Glamour Girls; A Film Cavalcade", Section 7, June 25, 1939, pp. 8-9, 15.

Film: Churchill, Douglas W.; "At 50 Chaplin Begins to Talk", Subtitle: Returning to the Screen, Charlie Chaplin Will Bring His Familiar Hat, Stick and Shoes, But He Will Break With His Long Tradition of Silent Pantomime. Section 7, July 30, 1939, pp. 10-12.

Film: Lejeune, C. A.; "By Their Movie Idols You Shall Know Them", Subtitle: A Study of Preferences — British and American. Section 7, August 6, 1939, pp. 6-7.

Film: Churchill, Douglas W.; "When Movie Stars Marry", Section 7, August 27, 1939, pp. 3, 19.

Theatre: Atkinson, Brooks; "Enter the Actor", Subtitle: He Faces a New Season Uncertain of His Job, But Certain of Another Crop of Stage-Struck youths. Section 7, September 10, 1939, pp. 9, 22.

Radio: Duffus, R. L.; "New Nerves That Stir the World", Subtitle: Modern Communication Makes Mankind Everywhere Quickly Sensitive to Any Distant Shock. Section 7, September 17, 1939, pp. 6-7, 20.

Film: Churchill, Douglas; "Pinnocchio Is Now 'Disneyed'", Subtitle: Another Figure from the Child's Universe Joins Snow White on the Screen, Invested With Life That Can Be Comprehended by the Adult's Literal Mind. Section 7, October 1, 1939, pp. 12-13.

Television: Schwartz, Daniel; "Television From Backstage", Subtitle: One of the Incredible Miracles of Science is Slowly Building Up Its Technique of

	Showmanship. Section 7, October 1, 1939, pp. 8-9, 14.
Press:	Birchall, Frederick T.; "Getting At the Facts Despite the Censor", Subtitle: A Foreign Correspondent Holds it Possible to Approach the Truth Through the Fog of Secrecy, Concentration, and Denial. Section 7, October 15, 1939, pp. 3, 18, 20.
Press: Propaganda:	Nevins, Allan; "Propaganda: An Explosive Word Analyzed", Subtitle: It is Domestic Propaganda, Not the Foreign Kind, Which is Most to Be Feared Today, Says an American Historian. Section 7, October 29, 1939, pp. 3, 18.
Film:	Crowther, Bosley; "Luring Hollywood", Section 7, November 5, 1939, p. 19.
Theatre:	Pemberton, Brock; "Broadway is Hit-Happy Again", Subtitle: The Young Theatrical Season, Coming as a New War Started Is Surprising Even the Managers. Section 7, November 5, 1939, pp. 6-7, 20.
Rhetoric:	Robbins, R. H.; "I Should Like to Ask the Speaker —", Subtitle: The Long-Silent America is at Last Finding His Voice and Joining Again in Old Town-Meeting Debate. Section 7, November 5, 1939, pp. 5, 17.
Theatre:	Pemberton, Brock; "Hits — And Why They Are", Subtitle: After "'Abie's Irish Rose" Comes "Tobacco Road" to Spur Broadway's Gust for the Hardy Perennials of the Drama. Section 7, November 12, 1939, pp. 6-7, 18.

Rhetoric: Bracker, Milton; "Free Speech Rodeos", Subtitle: At Columbus Circle and Union Square the Right to Sir an Opinion on any Subject Receives Nightly Exercise. Section 7, November 19, 1939, pp. 8, 27.

Radio: Robbins, R. H.; "The Adam of Gag Men", Subtitle: Joe Miller's Joke Book is 200 Years Old; How Joke-Smithing is a Big Business. Section 7, November 26, 1939, pp. 6, 24.

Press: Devree, Howard; "Nine Prints of the Year", Section 7, December 3, 1939, pp. 12-13.

Radio: Crisler, Ben; "Tin Pan Cavalcade", Subtitle: War Offers a Fresh Inspiration to the Song Writers, Who, However, Must Be Allowed to Carry On In Their Peculiar Way. Section 7, December 7, 1939, pp. 10-11, 19.

Film: Nugent, Frank S.; "Gone With, Etc. — or the Making of a Movie", Section 7, December 10, 1939, pp. 6-7, 17-18.

Film: Lejeune, C. A.; "So This Was Life in 1939!", Subtitle: If the Wise Men of 3939 Unearth Our Movies, They Will See a World Strange Even to Us Who Live In It. Section 7, December 31, 1939, pp. 8-10.

Year 1940

Film: Churchill, Lillian; "Modes a la Movies", Subtitle: Costume Films Bring Back Fashions of

Years 1931-1940 — 75

	Long Ago. Section 7, January 7, 1940, pp. 8-9, 18.
Film:	Nugent, Frank S.; "Movie Humor — No Laughing Matter", Subtitle: The Laws of Comedy as Worked Out in the Studios Cannot Always Allow for the Unknown Quantity of the Audience. Section 7, March 3, 1940, pp. 6, 13.
Film:	Churchill, Douglas W.; "The Youthful Stars That Mostly Wane", Section 7, May 26, 1940, pp. 8-9, 21.
Film:	MacKenzie, Catherine; "Movies and the Child: The Debate Rages On", Subtitle: Good and Bad Effects of Popular Films Presented. Section 7, June 23, 1940, pp. 9, 20.
Radio:	MacKenzie, Catherine; "Child and Parent", Subtitle: Radio Survey. Section 7, June 30, 1940, p. 23.
Film:	Churchill, Douglas W.; "The Hollywood Span of Life", Section 7, July 7, 1940, pp. 6-7, 15.
Film:	MacKenzie, Catherine; "Child and Parent", Subtitle: Young Reviewers. Section 7, July 7, 1940, p. 19.
Film:	Crowther, Bosley; "Double Feature Trouble", Section 7, July 14, 1940, pp. 8, 20.
Film:	Crowther, Bosley; "Realistic Stepchild of the Movies", Subtitle: The Documentary Film, Which Deals With Things As They Are, Is Forging Ahead, Sometimes at the Expense of "Art". Section 7, August 25, 1940, pp. 12-13.

Film: Gelder, Robert Van; "Chaplin Draws a Keen Weapon", Subtitle: "What is More Effective," he says of His New Picture, "Than to Laugh at These Fellows Who Are Kicking Humanity Around?". Section 7, September 8, 1940, pp. 8-9, 22.

Film: Crowther, Bosley; "Cavalcade of Movie Comics", Section 7, October 20, 1940, pp. 6-7.

Film: Bergman, Lewis; "Added Feature: The Movie Audience", Section 7, December 1, 1940, p. 9.

Year 1941

Radio: Cobb, Jane; "Living and Leisure", Section 7, January 5, 1941, p. 15.

Radio: Cobb, Jane; "Living and Leisure", Subtitle: Critics. Section 7, January 26, 1941, p. 20.

Theatre: Shalett, Sidney M.; "Theatre On Skates", Subtitle: Rising From Nothing in a Few Years, Ice Spectacles Now Fill the Big Studio. Section 7, January 26, 1941, pp. 14-15, 27.

Radio: Richardson, Dow; "The Battle of Music", Section 7, February 9, 1941, p. 23.

Film: Crowther, Bosley; "Male Movie Stars Outshine the Female", Section 7, February 16, 1941, pp. 10-11, 17.

Film: Valentine, Elizabeth R.; "Are Movies Good or Bad for Them?", Subtitle: The Young Critics, After the Matinee, Say What Is On Their Minds, But Fail to Decide an Old Debate. Section 7, March 30, 1941, pp. 8-9, 30.

Film: Lejeune, C. A.; "Making Movies Amid the Blitz", Subtitle: British Studios Continue to Produce Pictures and Let Bombs Fall Where They May. Section 7, May 11, 1941, pp. 15, 24.

Advertising: Desfor, Harold D.; "The Housewife: Great Quizee", Subtitle: She is Becoming Hardened to the Polls Which Seek Her Views on all Sorts of Questions and Her Likes and Dislikes. Section 7, June 16, 1941, pp. 12, 25.

Film:	Crowther, Bosley; "It's a Far, Far, Cry From Valentino Days", Section 7, June 22, 1941, pp. 6-7, 25.
Propaganda:	Hitler, Adolph; "The Art of Propaganda", Subtitle: Excerpts from "Mein Kampf". Section 7, June 22, 1941, p. 3.
Film:	March, Joseph Moncure; "One Minute on the Screen — Or Two Days on the Lot...", Section 7, September 28, 1941, pp. 6-7, 29, 31.
Film:	March, Joseph Moncure; "Star-Gazing in Hollywood", Subtitle: When the Great Producer Asks "Who is that girl?" the Wheels Are Started for a Dream Career — He Hopes. Section 7, October 12, 1941, pp. 10-11, 29, 30.
Film:	March, Joseph Moncure; "Nemesis — Alias Hollywood Agent", Subtitle: Actors, Writers, Directors Find It Hard to Shake Him, Once They Sign Contracts. Section 7, December 7, 1941, pp. 14, 31.
Radio: Propaganda:	Phillips, Cabell; "War of the Air Waves", Subtitle: Against the Tide of Words Launched Against Us by Axis Powers We Have Created a Huge Defense. Section 7, December 28, 1941, pp. 12, 19.

Year 1942

Radio:	Hutchens, John K.; "Serious Business, This Radio Humor", Subtitle: So Actors Who Go On the Air Resolved to Be Funny Work Out Their

Technique Carefully. Section 7, March 15, 1942, pp. 16-17, 29.

Radio: Hutchens, John K.; "Tricky Ad Lib", Subtitle: Those Spontaneous Quips Over the Air May Be Funny, But They Are Serious Business for the Fred Allens and Bob Hopes Who Must Take Them. Section 7, May 24, 1942, pp. 16-17, 29.

Radio: Woolf, S. J.; "Corwin Presents — Britain At War", Subtitle: Norman Corwin, American Poet and Dramatist, Created a New Radio Technique. Today He Uses His Method to Tell Britain's Story to Britons. Section 7, August 9, 1942, pp. 13, 27.

Radio: Hutchens, John K.; "Who Thought Up The Quiz Show?", Subtitle: This Isn't the $64 Question, But It Is One Many People Have Tried (Unsuccessfully) to Answer. Meanwhile the Quiz Mills Grind On. Section 7, August 23, 1942, pp. 12-13, 31.

Radio: Hutchens, John K.; "The Secrets of a Good Radio Voice", Section 7, December 6, 1942, pp. 26-27, 39.

Year 1943

Film: Nugent, Frank S.; "Double, Double, Toil and Trouble", Subtitle: Does Hollywood Really Want to Get Rid of the Double Feature? Do the Exhibitors? It Seems Not. And Here are the Reasons Why They Don't. Section 7, January 17, 1943, pp. 11, 21.

Film:	_____; "Stage Door Canteen in Movies", Section 5, January 31, 1943, p. 38.
Radio:	Hutchens, John K.; "Are Soap Operas Only Suds?", Subtitle: Twenty Million Women Listen to the Serials Daily and In Them Find a World of Dreams — Is the Effect Good or Bad?. Section 6, March 28, 1943, pp. 19, 36.
Press:	Long, Tania; "The Free Press of Enslaved Europe", Subtitle: One Thousand Underground Newspapers are Weapon That Harrasses the Nazi Rulers. Section 6, May 16, 1943, pp. 20-21, 36.
Film:	Crowther, Bosley; "The Ten Best Films", Subtitle: Here is a Critic's List of Those He Found "Most Thoroughly Gratifying and Artistically Respectable". Section 6, May 30, 1943, pp. 12-13, 21.
Film:	_____; "'This is the Army' On the Screen", Section 6, June 27, 1943, pp. 12-13.
Film:	_____; "Undersea Film for the Navy", Section 6, July 11, 1943, p. 35.
Film:	Robinson, Florett; "The Hiss-s-s-s-s Through the Years", Subtitle: Styles in Movie Villains Change, But Whether Western Desperados, City Slickers or Japs, They're All Bad Men. Section 6, August 15, 1943, pp. 16-17.
Film:	MacKenzie, Catherine; "Parent and Child", Subtitle: War Films for Youngsters. Section 6, September 5, 1943, p. 24.
Film:	_____; "'Madame Curie' On the Screen", Section 6, September 26, 1943, p. 18.

Film:	Nugent, Frank S.; "Super-Duper Epic: Hollywood Canteen", Subtitle: 7,000 Movie Stars and Extras — Count Them, 7,000 — Have Made Its First Year Something to Be Proud Of. Section 6, October 17, 1943, pp. 16-17.
Theatre:	Simonson, Lee; "Prescription for an Ailing Theatre", Subtitle: Lee Simonson Suggests That Successful Plays Be Taxed to Pay for Those That Would Make the Stage Once More a National Institution. Section 6, November 14, 1943, pp. 16, 39.
Film:	Woolf, S. J.; "The Story Makes the Movie", Subtitle: So Declares Samuel Goldwyn, Who Winds Up Thirty Years as a Producer Believing in Fewer and Better Pictures. Section 6, November 14, 1943, pp. 18, 46.
Film:	Hutchens, John K.; "Tracy, Superman, etc. all Go to War", Subtitle: These Dauntless Lads Were Never So Busy and the Debate Over Their Influence on Children Flows on Relentlessly. Section 6, November 21, 1943, pp. 14, 42-43.
Press:	Craven, Thomas; "The March of Humor", Section 6, December 5, 1943, pp. 10-11.
Film:	Woolf, S. J.; "Highest Paid Movie Actress", Subtitle: Ginger Rogers Gives Her Recipe for Success in Hollywood — It is Intelligence, Adaptability, Capacity for Hard Work. Section 6, December 5, 1943, pp. 18, 45.
Press:	Brook, H. I.; "Shrine of a Basic Freedom", Subtitle: St. Paul's Eastchester is a Memorial to a Momentous Battle for the Freedom of the

Press. Section 6, December 12, 1943, pp. 20, 46.

Year 1944

Film: _____; "'Oscars' for '43", Section 6, March 12, 1944, p. 15.

Radio: Hutchens, John K.; "Crime Plays — On the Radio", Subtitle: Though Some Critics Deplore Chills, Thrills, and Horrors, Apparently They Are Here to Stay. Section 6, March 19, 1944, pp. 16-17, 31.

Film: _____; "Wilson on the Screen", Section 6, March 26, 1944, pp. 16, 17.

Film: Crowther, Bosley; "From Peep Show to Technicolor", Subtitle: The Kinetoscope's Flickering Image of 50 Years Ago Was the Fateful Forerunner of All Motion Pictures. Section 6, April 23, 1944, pp. 15, 38.

Film: Nugent, Frank S.; "Film Men of the Air Force", Subtitle: Their Job is to Make the Training and Combat Films That Help Pilots to Understand Planes and Fighting Tactics. Section 6, April 30, 1944, pp. 14, 30.

Advertising: Berger, Meyer; "From White Way to Color Canyon", Subtitle: Sign Man's Vision of a Broadway Painted With Lights in the Winslow Homer Manner. Section 6, June 4, 1944, pp. 34-36.

Years 1941-1950 — 83

Radio: _____; "Favorite Gags of Funny Men", Section 6, June 11, 1944, p. 39.

Film: _____; "Woodrow Wilson — A Screen Biography", Section 6, June 18, 1944, pp. 18-19.

Radio: Hutchens, John K.; "His Humor: Radio Showman", Subtitle: Mayor La Guardia's Technique Is 'Wrong' But He Has Won a Huge Sunday Audience. Section 6, July 16, 1944, pp. 14, 41.

Radio: Cook, Lilyn M.; "The Mayor", Section 6, July 30, 1944, p. 2.

Radio: Hopkins, Arthur; "Looking Toward a People's Theatre", Subtitle: A Veteran Producer Makes Predictions Based on His Current Radio Experiments. Section 6, July 30, 1944, pp. 17, 33.

Film: Nathan, Paul S.; "Hunting With a Movie Scout", Subtitle: His Search for Talent Gives Him a Chance to Study the Relationship Between Hollywood and the Theatre. Section 6, August 6, 1944, pp. 17, 35.

Film: _____; "Hollywood Grows a Tree in Brooklyn", Section 6, August 6, 1944, pp. 14-15.

Film: Morgansen, Thomas G.; "Screen Rights", Section 6, August 20, 1944, p. 36.

Film: Crowther, Bosley; "When Satire and Slapstick Meet", Subtitle: Preston Sturges Likes to Mix Shrewd Comment on American Foibles With the

Mad Action of the Old "Keystone Style". Section 6, August 27, 1944, pp. 14-15, 37.

Radio: Hutchens, John K.; "Mr. Kilocycle Twists the Dials", Subtitle: And Speaks his Mind Freely About His Radio Likes and Dislikes. Section 6, September 3, 1944, pp. 18-19.

Film: _____; "Bob Hope's Seven Faces", Section 6, September 10, 1944, p. 24.

Radio:
Rhetoric: Bender, James F.; "The Two Men: A Radio Analysis", Subtitle: A Speech Expert Finds Roosevelt and Dewey Equally Matched As Air Orators. Section 6, September 17, 1944, pp. 11, 36.

Radio: Askenas, Ruth; "Radio Personalities", Section 6, October 8, 1944, p. 23.

Advertising: Graham, Al; "Jingle or Jangle", Subtitle: Sponsored Ditties Fill the Air — Some Folks Like Them, Some Despair. Section 6, October 29, 1944, pp. 26-27, 44.

Press:___Morgansen, Thomas G.; "Country Editor", Section 6, October 29, 1944, p. 22.

Press: Penton, Brian; "Problem: The Expert", Subtitle: He is Needed and Yet How is He to be Fitted Into the Working of Democracy?. Section 6, December 10, 1944, pp. 13, 44-45.

Film: _____; "Winged Victory", Section 6, December 17, 1944, p. 16.

Years 1941-1950 — 85

Film: _____; "Song to Remember", Section 6, December 31, 1944, p. 20.

Year 1945

Film: Stanley, Fred; "Fitzgerald Meets Fame — And He Follows", Subtitle: The Limelight Focuses Fiercely on the Actor and He Finds It "Down Right Boring". Section 6, January 14, 1945, pp. 14, 38.

Newspaper: _____; "GI News in the Pacific", Section 6, January 14, 1945, p. 41.

Radio: Bender, James F.; "Voices on the Air", Section 6, February 4, 1945, p. 38.

Radio: Durand, Lionel J.; "The Voice of the Wehrmacht", Section 6, February 11, 1945, p. 23.

Film: Markel, Helen; "Goldilocks Grows Up, But Definitely", Subtitle: Portrait of a Chick Named Shirley Temple — Who Tells How She Evolved From Gurgling to Glamor. Section 6, February 11, 1945, pp. 18, 35.

Censorship: Price, Bryon; "The Censor Defends the Censorship", Subtitle: Bryon Price Replies to Those Who Complain That Too Much News Is Kept From the Public. Section 6, February 11, 1945, pp. 11, 32-33.

Communication: MacLeish, Archibald; "People Must Speak to People", Subtitle: "If They Know Each Other" Mr. MacLeish says, "They Will Do Away With

	Misunderstanding". Section 6, February 18, 1945, p. 9.
Film:	Nugent, Frank S.; "How Long Should a Movie Be?", Subtitle: Hollywood Has Debated the Question for Months and the Experts There Are Still at a Loss for the Answer. Section 6, February 18, 1945, pp. 18-19.
Radio:	Bender, Jane F.; "Correction", Subtitle: To The Editor. Section 6, March 11, 1945, p. 21.
Censorship:	Cooper, Kent; "To Prevent War — No News Blackout", Subtitle: We Must Spend the Truth: says Kent Cooper and Make It a Shield to Guard World Peace. Section 6, March 11, 1945, pp. 12, 33, 35.
Film:	Weil, Henry; "Movie Fan's Reaction to Article on 'How Long Should a Movie Be?'", Subtitle: To the Editor. Section 6, March 11, 1945, p. 21.
Radio:	Clark, Ernest R.; "Radio Announcers", Section 6, March 18, 1945, p. 44.
Film:	Stanley, Fred M.; "Oscar: His Life and Times", Subtitle: He is the Academy Award for the Best Film Work — Just Now His Claim to Fame is Being Debated in Hollywood. Section 6, March 18, 1945, pp. 18-19, 53-54.
Film:	_____; "Tallulah the Great", Section 6, March 18, 1945, p. 28.
Film:	Pryor, Thomas M.; "Stars in New York", Section 6, April 1, 1945, p. 46.

Years 1941-1950 — 87

Film: Goldwyn, Samuel; "Future Challenges in the Movies", Subtitle: Mr. Goldwyn says They Must Educate as Well as Entertain and These Two Roles Do Not Conflict. Section 6, April 22, 1945, pp. 14, 39.

Radio:
Rhetoric: Bender, James F.; "The Truman Voice — 'General American'", Subtitle: The President Speaks the Tongue of Ninety Million of Us — with Touches of the South. Section 6, April 29, 1945, p. 17.

Radio: Reznick, Sidney; "It's Funny But —", Section 6, May 13, 1945, p. 23.

Press: Thompson, Robert L.; "Portrait of a Tar-Heel Editor", Subtitle: Josephus Daniels at 83 is Still the Liberal Fighting for His Beliefs and His Prejudices. Section 6, May 20, 1945, pp. 16, 42.

Film: _____; "Adano's Bell Rings Again", Section 6, May 20, 1945, p. 17.

Film: _____; "Rhapsody in Blue", Section 6, June 3, 1945, p. 24.

Film: Crowther, Robert; "It's the Fans Who Make the Films", Subtitle: Their "Want to See" Can Be Charted and Used As a Guide For the Producers. Section 6, June 24, 1945, pp. 14, 29-30.

Film: Crowther, Bosley; "Hollywood's New Fair-Headed Boys", Subtitle: It's the Youthful, Not the Sophisticated, Type That Gives Today's Movie Fans Their Romance and Heart-Throbs. Section 6, July 15, 1945, pp. 14-15, 19.

Film:	_____; "Crime Certainly Pays on the Screen", Subtitle: The Growing Crop of Homicidal Films Poses Questions for Psychologists and Producers. Section 6, August 5, 1945, pp. 17, 37.
Radio:	
Television:	W. K.; "Video Bars Hefty Singer", Section 6, August 19, 1945, p. 29.
Film:	_____; "Hollywood Rides Again", Section 6, August 19, 1945, pp. 16-17.
Film:	Berger, Oscar; "Hollywood Sketch Book", Section 6, September 16, 1945, p. 25.
Advertising:	Waggoner, Walter M.; "The Shape of Things and Goods to Come", Subtitle: A Bright New World Lies Ahead for the Civilian as Store Shelves Fill Up Again. Section 6, September 16, 1945, pp. 14, 45-46.
Film:	Carew, Dudley; "Hollywood Indicted: A British Viewpoint", Subtitle: The Trend, Despite Lapses, Is Held to Be Toward Better Pictures and Better Taste. Section 6, September 30, 1945, pp. 16, 50.
	Film: ____Newton, E.J.; Liebman, Pearl; Hoffman, Mary Ellen; Bond, Catherine; Hastings, Grace; Morgansen, Thomas; Levin, M. E.; "Letters", Section 6, October 14, 1945, p. 20.
Radio:	d'Alessio, ; "Telsiretims", Subtitle: (cartoons). Section 6, October 21, 1945, p. 28.

Radio:	Shearer, Lloyd; "It's the Gag That Gets the 'Boff'", Subtitle: The Story of How Jokes are Made for the Radio Comedians and How They Get a "Boff" (laugh) From the Audience. Section 6, October 21, 1945, p. 18.
Film:	_____; "Facts and Footnotes", Section 6, October 21, 1945, p. 35.
Film:	Ball, Joseph M.; "Labor and the Law: A Challenge by Ball", Subtitle: All Citizens, the Senator Urges, Should Accept Responsibility in Preventing Strike Disorders. Section 6, October 28, 1945, pp. 9, 48.
Film:	Greenbaum, Lucy; "A Sinatra in a Sombrero", Subtitle: Singing Roy Rogers and His Partner, Trigger, Keep the Western Riding High. Section 6, November 4, 1945, p. 42.
Propaganda:	Benton, William; "Self-Portrait by Uncle Sam", Subtitle: The State Department Is Making a New Effort to Give the World a Realistic Picture of America. Section 6, December 2, 1945, pp. 13, 45-46.
Film:	Nugent, Frank S.; "That Phenomenon Named Bergman", Subtitle: With Three of Her Pictures on Broadway at One Time, the "Off-Beat" Girl is Hollywood's Most Desired Woman. Section 6, December 16, 1945, pp. 14-15, 36-37.
Film:	Shearer, Lloyd; "What's in a Name? Ask Hollywood", Subtitle: There is Method in the Movie Mania to Change the Title and It Is Always Very Complicated. Section 6, December 30, 1945, pp. 12, 26.

Year 1946

Film: Barry, Iris; "Challenge of the Documentary Film", Subtitle: We Need This Instrument to Supplement Our Education and Extend Our Horizon. Section 6, January 6, 1946, pp. 16-17, 46.

Film: Crowther, Bosley; "Living Biographies, Hollywood Style", Section 6, January 20, 1946, pp. 24-25, 46.

Film: Deitz, Howard; "Must the Movies be 'Significant'?", Subtitle: They Can Entertain and at the Same Time Have Real Meaning, Says Howard Deitz. Section 6, January 27, 1946, pp. 18, 44.

Radio: Burger, H. H.; "Operation Annie: Now It Can Be Told", Subtitle: Here is the Story of an American Radio Station That Comforted the Germans — and Hoaxed Them. Section 6, February 17, 1946, pp. 12-13, 48, 50.

Film: Nichols, Lewis; "Gallery of Leading Ladies", Subtitle: Portraits From the Broadway Group Noted for Beauty and Other Graces. Section 6, March 3, 1946, pp. 20-21.

Radio: Gould, Jack; "They Say the Right Thing at the Wrong Time", Subtitle: The Radio Stooge's Job is to Give Mr. Big His Come Uppance to the Joy of One and All. Section 6, March 24, 1946, pp. 22-23, 60-61.

Film:	Woolf, S. J.; "Hammerstein the Second", Subtitle: Grandson of Oscar the First, He Gave Up a Career That Took Him to "Oklahoma!" and Beyond. Section 6, March 31, 1946, pp. 26-27.
Censorship:	Ethrige, Marc; "The Blackout of News in Eastern Europe", Subtitle: If We Are to Understand Each Other, Says an Observer, Dispatches Must Move Freely. Section 6, April 14, 1946, pp. 10, 53-55.
Radio:	Morgan, Henry; "What's Wrong With Radio? 'The Audience'", Subtitle: We Could Have Better Shows, Henry Morgan Says, If the Listener Would Listen to Them. Section 6, April 21, 1946, pp. 12, 59-60.
Film:	Schwartz, Daniel; "The Present and Future of Shakespeare", Subtitle: Lawrence Olivier Talks of the Bard's Popularity on the Stage and of his Future Movie Audience. Section 6, May 12, 1946, pp. 22-23, 58.
Film:	Woolf, S. J.; "Sharpshooting Singer from Astoria", Subtitle: Miss Merman Sits for Her Portrait and Talks About the Roles She Had Before She Got a Gun. Section 6, June 2, 1946, pp. 22, 57.
Radio:	_____; "Radio's 'Best Gags'", Section 6, June 2, 1946, p. 31.
Film:	_____; "Cleopatra and Caesar", Section 6, June 21, 1946, pp. 18-19.
Film:	Nugent, Frank S.; "'Forever Amber' or 'Crime Doesn't Pay'", Subtitle: In the Hollywood

Version, the Moral Lesson Will Be Underscored; Amber Will Suffer for Her Sins. Section 6, August 4, 1946, pp. 12, 44.

Film: Macgowan, Kenneth; "Some Gleams of Hope From Hollywood", Subtitle: They Promise Better and More Mature Films, But Progress in Raising Standards is Slow. Section 6, August 11, 1946, pp. 20, 38-39.

Newspaper: Middleton, Drew; "A Week's News as Russia Got It", Subtitle: The Soviet Citizen Learned That His Country Faces International Cabals at Paris and That at Home Has Much to Be Thankful For. Section 6, August 18, 1946, pp. 10, 50.

Radio: Free, Lloyd; "What Can Be Done to Improve Radio?", Subtitle: The Fight Begun on "Excessive Commercialism" is One in Which Listeners Take a Hand. Section 6, August 25, 1946, pp. 9, 50, 52.

Newspaper: Milne, A. A.; "Blue Eyes — I Love You Only — Michael", Subtitle: Every Entry in the "Agony Column" of the London Times Tells a Story to the Perceptive Reader. Section 6, September 1, 1946, pp. 12, 44.

Film: _____; "Dietrich Returns", Section 6, September 22, 1946, p. 37.

Film: _____; "The Jolson Story", Section 6, October 13, 1946, pp. 30-31.

Film: _____; "Presidential Stars", Section 6, October 20, 1946, p. 36.

Film: Nugent, Frank S.; "Mr. Hitchcock Discovers Love", Subtitle: Romance Pays Better Than Crime, He Finds so He Gives the Audience Both. Section 6, November 3, 1946, pp. 12-13, 63-64.

Film: Sherwood, Robert E.; "They're Film Writers, Not Juke Boxes", Subtitle: And says Robert Sherwood, They Should Have Authority Equal to Their Responsibilities. Section 6, December 1, 1946, pp. 15, 50.

Film: Crowther, Bosley; "The Evolution of a Movie Kiss", Subtitle: It Has Passed Through Startling Phases Since Its Casual Discovery in the Silent Film Era. Section 6, December 22, 1946, pp. 21, 434.

Year 1947

Newspaper: Baxter, Beverly; "Britain's Newspaper Phenomenon", Subtitle: News of the World, With Its Mixture of Crime Stories and Serious Comment, Has Captured More Than Seven Million Readers. Section 6, January 5, 1947, pp. 10, 26-27.

Radio: _____; "About — Radio Trances", Section 6, January 5, 1947, p. 2.

Theatre: Funke, Lewis; "Broadway Husband-and-Wife Teams", Section 6, January 12, 1947, pp. 18-19.

Press: _____; "About — The Press", Section 6, January 19, 1947, p. 4.

Rhetoric: Brown, John L.; "Chief Prophet of the Existentialists", Subtitle: Sartre of the Left Bank Has a Philosophy That Provokes Both Sermons and Fistfights. Section 6, February 2, 1947, pp. 20-21, 50, 52.

Rhetoric: Daniell, Raymond; "'Indomitable' or 'Incorrigible'?", Subtitle: To His Supporters, Winston Churchill is a Rock Amid Destructive Currents; To his Critics He is a Man Who Outlived His Time. Section 6, February 9, 1947, pp. 16, 42-43.

Books: Langer, Lawrence; "Mr. Shaw Discussed Mr. Shaw et Al.", Subtitle: The Sage of Ayott St. Lawrence Finds That, at 90, It's Rather Hard to Get New Ideas. Section 6, February 16, 1947, pp. 11, 60-61.

Theatre: Hopkins, Arthur; "Mr. Hopkins Looks at the Theatre", Subtitle: The Producer Finds Many Things Awry, But He Can Still Gaze Hopefully Into the Future. Section 6, March 2, 1947, pp. 18, 58-60.

Telephone: Berger, Meyer; "At the White House Switchboard", Subtitle: Chief Operator "Hackie," Who has Handled Many Telephone Messages for President Roosevelt and Truman, Recalls Moments of High Drama. Section 6, March 23, 1947, pp. 20, 63-65.

Film: Brady, Thomas F.; "'Bluebeard' Chaplin", Section 6, March 30, 1947, pp. 24-25.

Television: Gould, Jack; "The Paradoxical State of Television", Subtitle: The Video Art Has Made Strides Since the War, Yet Nobody Seems to

	Know Where it is Going. Section 6, March 30, 1947, pp. 14, 34-35.
Film:	Shearer, Lloyd; "Recipe for a Movie Star", Subtitle: Obstinacy and Intelligence Are the Qualities Which Won an "Oscar" for Miss de Havilland. Section 6, March 30, 1947, p. 17.
Film:	Nugent, Frank S.; "Cavalcade of Hollywood Heroes", Section 6, May 4, 1947, pp. 12-13, 60-61.
Film:	Mason, James; "A 'Villain' Turns Hero-Worshiper", Subtitle: James Mason, Something of a Hater on the Screen, Tosses Bouquets to Six Actors. Section 6, May 25, 1947, pp. 20, 50.
Film:	Woolf, S. J.; "J. Arthur Rank Presents — Himself", Subtitle: In America on a Sentimental — and Practical — Visit, He Gives His Credo on Movie-Making. Section 6, June 1, 1947, pp. 17, 52-53.
Film:	Middleton, Drew; "The Party Line Guides Russia's Movies", Subtitle: Even the Love Story, Like the Documentary, Always Ends With an Idealogical Punch Line. Section 6, July 27, 1947, pp. 12-13, 31, 33.
Film:	Crowther, Bosley; "Hollywood Versus New York", Subtitle: The New Proposal to Bring a Large Part of the Movie Industry Here Revives Many Old Arguments. Section 6, August 3, 1947, pp. 10-11, 17-18.
Rhetoric:	Hartley, Rev. Lyman Richard; "Women as Ministers: The Pros and Cons", Subtitle: The Presbyterians Are Voting on an Issue That Has

Developed Pointed Arguments. Section 6, August 13, 1947, pp. 19, 59.

Film: Lejeune, C. A.; "Can Piccadilly Do Without Hollywood?", Subtitle: Yes, say Britons — They'll Take Mason and Mills Against Gable and Musicals Any Day. Section 6, August 24, 1947, pp. 16-17, 32.

Film: Goldwyn, Samuel; "World Challenge to Hollywood", Subtitle: A Leading Producer Says Our Films Can be the Best Propaganda for the American Way of Life Because They Have No Propaganda Motive. Section 6, August 31, 1947, pp. 8, 30.

Film: Karpt, Ruth; "School of the Cinema", Subtitle: Paris is the home of a Pioneering "University" Devoted to Technical Studies in Movie-Making. Section 6, October 19, 1947, pp. 33-34.

Press:
Books: Nevins, Allan; "Ten Million Readers, 23 Million Books", Subtitle: In Fifty Years That Many People Have Used That Many Volumes at Our "National Library". Section 6, October 26, 1947, pp. 15, 61.

Film: Shearer, Lloyd; "GWTW: Superschool Saga of an Epic", Subtitle: Scarlett O'Hara and Rhett Butler Still Pull 'Em Into the "Most Successful" Picture of All. Section 6, October 26, 1947, pp. 22-23, 53, 55-56.

Film: Schumach, Murray; "A Director Named 'Gadge'", Subtitle: That is the Nickname of Elia Kazan, a Fiery Man With a Long List of

	Broadway and Hollywood Hits. Section 6, November 9, 1947, pp. 18, 54-56.
Rhetoric:	Woolf, S. J.; "'Slow-Easy,' says a Speech Doctor", Subtitle: That is the Slogan Used by Dr. Greene, Who for Thirty Years Has Helped the Handicapped Toward Normal Speech. Section 6, November 16, 1947, pp. 20, 64-66.
Theatre:	Nichols, Lewis; "The Nine Cold Men of Broadway", Subtitle: They Are the Critics and There are Some Who Hold Them in Contempt for Dissenting Opinions. Section 6, November 18, 1947, pp. 17, 49-52.
Theatre:	Geddes, Norman Bel; "Design for a New Kind of Theatre", Subtitle: A Complete Revolution — Artistic, Economic, and Functional — Is Proposed for the Playhouse. Section 6, November 30, 1947, pp. 24-25, 56-57, 59.
Film:	Mason, James; "Mr. Mason Names Five 'Six Best Actresses'", Subtitle: Rating the Cinema Ladies, He Gives Good Reasons for His Choices — and for Omissions. Section 6, November 30, 1947, pp. 17, 53-54.
Film: Radio:	Samuels, Gertrude; "Too Much Murder — Or Not Enough?", Subtitle: Movies, Radio and Comic Books Raise an Issue concerning the Mind of the Child. Section 6, November 30, 1947, pp. 15, 34-35, 37.
Film:	Nugent, Frank S.; "Writer or Director — Who Makes the Movies", Section 6, December 21, 1947, pp. 16-19.

Year 1948

Magazine: Lewis, R. C.; "Inquiry Into College Humor", Subtitle: Time Doesn't Change the Campus Magazine... The Old Jokes Still Do Valiant Service, the Familiar Parodies Reappear. Section 6, January 4, 1948, pp. 10-11, 18.

Film: Campbell, Kenneth; "And Now It's 'The Cocteau Touch'", Subtitle: The French Producer and Author Puts His Cachet on Movies That Dramatically Mix Factored Dreams. Section 6, January 11, 1948, pp. 18, 45.

Radio: Nichols, Lewis; "Lament for the Age of Clowns", Subtitle: The Great Conditions of Yesteryear Were to Be Seen As Well as Heard — And Then Came Radio. Section 6, February 1, 1948, pp. 12-13.

Film: _____; "Mister Roberts", Section 6, February 8, 1948, pp. 12-13.

Communication: _____; "People Who Read and Write", Section 6, February 8, 1948, p. 8.

Film: Boutillier, Peggy Le; "The Pearl", Section 6, February 15, 1948, pp. 34-35.

Film: _____; "Bergman as Joan", Section 6, February 26, 1948, pp. 12-13.

Film: _____; "Epic of Europe's Lost Children", Section 6, March 14, 1948, pp. 22-23.

Theatre:	Baxter, Beverly; "Broadway Hits May Be Piccadilly Flops", Subtitle: And Vice-Versa, of Course — Here a British Playwright Gives an Accounting for Tastes. Section 6, March 28, 1948, pp. 18-19, 46-47.
Books:	_____; "On Russian Books", Subtitle: A Discussion of the Content and Purpose of Children's Reading Matter in the U.S.S.R.. Section 6, April 4, 1948, p. 2.
Film:	Nichols, Lewis; "The Actor's Life — More Kudos Than Cash", Subtitle: There Must Be Easier Ways of Making a Living, But Our Thespians Keep Sacrificing for Art. Section 6, April 14, 1948, pp. 24, 57-59.
Theatre:	_____; "Europe's Theatre — In Four Capitals", Section 6, April 14, 1948, pp. 16-17.
Theatre:	Woolf, S. J.; "Henry Fonda Gives a Receipe for a Hit", Subtitle: Take Believable Characters in a Believable Setting, Take — Well, Take "Mister Roberts". Section 6, April 25, 1948, pp. 20, 56, 58-59.
Communication:	Nevins, Allan; "University City Within the City", Subtitle: The Columbia That Eisenhower Takes Over is a Metropolis of Learning — and of "Personality". Section 6, June 6, 1948, pp. 22-23, 48, 50-51, 53.
Film:	Wood, Thomas; "Bing Crosby, Mousetrap Builder", Subtitle: He Sponsors a Better Mouse Catcher, Though the World is Already Clamoring at his Door. Section 6, June 6, 1948, pp. 17, 66-67.

Rhetoric:	Gould, Jack; "Portrait of a Candidate, Down-East Style", Subtitle: Neil Bishop of Sagadahoe, Maine, Running for Governor, Pays Little Mind to the Usual Fixin's. Section 6, June 13, 1948, pp. 17, 61.
Rhetoric:	Meiklijohn, Alexander; "Everything Worth Saying Should Be Said", Subtitle: An Educator Says We Talk of Free Speech, But Hedge That Freedom With Too Many Reservations. Section 6, July 18, 1948, pp. 8, 32.
Film:	Brennan, Frederick H.; "Memo to the Moguls of Hollywood", Subtitle: An Insider Says Mass Production, Plus Too Many Brass Hats, Are Reasons for Industry's Plights. Section 6, July 25, 1948, pp. 14, 36-37.
Television:	Gould, Jack; "Family Life, 1948 A.T. (After Television)", Subtitle: Privacy Goes Out the Window When the Video Party Enters Through the Door. Section 6, August 1, 1948, pp. 12-13.
Radio:	Gould, Jack; "Jack Benny or Jackpot?", Subtitle: The FCC Has Decided That Radio Must Choose Between Entertainment and Give-Away Shows. Section 6, August 15, 1948, pp. 16, 39, 41.
Film:	_____; "Hoss Opera Rides Again", Section 6, September 18, 1948, pp. 24-25.
Rhetoric:	Davison, W. Phillips; "Why People Vote — And Why They Don't", Subtitle: On the One Hand It May Be Habit or a Candidate's Appeal — On the Other, Apathy, Laziness, or the Law. Section 6, September 19, 1948, pp. 10, 54-57.

Rhetoric:	Williamson, Samuel T.; "Dissertation on Speeches and Speakers", Subtitle: In This Long Season of Hortatory Oratory, It Behooves the Men Who Note Certain Ideals. Section 6, October 3, 1948, pp. 20, 30-31, 33.
Theatre:	Schumach, Murray; "A Texas Tornado Hits Broadway", Section 6, October 17, 1948, pp. 19, 59-60.
Rhetoric:	Schwarzschild, Leopold; "That American Disease, 'Electionitis'", Subtitle: It is an Affliction That Strikes Us Too Often, Lasts Too Long and Has Too Many Harmful Effects. Section 6, October 24, 1948, pp. 12-13.
Rhetoric:	Phillips, Cabell; "The Lengthening Shadow of Huey Long", Subtitle: His Brother is Governor, His Son is the New Senator — They Emulate Both Him and His Ideas. Section 6, November 7, 1948, pp. 14, 74-75, 79.
Film:	Lowry, Walker; "Movies With a Latin Accent", Subtitle: South of the Rio Grande The Screen Turns Up Some Surprises for North Americans — Including Some Non-Hollywood Merit. Section 6, November 14, 1948, pp. 19, 79.
Radio:	Gould, Jack; "How Comic Is Radio Comedy?", Subtitle: It is Suffering From, Among Other Things, Monotony, Under-Nourishment, and "Repeats". Section 6, November 21, 1948, pp. 22, 64, 66-68.
Press:	Schwartz, Henry; "'News' — In Moscow and New York", Subtitle: A Comparison of What the Papers Print and How They Handle It in the

Two Cities on the Same Day. Section 6, November 21, 1948, pp. 10, 31-32.

Press: Lieberman, Henry R.; "The Correspondent Versus the News in China", Subtitle: It Was Never More Important That The Facts Be Made Known — But They Are Elusive. Section 6, December 5, 1948, pp. 11, 69.

Press: Salisbury, Harrison E.; "Russia Tightens the Iron Curtain on Ideas", Subtitle: A Barrage of Censure Has Been Aimed at All, in Russia and Out, Who Follow Western Thought — Why?. Section 6, December 26, 1948, pp. 9, 30-31.

Year 1949

Communication: Myers, Robert Cobb; "Vital Part of the Poll Question", Subtitle: The Election Forecasts Have Had All the Attention But What About the Polls on the Issues of our Time?. Section 6, January 2, 1949, pp. 8, 31.

Film: _____; "The Quiet One", Section 6, January 2, 1949, pp. 24-25.

Film: Beal, Sam; "Plan for Hollywood — By Schary", Subtitle: MGM's un-Hollywoodlike "wonder boy" says Studio Must Meet Audience Demand, But With Steady Change, Not Wild Innovation. Section 6, February 6, 1949, pp. 16, 26-27.

Film: Goldwyn, Samuel; "Hollywood in the Television Age", Subtitle: Movies, which Cannot Lick Video, Must Join It, says Samuel Goldwyn, For

Years 1941-1950 — 103

Great Things. Section 6, February 13, 1949, pp. 15, 44, 47.

Film: Colton, Helen; "Top Dog in Hollywood", Subtitle: Canine Star Lassie "The Bark", is Putting the Bite On the Box Office Dollar In Grrr-eat Fashion. Section 6, February 27, 1949, pp. 20-21, 32, 34.

Communication: Gallup, George; "The Case for the Public Opinion Polls", Subtitle: A Leading Analyst Answers Critics Who Challenge Sampling Techniques, Evaluation, and Influence. Section 6, February 27, 1949, pp. 11, 55, 57.

Communication: Foote, Robert O.; "Integrity", Subtitle: To the Editor. Section 6, March 20, 1949, p. 4.

Radio: _____; "Japanese Hamlet", Section 6, March 20, 1949, p. 38.

Television: Daley, Arthur; "When the Ringside Becomes the Fireside", Subtitle: Does TV Help Sports or Will the Armchair Ruin the Box Office? Here Are the Major Viewpoints. Section 6, March 27, 1949, pp. 17, 58-59.

Film: Toledano, Edward; "Supercolossal, Arab Style", Subtitle: The Movie Makers of Cairo Know How the Customers Want Their Romance. Section 6, March 27, 1949, pp. 50, 53-54.

Advertising: _____; "London's Light's Return", Section 6, April 10, 1949, p. 17.

Film: Crowther, Bosley; "Youngest Generation of Movie Stars", Subtitle: A group of remarkable talented youngsters, cast in key dramatic roles, has commanded unusual attention in recent and forthcoming films. Here are some of the striplings who are making names for themselves. Section 6, April 17, 1949, pp. 18-19.

Film: Marashian, O. M.; "Arab Movies", Subtitle: To the Editor. Section 6, April 17, 1949, p. 2.

Film: Rashid, Albert; "Arab Films", Subtitle: To the Editor. Section 6, May 1, 1949, pp. 2, 4.

Newspaper: Waring, Houston; "The Big Job of the Small-Town Editor", Subtitle: He must make plain to Main Street the meaning of problems and events in the far-off places. Section 6, May 15, 1949, pp. 7, 49-51.

Television: Gould, Jack; "What is Television Doing to Us?", Subtitle: A Survey of the Various Surveys Dealing With the Effects of the New Medium on Family Life. Section 6, June 12, 1949, pp. 7, 24, 26-28.

Television: O'Shea, Ruth; "Colossal", Subtitle: To the Editor. Section 6, July 3, 1949, p. 2.

Press: Leviero, Anthony; "Press and President: No Holds Barred", Subtitle: The White House Weekly Conference is an Exercise in Democracy As Well As a Prime Source of News. Section 6, August 21, 1949, pp. 10, 51-52.

Press: Powell, Theodore; "Press and President", Subtitle: To the Editor. Section 6, September 4, 1949, p. 2.

Film: _____; "World War II on the Screen", Section 6, September 11, 1949, pp. 24-25.

Radio:	Kantor, Ken; "Uncle Come-Come", Subtitle: Joe Kirakawa teaches English by Radio to Japan's Millions. Section 6, September 25, 1949, pp. 70-79.
Film:	Copeland, Aaron; "Tip to Movie Goers: Take off Ear-Muffs", Subtitle: There's Music on the Soundtract, Too, and You're Missing Too Much Of It, A Film Composer Advises. Section 6, November 6, 1949, pp. 28-32.
Film:	_____; "The Bicycle Thief", Section 6, December 4, 1949, pp. 24-25.
Television:	Doty, Roy; "Vision and Television", Subtitle: Here Are Six Rules For Visual Video Comfort, as Laid Down by the American Optometric Association. Section 6, December 11, 1949, p. 20.
Film:	_____; "Bringing Down a Temple", Section 6, December 11, 1949, p. 62.
Film:	_____; "Bergmen's Stombili", Section 6, December 25, 1949, pp. 14-15.
Film:	_____; "Hollywood Technique", Subtitle: To the Editor. Section 6, December 25, 1949, p. 2.

Year 1950

Film:	Freeman, Don (artist); "Hollywood and Vine", Subtitle: The Thinking, Politics, mores and folkways of a world have changed greatly in a

half century and Hollywood has been a heavy contributor to the process. But at one famous crossroad, Hollywood and Vine, nothing has changed but the styles. Here is an artist's conception of the spot where above all others, clothes mark the man. Section 6, January 1, 1950, p. 11.

Television: Whiteside, Thomas; "An Old Vic for New York", Subtitle: Maurice Evans, in the role actor-Manager, seeks a loyal following here for city center. Section 6, January 1, 1950, pp. 10, 25.

Film: Brut, Harvey; "Give the Public What I Like", Subtitle: So says Britain's Carol Rud whose recent hits prove critics and moviegoers agree with him. Section 6, January 15, 1950, pp. 18, 19.

Books: Holbrook, Stewart; "Lament for the Lost Art of Lying", Section 6, February 5, 1950, pp. 18, 51, 52, 53, 54.

Radio: Musgrave, Francis and Watkins, Harold; "The BCC Calling", Subtitle: The Voice of Britain Has a Military Accent. Section 1, February 19, 1950,

Film: _____; "Hollywood Shoots For the Moon", Section 6, February 19, 1950, pp. 47, 48.

Television: Barclay, Dorothy; "Comic Books and Television", Section 6, March 5, 1950, p. 43.

Newspaper: Bracker, Milton; "Peron's Challenge to Free Press", Subtitle: Argentina's Dictator Controls Most Newspapers but La Prensa and La Nacion

Years 1941-1950 — 107

	Still Resist Him. Section 6, March 5, 1950, pp. 14, 41, 42, 43.
Newspaper:	Moses, Robert; "Broadside Against Billboards", Section 6, March 5, 1950, p. 14.
Newspaper:	Pearson, Hayin S.; "From Our Country Correspondent", Subtitle: Sending Problem Stirs Up the Selectmen, but All is Peaceful Now. L. Adams says He Saw Black Panthers Tracks. Section 6, March 12, 1950, p. 22.
Film:	_____; "Fred Astaire and ...", Subtitle: Hollywood's Nimble Footed Star Adds Two More to His Growing List of Movie Dancing Partners. Section 6, March 12, 1950, pp. 40, 41.
Film:	_____; "Personalities", Section 6, March 12, 1950, pp. 32, 33.
Film:	Goldwyn, Samuel; "Television's Challenges to the Movies", Subtitle: It Offers Serious Competition Mr. Goldwyn says, and Hollywood Must Meet the Problem Promptly. Section 6, March 26, 1950, pp. 17, 40, 42, 44.
Television:	Markel, Lester; "The Great Need — An Informed Opinion", Subtitle: We Have All the Equipment At Hand For Guidance and Leadership, but We Must Put It To Use Now. Section 6, April 9, 1950, pp. 7, 48.
Film:	Schary, Dore; "Exploring the Hollywood Myth", Subtitle: A Realistic Study of the Movie Capital Shows It Is By No Means a Typical Community, Yet it is Far From the Popular Stereotype. Section 6, April 9, 1950, pp. 14, 40, 41.

Television:	Baldwin, Hanson W.; "At Okinawa", Section 6, April 16, 1950, pp. 6, 8.
Film:	_____; "Roles Across the Sea", Section 6, April 16, 1950, p. 20.
Film:	Barclay, Dorothy; "A Boy's Life Drama", Section 6, April 23, 1950, p. 48.
Film:	_____; "Rebirth of a Star", Section 6, April 23, 1950, pp. 26, 27.
Television:	Barber, Red; "The Turmoil Behind the Baseball Telecast", Subtitle: He is sports director of C-B-S radio and T.V. Red Barber, in the midst of it, finds that he is not the free man that he was with only a "mike". Section 6, April 30, 1950, p. 58.
Television:	Gould, Jack; "T. V. Daddy and Video Mama: A Dirge", Subtitle: What Hopalong and the rest do to children is nothing to what they are doing to parents. Section 6, May 14, 1950, pp. 20, 56.
Film:	Lauterbach, Richard E.; "The Ways of Chaplin's Appeal", Subtitle: Just as he did 25 years ago, the incomparable little tramp still mirrors the trials, tribulations, pathos, and comedy of mankind. Section 6, May 21, 1950, pp. 24, 25.
Film:	_____; "Of Men and Wheel Chairs", Section 6, May 28, 1950, pp. 44, 45.
Film:	Laurette, Talor; "Dream's In Glass", Section 6, June 4, 1950, pp. 58, 59.
Newspaper:	Schwartz, Harry; "Russia Has a Paper Curtain Too", Subtitle: Her Newspaper and Magazines are Notable for What They Do Not Tell About

	Conditions. Section 6, June 4, 1950, pp. 17, 54, 55, 56, 57.
Theatre:	Franklin, Rebecca; "The Newest Theatre is the Oldest", Section 6, June 11, 1950, pp. 22, 23, 57, 58.
Rhetoric:	Carter, Hodding; "Hushpuppies, Stew — And Oratory", Subtitle: Southern Politicians Must Be Showmen Too, but Behind Their Act is Deadly Seriousness. June 18, 1950, pp. 12, 13, 46, 47.
Radio:	Rosenthal, A. M.; "Antenna Most of Babel", Subtitle: The United Nations News Broadcast Service Talks in Twenty-Seven Languages, Twenty-Four Hours of Day. Section 6, July 23, 1950, p. 14.
Film:	Brady, Thomas F.; "Hollywood Goes More Thataway", Section 6, August 20, 1950, pp. 24, 25.
Film:	_____; "Maugham's Trio", Section 6, September 24, 1950, pp. 76, 77.
Film:	Cullman, Marguerite W.; "Double-Feature Movie and Moonlight", Subtitle: A great new force, the movie drive-in alters some of America's habits and the landscape. Section 6, October 1, 1950, pp. 22, 68, 69, 72.
Film:	_____; "American Victoria", Section 6, October 15, 1950, pp. 58, 59.
Film:	Hitchcock, Alfred; "Core of the Movies — The Chase", Subtitle: Physical or Psychological, It is the Substance of the Drama from "Hamlet" to

	boy-pursues-girl, says Mr. Hitchcock. Section 6, October 29, 1950, pp. 22, 44, 45, 46.
Film:	Crowther, Bosley; "A Movies on B Budget", Subtitle: A New Hollywood Genius Stanley Kramer, Combines Films of High Artistic Content with Low Financing. Section 6, November 12, 1950, pp. 24, 25.
Advertising:	Moses, Robert; "A Broadside Against Billboards", Subtitle: Mr. Moses Argues For Strict Regulation of Outside Advertising to Protect Scenery. Section 6, November 12, 1950, pp. 15, 60, 62, 63.
Television:	Kalb, Bernard; "Toreros On Television", Subtitle: Mexico's New Video is a Gift to Bull Fight Fans. Section 6, November 19, 1950, pp. 76, 78.
Film:	_____; "Seven Days To Noon", Section 6, December 3, 1950, pp. 28, 29.
Television:	Herrmann, Helen Markel; "Folk Humorist From Brooklyn", Section 6, December 17, 1950, pp. 14, 26, 28, 80.
Television:	Pepis, Betty; "Improving the View", Section 6, December 31, 1950, pp. 18, 19.
Advertising:	Sullivan, Frank; "Why Not A Spinach Week, Too?", Subtitle: You May Not Know It but This Year Had 122 Weeks Devoted to Extolling Nearly Everything From Scallions to Brotherly Love. Section 6, December 31, 1950, pp. 12, 26.

Year 1951

Television: _____; "British Views", Section 6, January 14, 1951, p. 12.

Television: Taylor, Telford; "Finding A Place For Education on TV", Subtitle: The Use of Tax Money and Private is Urged to Finance Non-Commercial Channels. Section 6, January 28, 1951, pp. 9, 14, 15.

Television: Reisner, Konrad; "Letters", Subtitle: Educational TV Telford Taylor's Tending a Place for Education on TV. Section 6, February 18, 1951, p. 4.

Film: Salisbury, Harrison E.; "What They Read and Saw in Moscow", Subtitle: Best Sellers and Hit Plays Reveal That Home Problems are Close to the Russians Hearts. Section 6, February 18, 1951, p. 20.

Television: Millstein, Gilbert; "Bringing Things To A Berle", Subtitle: Uncle Miltie Discusses the Art of Being Funny. Section 6, April 8, 1951, pp. 17, 79.

Film: _____; "The Medium of Film", Subtitle: The photographs on these pages are from The Medium, Gian-Carlo Menotti's English language opera converted into a motion picture soon to be released. Filmed in Italy under the diretion of the composer librettist, it has been expanded to include several exterior shots, notably a carnival sequence, to which Menotti wrote twenty minutes of new music. Again the 1947 stage success control to Marie Powers is starred and

Leo Coleman plays the mute. Section 6, April 8, 1951, pp. 60, 61.

Television: Taylor, Telford; "The Issue Is Not, But Fair Play", Subtitle: Television is only the medium; the need is for higher standards in Congressional hearings. Section 6, April 15, 1951, pp. 12, 67, 68.

Television: Churchill, Allen; "Close-up of the Undizzy Mr. Dean", Subtitle: As a telecaster, he pitches the language as spectacularly as he pitched baseball. Section 6, April 22, 1951, pp. 15, 54.

Radio: Feldman, Sidney; "Mars Calling", Subtitle: America's radio hams are closely linked with the army and air force. Section 6, April 22, 1951, pp. 44, 45.

Television: Katz, Alvin; "TV Covered Walls", Subtitle: College courses, it is announced in the press, are to be conducted on television and the idea offers some interesting possibilities. Here are a number of such developments, as conceived by the artist. Section 6, April 29, 1951, p. 20.

Television: Gould, Jack; "What TV Is — And What it Might Be", Subtitle: Programs lack originality and variety, but news and education offer cues for the future. Section 6, June 10, 1951, pp. 18, 22, 23, 24.

Television: Rudish, Leslie; "Letters", Subtitle: Critics. Section 6, June 24, 1951, p. 6.

Film: _____; "A Streetcar Named Desire", Section 6, July 22, 1951, pp. 34, 35.

Years 1951-1960 — 113

Film: _____; "Drieser's Tragedy", Section 6, July 29, 1951, p. 35.

Communication: Webster, Margaret; "Why Shakespeare Goes Right On", Subtitle: A producer appraises the premier playwright of Broadway, the road movies, radio, and television. Section 6, August 12, 1951, pp. 10, 24, 26.

Newspaper: _____; "Moscow Parable: The Human Octopus", Subtitle: A Story of communist favoritism and deceit translated from a Russian youth publication. Section 6, August 12, 1951, p. 17.

Film: _____; "India's Magic In The River", Subtitle: The River, filmed in color along a branch of the Ganges, will bring to the New York screen a twofold picture of life in India. Director Jean Renoir has set Rumer Godden's drama of love and a group of growing British children against a documentary background which captures the haunting and majestic mood of India's sacred stream. Memorably photographed the emphasis of the United Artists Release is on river people and Hindu ways unchanged for centuries. Section 6, August 19, 1951, p. 25.

Newspaper: Nevins, Allan; "1851-1951: Panorama of New York's Press", Subtitle: The development of the metropolitan newspaper has mirrored the growth and change of America. Section 6, September 16, 1951, pp. 14, 15, 28, 30, 32.

Film: _____; "An American in Paris", Section 6, September 16, 1951, pp. 70, 71.

Television:	Peck, Ira; "Quiz Shows Are No Clue to the I.Q.", Subtitle: Extroverts hit the jackpot with audiences which crave entertainment, not education. Section 6, October 7, 1951, pp. 22, 23.
Television:	_____; "At Democracy's Grassroots", Subtitle: Photographs by Sam Talk. Section 6, October 7, 1951, p. 25.
Television:	_____; "People in the News", Subtitle: Photographs. Section 6, November 11, 1951, pp. 18, 19.
Television:	Barclay, Dorothy; "Parent and Child", Subtitle: Teenagers Go Their Accustomed Way. Section 6, November 18, 1951, p. 52.
Radio:	Gander, L. Marsiand; "Britain's Highbrow Third", Subtitle: The BBC is proud of this radio experiment in cultural expression after catering five years to the tastes of an intelligent minority. Section 6, December 9, 1951, pp. 22, 78.
Radio:	Hewson, E. Wendell; "Third Program", Subtitle: Marsiand Gander's article Britain's Highbrow Third and Lowell Institute's new FM station WGBH. Section 6, December 23, 1951, p. 2.
Television:	Knott, Seymour H.; "Letters to the Editor", Subtitle: Urges non-commercial cultural network under government control. Section 6, December 30, 1951, p. 4.

Year 1952

Theatre: Funke, Lewis; "First-Night Flutters", Section 6, January 6, 1952, p. 17.

Television: Javits, Jacob K.; "Case For Televising Congress", Section 6, January 13, 1952, pp. 12, 13.

Rhetoric: Rosenthal, A. M.; "The Bear That Talks in Proverbs", Subtitle: (Russia). Section 6, January 27, 1952, p. 14.

Television: Adler, Barbara S.; "'Unexpendables' of Video", Section 6, February 3, 1952, p. 20.

Radio: _____; "First Lady of the Voice of America", Section 6, February 3, 1952, p. 14.

Film: _____; "Exciting Voyage of African Queen", Section 6, February 10, 1952, pp. 20, 21.

Film: Pryor, Thomas M.; "How Mr. Chaplin Makes a Movie", Section 6, February 17, 1952, pp. 18, 19, 22.

Television: Cherne, Leo M.; "Biggest Question on TV Debates", Section 6, March 2, 1952, pp. 14, 35, 36.

Television: Gould, Jack; "TV at the Crossroads: A Survey", Subtitle: Here is a report on the good and bad of TV's 6 years and a look to the future. Section 6, March 9, 1952, pp. 12, 13, 49, 50.

Film: Crowther, Bosley; "Hollywood Accents the Downbeat", Section 6, March 16, 1952, pp. 22, 38.

Theatre: Millstein, Gilbert; "The Ratiocinating Mr. Burrows", Section 6, March 16, 1952, pp. 20, 33.

Rhetoric: Woodward, A. C.; "A Spade Is a Spade Is a Maybe", Section 6, March 16, 1952, pp. 13, 54.

Music: Gumpert, Martin; "Toscanini's Secret: Keep Growing", Section 6, March 23, 1952, pp. 12, 19.

Film: Laughton, Charles; "How Mr. Laughton Became the Devil", Section 6, March 23, 1952, p. 21.

Film: Watts, Stephen; "Guinness Is What Guinness Acts", Section 6, April 6, 1952, pp. 18, 48.

Theatre: Tyman, Kenneth; "Why London Likes Our Musicals", Section 6, April 13, 1952, pp. 18, 19.

Newspaper: Davis, Kenneth S.; "Wit and Wisdom By Will White", Section 6, April 20, 1952, p. 13.

Film: Gilroy, Harry; "Hollywood Can't Change Shirley Booth", Section 6, April 27, 1952, pp. 15, 24.

Theatre: Louchheim, Aline B.; "Director Having A Wonderful Time", Subtitle: (Josh Logan). Section 6, June 15, 1952, pp. 22, 38.

Books: White, Theodore H.; "Victor Huga Again Is a Storm Center", Section 6, June 22, 1952, pp. 10, 26.

Film:	_____; "Hollywood on the Remake", Section 6, July 20, 1952, pp. 22, 23.
Theatre:	Millstein, Gilbert; "Summer Theatre vs. Broadway", Section 6, August 3, 1952, pp. 20, 25.
Music:	Newman, Ernest; "An English AND Universal Music", Section 6, August 12, 1952, pp. 20, 28.
Film:	Crowther, Bosley; "The Ten Best of Forty Years", Section 6, August 17, 1952, pp. 22, 23.
Books:	Russell, Bertrand; "The Faultless Max At 80", Subtitle: (Max Beerbohm). Section 6, August 24, 1952, pp. 18, 41.
Newspaper:	Monroe, Elizabeth; "Behind the Headlines on the Middle East", Subtitle: There are basic factors of poverty, pride and power shifts in that region's current unrest. Section 6, September 14, 1952, pp. 9, 54, 56.
Rhetoric:	Hershfield, Harry; "The Ad Lib — Quip That Stings", Section 6, September 21, 1952, pp. 17, 57.
Books:	Schmidt, Dana Adams; "Israel Uses the Bible as a Diving Rod", Section 6, September 21, 1952, pp. 14, 26.
Rhetoric:	Smith, T. V.; "The Serious Problem of Campaign Humor", Section 6, September 28, 1952, pp. 11, 51.

Theatre:	_____; "Curtain Going Up", Subtitle: (Photos). Section 6, September 28, 1952, pp. 18, 19.
Film:	Millstein, Gilbert; "Bette Davis Turns From Buskin to Bumps", Section 6, October 19, 1952, pp. 22, 73.
Music:	Crozier, Eric; "He Puts England on the Opera Map", Subtitle: (Benjamin Britten). Section 6, October 26, 1952, pp. 20, 44.
Film:	Samuels, Gertrude; "The Director — Hollywood's Leading Man", Section 6, October 26, 1952, pp. 22, 23.
Television:	Bendiner, Robert; "How Much Has TV Changed Campaigning?", Section 6, November 2, 1952, pp. 13, 70.
Music:	_____; "Overture To The Opera", Section 6, November 9, 1952, pp. 12, 13.
Television:	_____; "The Show Behind the Television Show", Section 6, November 23, 1952, pp. 24, 25.
Theatre:	Clurman, Harold; "Actors in Style — And Style in Actors", Section 6, December 7, 1952, pp. 26, 27, 36.
Film:	Tyman, Kenneth; "Claire Bloom in the Limelight", Section 6, December 14, 1952, pp. 17, 44.
Film:	Crowther, Bosley; "McBoing Boing, Magoo and Bosustow", Subtitle: (Animated Film Cartoons). Section 6, December 21, 1952, pp. 14, 15, 23.

Year 1953

Theatre: _____; "Broadway Preview — 1953", Section 6, December 28, 1952, pp. 10, 11.

Television: Gilroy, Harry; "A Peep At Mr. Peepers — and Wally Cox", Subtitle: The shy teacher and the new TV star are deceptively alike — but is a $1,500-a week quality that's different. Section 6, January 11, 1953, p. 14.

Newspaper: Salisbury, Harrison E.; "Man, Dig That Stilyag", Subtitle: With reet pleat and drape shape he may be real George, but he's a square to the Soviet press. Section 6, January 11, 1953, p. 18.

Press: Sulzberger, Arthur Hays; "Have We The Coverage to Be Free?", Subtitle: A plea that we not allow fear of totalitarianism from the left or from the right, so stifle our freedom of expression. Section 6, February 15, 1953, pp. 12, 45, 46.

Television: Millstein, Gilbert; "The Four Red Buttons and How They Grow", Subtitle: Out of club dates, the Catskills and Burlesque come television Rocky, Maggy, Reeglefarvers, and the Kuphe Red. Section 6, February 22, 1953, pp. 14, 24.

Television: Gould, Jack; "Why Millions Love Lucy", Subtitle: In the comical trials of Lucy and Ricky Riccardo TV audiences recognize the exasperations and warmth of their own lives. Section 6, March 1, 1953, p. 16.

120 — *Mass Media: Marconi to MTV*

Press: _____; "Have We The Courage To Be Free?", Subtitle: Here are reactions to a statement concerning our basic liberties. Section 6, March 1, 1953, p. 34.

Television: Bendiner, Robert; "TV Moved Into the Classroom", Subtitle: Fewer and better teachers could revolutionize education experts argue, although others costs are formidable. Section 6, March 8, 1953, pp. 9, 49, 52.

Television:
Radio:
Music: Taubman, Howard; "Why More and More Like Opera", Subtitle: Because, this critic says, it is an expression of heart to heart emotions as Americans — with the help of radio and TV — are finding out. Section 6, March 8, 1953, pp. 18, 61, 62.

Television: Riechenthal, Gene; "Letters", Section 6, March 22, 1953, p. 6.

Television: Barclay, Dorothy; "Art for the Family — Via Television", Section 6, April 12, 1953, p. 52.

Theatre: Martin, John; "The Dancer As An Artist", Subtitle: Jose Limon, who returns to Broadway this week, has brought new range to ballet. Section 6, April 12, 1953, pp. 19, 34, 35.

Theatre: Ward, Barbara; "The Spell He Casts Is the Spell of Life", Subtitle: Shakespeare's hold on people everywhere has the power of reality itself. Section 6, April 19, 1953, pp. 14, 15, 39, 42, 46.

Film:	_____; "Paris Ballet On the Movies", Section 6, April 19, 1953, p. 30.
Press:	Cole, Malvine; "Goodbye, Central!", Subtitle: But in Jamaica, it, the dial tone, can hardly expect to replace the irreplaceable Mrs. Perry. Section 6, April 26, 1953, pp. 63, 64.
Press:	Commanger, Henry Steele; "A Fighting Printer — And a Free Press", Section 6, April 26, 1953, pp. 13, 63, 64, 65, 67.
Television:	Mitgang, Herbert; "TV (The Business) Lexicon", Section 6, April 26, 1953, p. 49.
Television:	Gould, Jack; "A Primer of TV Comics", Subtitle: A Critic at considerable risk, compiles a highly personal appraisal of some of video's many comedy stars. Section 6, May 3, 1953, pp. 12, 37, 39, 42, 44.
Press:	Sulzberger, C. L.; "From a Foreign Correspondent's Notebook", Subtitle: An overseas reporter who has covered most of the big events since the war records some little ones behind the headlines. Section 6, May 10, 1953, pp. 14, 44, 45, 46, 48.
Broadcasting:	Leverett, Norman; "Letters", Subtitle: Royal Broadcast. Section 6, June 7, 1953, p. 6.
Television:	Pepis, Betty; "TV Takes Cover", Section 6, June 7, 1953, pp. 52, 53.
Books:	Samuels, Gertrude; "Light in Darkness", Subtitle: Recorded books have opened new and triumphant vistas for the blind. Section 6, June 7, 1953, pp. 45, 46.

Film: Crowther, Bosley; "Picture of Hollywood in the Depths", Subtitle: The depths are three-dimensional and the movie industry is going through an anxious period of floundering in them. Section 6, June 14, 1953, pp. 17, 64, 66.

Film: Trumbull, Robert; "Movies Are Booming — In Bombay", Subtitle: And India's stars, not Hollywood's are drawing the largest pay and audiences in the world. Section 6, July 15, 1953, pp. 14, 15, 17.

Television: Bracker, Milton; "No Question About Quiz Shows", Subtitle: Their smash popularity on TV attests to our unquestionable thirst for the knowledge that we already know all the answers. Section 6, July 26, 1953, pp. 16, 17, 39.

Film: Addams, Charles; "Movie Monster Rally", Section 6, August 9, 1953, pp. 16, 17.

Television: Gould, Jack; "Europe's TV Picture — And Ours", Subtitle: Our programs stand out in pace and diversity, this critic finds. The contrast abroad is quality and intellectual stimulus. Section 6, August 23, 1953, pp. 22, 23, 52, 53.

Film: Jamison, Barbara Berch; "From Here to Maturity", Subtitle: Burt Lancaster has completed the long haul from punk kid to finished actor — and learned a lot along the way. Section 6, August 23, 1953, pp. 20, 31.

Television: _____; "TV Goes to War", Subtitle: The Military tries a new technique for checking the front behind the lines. Section 6, August 23, 1953, p. 29.

Public Relations:	Childs, Marquis W.; "Public Relations Along the Potomac", Subtitle: A businessman administration takes on the unfamiliar responsibility of keeping the press and the voters adequately informed. Section 6, August 30, 1953, pp. 12, 29, 31.
Theatre:	Peck, Seymour; "Theatre Preview — Beautiful Season?", Section 6, August 30, 1953, pp. 22, 23.
Public Relations:	Klein, Allen; "Letters", Subtitle: "Good Performance". Section 6, September 6, 1953, p. 4.
Theatre:	_____; "The Confidential Clerk", Section 6, September 6, 1953, pp. 36, 37.
Film:	Jamison, Barbara Berch; "Of Mouse and Man, Mickey Reaches Twenty-Five", Subtitle: Time has shown his step, but Walt Disney's remarkable rodent has come smiling through depressin, H bombs and A-bombs. Section 6, September 13, 1953, pp. 26, 27.
Theatre:	Millstein, Gilbert; "First of the Red Hot Mamas", Subtitle: After fifty years in show biz, Sophie Tucker has taken on the aspect of a national institution for a great many admirers. Section 5, September 27, 1953, p. 19.
Film:	Peck, Seymour; "Movie Scenarios: The Bible", Section 6, October 11, 1953, pp. 32, 33.
Broadcasting:	Millstein, Gilbert; "He Makes Crime Gay", Section 6, October 18, 1953, pp. 14, 15.

Broadcasting: Berger, Meyer; "That Strange Hi-Fi Set", Subtitle: It is a machine and a society both tuned to a frantic pitch. Section 6, November 15, 1953, pp. 19, 54.

Television: Gould, Jack; "TV's Top Comediennes", Section 6, December 27, 1953, pp. 16, 17.

Year 1954

Television: Gould, Jack; "Television Tube Bites Television Critic", Subtitle: He finds television is no medium as seen from the repairman's side. Section 6, January 3, 1954, p. 14.

Film: Jamison, Barbara Berch; "And Now Super-Colossal Headaches", Subtitle: Hollywood today is beset by more perils than Pauline and yet, with enough aspirin, you can still make money. Section 6, January 10, 1954, pp. 20, 21, 47, 48.

Film: Bankhead, Tallulah; "Not 3-D, But No-T", Subtitle: No-T means no talking, Tallulah Bankhead explains, and she advised Hollywood to go back where it came from: the silents. Section 6, January 31, 1954, pp. 14, 27.

Television: Gould, Jack; "Television Takes to Color", Section 6, February 8, 1954, pp. 16, 17.

Television: _____; "TV's Eye is Everywhere", Section 6, February 14, 1954, pp. 50, 51.

Television: Barclay, Dorothy; "Making the Most of Television", Section 6, February 21, 1954, p. 34.

Years 1951-1960 — 125

Television:	Millstein, Gilbert; "TV's No. 1 Second Comedian", Subtitle: Art Carney is to Jackie Gleason what tonic is to gin and tonic. Section 6, April 18, 1954, p. 19.
Television:	Gould, Jack; "TV Techniques on the Political Stage", Subtitle: A critic urges that public figures be seen as God rather than TV made them. Section 6, April 25, 1954, pp. 12, 42, 44.
Newspaper:	Reynolds, William; "A Line of Type that Revolutionized Printing", Subtitle: A young German immigrant named Mergenthaler, born a century ago this week, invented a mechanical typecaster and thus brought Gutenberg and Co. up to date. Section 6, May 9, 1954, p. 26.
Television:	Cotler, Gordon; "That Strange TV Studio Audience", Subtitle: Eager multitudes — of all ages and mostly feminine — vie for a real life glimpse of their electronic idols. Section 6, May 16, 1954, pp. 19, 39.
Film:	Jamison, Barbara Berch; "If At First You Do Succeed", Subtitle: Make them, make them again — that is the course Hollywood follows with its box office hits of years gone by. Section 6, June 20, 1954, pp. 20, 21, 43.
Television:	Cherne, Leo; "What Should be Television?", Subtitle: The new McCarthy inquiry is blacked out, yet there is a strong case, an expert says, for televising such events. Section 6, August 22, 1954, pp. 7, 25, 27, 29, 30, 32.
Television:	_____; "Coming Attractions on TV", Section 6, August 29, 1954, pp. 20, 21.

Television:	Seldes, Gilbert; "A Clinical Analysis of TV", Subtitle: An observer offers a not wholly laudatory view of the medium. It has evolved faster than expected, with results both awesome and awful to behold. Section 6, November 28, 1954, pp. 13, 55, 59, 60.
Rhetoric:	Burns, James MacGregor; "Debate Over Collegiate Debates", Subtitle: The affirmative: They clarify both sides of controversial issues. They lead to dishonesty because students may argue against their own convictions. Section 6, December 5, 1954, pp. 12, 30.
Film:	Peck, Seymour; "New Role for Actors Directory", Section 6, December 5, 1954, pp. 28, 29.
Television:	Warren, Constance; "TV Can Solve Our Educational Problem", Subtitle: The pressure of large enrollments on our colleges is increasing steadily; one answer, says an observer, may be televised higher learning. Section 6, December 19, 1954, pp. 16, 20, 21, 23, 24.

Year 1955

Television:	Millstein, Gilbert; "Portrait of an M. A. L.", Subtitle: Master of ad Lib., he is Steve Allen, a man with a clutch of small talents that add up to high degree of comedy. Section 6, January 9, 1955, pp. 17, 67, 68.
Television:	Marx, Arthur; "Number One Master of Timing", Subtitle: That, by common consent, is

	Jack Benny. He gets his laughs by knowing exactly when to speak a line — or to say nothing at all. Section 6, February 13, 1955, p. 17.
Film:	_____; "Marty in Movies", Section 6, March 20, 1955, p. 36.
Radio:	Gould, Jack; "Radio Has a Future", Subtitle: Reports of its demise are exaggerated, says a critic, provided it exploits its opportunities. Section 6, April 17, 1955, pp. 17, 61, 62.
Theatre:	Peck, Seymour; "Of 'Guys and Dolls'", Section 6, April 17, 1955, pp. 28, 29.
Theatre:	_____; "'Damn Yankees'", Section 6, April 17, 1955, p. 67.
Film:	_____; "Of Guys and Dolls", Section 6, April 17, 1955, pp. 28, 29.
Theatre:	Atkinson, Brooks; "Ten Top Moments of Broadway's Season", Section 6, April 24, 1955, pp. 26, 27.
Newspapers:	Baker, Russell; "'My Dear Constituent...'", Subtitle: Congress is in the newspaper business, too, with members writing regular bulletins to sway voters. Section 6, May 1, 1955, pp. 14, 47.
Theatre:	Gelb, Arthur; "School for Stars", Section 6, May 1, 1955, pp. 78, 79.
Theatre:	Martin, John; "Upbeat for Modern Dance", Section 6, May 1, 1955, pp. 28, 29.
Television:	Peck, Seymour; "TV to L. A.: Plays for Sale", Section 6, May 15, 1955, pp. 26, 27.

Theatre:	_____; "'A Musical Seventh Heaven'", Section 6, May 15, 1955, p. 19.
Theatre:	_____; "'The Great Adventure'", Section 6, May 15, 1955, p. 25.
Film:	S.P.; "'Mister Roberts'", Section 6, May 22, 1955, pp. 66, 67.
Television:	Schumach, Murray; "Muni's Second Fling with Fame", Subtitle: From great renown on stage and screen in the thirties, he went into semi-retirement in the forties. Today, once more, his star shines bright on Broadway. Section 6, May 22, 1955, pp. 17, 78.
Theatre:	Bevan, Ian; "London's Shrine of Show Biz", Subtitle: Neither movies nor night clubs nor TV have dimmed the glitter of Vaudeville at the Palladium. Section 6, May 29, 1955, pp. 15, 47, 48.
Film:	_____; "Ferrer's 'Shrike'", Section 6, May 29, 1955, p. 50.
Film:	_____; "'Umber to D.'", Section 6, June 5, 1955, p. 31.
Theatre:	Peck, Seymour; "Summer Theater Takes to the Tents", Section 6, June 12, 1955, pp. 24, 25.
Film:	Pryor, Thomas M.; "Hollywood's Search for Stars", Subtitle: There is a new crisis in cinema with most of the screen's front-rank names in the middle age, the industry must find fresh young talent fast. Section 6, June 12, 1955, pp. 14, 15, 26.

Film:	Crowther, Bosley; "When Movies Were Very Young", Section 6, June 19, 1955, pp. 62, 63.
Theatre:	Millstein, Gilbert; "Upbeat For A Song-Writing Duo", Subtitle: Ross and Adler, Broadway's hottest young composers, are rallying - from the effects of fame-bronchiectasis and prosperity-induced depression. Section 6, June 19, 1955, pp. 20, 31, 31.
Film:	Kempe, Richard; "'Hollywood's Need'", Section 6, June 26, 1955, p. 4.
Film:	_____; "The Family 'Drives In'", Section 6, June 26, 1955, p. 16.
Oratory:	Egan, Leo; "Harriman Becomes 'The Guv'", Subtitle: Political success has changed him from a diffident to a folksy, speech-making — and ambitious — public figure. Section 6, July 3, 1955, pp. 12, 13, 27.
Film:	_____; "Bette As Bess", Section 6, July 3, 1955, p. 31.
Theatre:	_____; "Kidd On His Toes", Section 6, July 10, 1955, pp. 20, 21.
Film:	_____; "Life In '1984'", Section 6, July 10, 1955, pp. 44, 45.
Theatre:	_____; "Shakespeare By the Oliviers", Section 6, July 10, 1955, p. 16.
Theatre:	_____; "World Theatre Jamboree", Section 6, July 17, 1955, pp. 18, 19.

Theatre: _____; "Britain's Ritual Molds Her Theatre", Section 6, July 24, 1955, pp. 16, 17.

Theatre: Atkinson, Brooks; "An Enduring Drama of Man's endurance", Subtitle: First performed in a world at war, "The Skin of Our Teeth" has truths for today's world too. Section 6, August 7, 1955, pp. 26, 27.

Books: Duffus, R. L.; "Main Street Thirty-Five Years Later", Subtitle: The dingy Gopher Prairie (alis Sauk Centre, Minn.) of Sinclair Lewis and his heroine, Carol Kennicott, appears to a visitor a cleaner, greener and happier town today.. Section 6, August 7, 1955, pp. 24, 25, 62, 63.

Oratory: Smith, Merriam; "Evolution of Eisenhower As Speaker", Subtitle: His years in the White House have made the president a calm and confident orator. And the improvement in his speeches is his own doing, not "Madison Avenue's". Section 6, August 7, 1955, pp. 18, 66.

Film: _____; "Night of the Hunter", Section 6, August 7, 1955, p. 30.

Television: Millstein, Gilbert; "Its Creator Explains the Sixty-Four Thousand Dollar Appeal", Subtitle: A sense of reality, drama, audience identification, suspense, simplicity, and all that money go into the formula for a fabulously successful TV show. Section 6, August 21, 1955, p. 30.

Theatre: Tyman, Kenneth; "Edinburgh: 'Olympics' of the Arts", Subtitle: Attending the brilliant festival in that dear city, one wonders how culture blossoms there. Yet for three weeks a

	year it does — mightily. Section 6, August 21, 1955, pp. 26, 27, 33, 34.
Newspaper:	Durdin, Peggy; "One-Man Point Four Project", Subtitle: Here is the story of the publisher of the Philippine Free Press. His achievements offer a model in East-West cooperation. Section 6, August 28, 1955, pp. 14, 64, 67.
Theatre:	_____; "Enter a New Theatre Season", Section 6, August 28, 1955, pp. 28, 29.
Theatre:	_____; "Olivier As 'Titus'", Section 6, September 4, 1955, p. 20.
Theatre:	_____; "Diary of Anne Frank", Section 6, September 5, 1955, p. 41.
Books:	Kemler, Edgar; "The Bright Twilight of H. L. Mencken", Subtitle: The acerbic Baltimore writer and editor, 75 tomorrow, has made a comeback from his illness and finds once again that life can be enjoyed. Section 6, September 11, 1955, pp. 14, 44, 47, 49.
Television:	Levines, Harry; "Oh, The Pain of It!", Subtitle: The quiz show contestant must give the tax collector a piece of his prize. Section 6, September 11, 1955, p. 18.
Television:	_____; "Coming Attractions on TV", Section 6, September 11, 1955, pp. 28, 29.
Theatre:	_____; "Tiger At The Gates", Section 6, September 11, 1955, p. 20.
Television:	Giniger, Henry; "Bonjour Again, Maurice", Subtitle: On his return to this country, the

ineffable Chevalier will exercise his Gallic charm on two generations. Section 6, September 18, 1955, pp. 19, 74.

Film: _____; "Old Tales, New Movies", Section 6, September 25, 1955, pp. 28, 29.

Theatre: _____; "Mr. Smith Goes to Hollywood", Section 6, October 9, 1955, pp. 22, 23.

Theatre: _____; "No Time For Sergeants", Section 6, October 9, 1955, p. 38.

Film: Talese, Gay J.; "Then and Now", Subtitle: Once the symbol of wickedness and wile on the screen, Nita Naldi teaches "vamping" to a new generation. Section 6, October 16, 1955, p. 20.

Film: _____; "The Big Knife", Section 6, October 16, 1955, p. 25.

Theatre: _____; "New York: Stage For All The World", Section 6, October 30, 1955, pp. 28, 29.

Theatre: Millstein, Gilbert; "Unexceptionable Julie Harris", Section 6, November 6, 1955, pp. 14, 19, 20, 22.

Theatre: _____; "The Helen Hayes Theatre", Section 6, November 20, 1955, pp. 28, 29.

Theatre: Guthrie, Tyrone; "The World of Thorton Wilder", Subtitle: He is essentially a man of New England, writing about his own environment. But His plays are true to universal human experience. Section 6, November 27, 1955, pp. 26, 27, 64, 66, 67, 68.

Broadcasting:	_____; "U. N. On The Air", Section 6, November 27, 1955, p. 41.
Theatre:	Franklin, Rebecca; "What Future For Young Stars?", Subtitle: This season has seen some remarkable talented young people. Their chance for lasting success is measured against theatre history. Section 6, December 11, 1955, pp. 28, 29.
Theatre:	_____; "Theatre Boom On Broadway", Section 6, December 18, 1955, pp. 24, 25.
Television:	Lardner, John; "Sports on TV — A Critical Survey", Subtitle: On the field? Mr. Lardner tells why you can still take him out to the ball game. Section 6, December 25, 1955, pp. 10, 11, 27.
Film:	_____; "Picnic Goes To A Picnic", Section 6, December 25, 1955, p. 26.

Year 1956

Film:	Millstein, Gilbert; "Sir Danny Kids Knighthood", Section 6, January 1, 1956, pp. 20, 21.
Film:	Peck, Seymour; "Another Ride on a Carousel", Subtitle: With Oklahoma in 1943 Richard Rodgers and Oscar Hammerstein 2nd made over the American musical show. Their marvelously fresh, unconventional motions worked wonders again in 1945 with their second collaboration "Carousel". To many, Carousel was even finer

than Oklahoma for besides the lovely music and original lyrics and clever ballets that mark a Rogers and Hammerstein show, carousel has a highly unusual book. It was based on Lelion, the tragic comedy fantasy by Molnar which hardly seemed musical material to anybody. Carousel ran for more than two years on Broadway and now has been converted by Fox into a movie in the new cinemascope process. Here are scenes from the film, which opens next month at the Roxy. Section 6, January 8, 1956, pp. 68, 69.

Television: _____; "Re: U.K.-T.V.", Section 6, January 8, 1956, p. 27.

Film: _____; "Tamburlaine", Subtitle: Tyrone Guthrie, British Director whose bold staging of the Matchmaker and Six Characters in Search of an Author has greatly impressed New Yorkers, is now preparing a third cantry, Christopher Marlowe's Tamburlaine the Great. Section 6, January 8, 1956, p. 20.

Theatre: Millstein, Gilbert; "How To Produce A Play — Or How Not", Subtitle: All a man has to do is find script, theatre, money, stars, and director, line up theatre parties, keep losses down on the road — and get good notices. Section 6, January 16, 1956, pp. 26, 56, 58.

Film: _____; "Helen of Troy", Section 6, January 16, 1956, p. 22.

Theatre: _____; "Ponder Heart", Section 6, January 22, 1956, p. 44.

Television:	Millstein, Gilbert; "How To Relax The Como Way", Subtitle: A Golfing Man, the singer advises "walk slow, swing slow — and win". Section 6, January 30, 1956, pp. 19, 22.
Film:	_____; "Guinness And Friend", Section 6, January 30, 1956, p. 25.
Film:	Peck, Seymour; "Hits Then and Now?", Section 6, February 5, 1956, p. 22.
Television:	Cortesi, Arnaldo; "5,120,000 Lire Question", Section 6, February 12, 1956, p. 44.
Theatre:	_____; "Art (And Profits) Off-Broadway", Section 6, February 12, 1956, pp. 28, 29.
Theatre:	_____; "O'Neill's Journey", Section 6, February 20, 1956, p. 56.
Theatre:	_____; "The Magic Flute", Section 6, February 20, 1956, p. 39.
Theatre:	Peck, Seymour; "Sir Laurence Again Widens His Range", Section 6, February 26, 1956, pp. 14, 15, 37, 39.
Film:	_____; "Personalities", Section 6, February 26, 1956, p. 22.
Theatre:	Peck, Seymour; "A Musical Pygmalion", Section 6, March 4, 1956, pp. 28-29.
Photography:	Preston, Stuart; "Through Lautrec's Eyes", Section 6, March 18, 1956, pp. 28-29.
Theatre:	Peck, Seymour; "The Boom in Shakespeare", Section 6, March 25, 1956, pp. 28-29.

Television:	Gould, Jack; "Television Today — A Critic's Appraisal", Subtitle: Now in its ninth year, the arts' fabulous infant shows commendable progress in some fields, but is lagging badly in others. Here is a report card on the medium. Section 6, April 1, 1956, pp. 12-13, 36, 38.
Theatre:	Millstein, Gilbert; "Flowering of a 'Fair Lady'", Subtitle: In song and speech, Julie Andrews makes the transition from Shaw's "draggletailed guttersnipe" to a creature of passing radiance. Section 6, April 1, 1956, pp. 24, 47-49.
Magazine:	Fay, Gerald; "New Punch in 'Punch'", Subtitle: Under editor Malcolm Muggeridge, its humor has developed sharp claws. Section 6, April 29, 1956, pp. 26-27, 63-65.
Television:	Kenworthy, E. W.; "Campaign Special: TV or Train?", Subtitle: Will the five-minute spot doom the whistle spot? That remains to be seen. Both parties are concentrating on TV this year. Section 6, April 29, 1956, pp. 13, 30-36.
Theatre:	Peck, Seymour; "The Temple of 'The Method'", Subtitle: Many of tomorrow's stars — and quite a few of today's — are developing their talents through the remarkable teachings of the Actor's Studio. Section 6, May 6, 1956, pp. 26-27, 42-28.
Film:	Peck, Seymour; "Quest for 'Moby Dick'", Section 6, May 13, 1956, pp. 30-31.
Television:	Gould, Jack; "Television In 'Endsville'", Section 6, May 20, 1956, pp. 66-67.

Theatre:	Millstein, Gilbert; "The Greater Loesser", Subtitle: The composer-lyricist-author of "Most Happy Fella" gives musical comedy the once-over seriously. Section 6, May 20, 1956, pp. 20, 22.
Television: Advertising:	Schumach, Murray; "TV: Love That 'Soft Sell'", Subtitle: Low-pressure advertising with a touch of wit, is gaining rapidly in a world overrun by the loud, hard commercial. Section 6, May 27, 1956, pp. 26-27.
Film:	Peck, Seymour; "... Based on the Broadway Play ...", Section 6, June 3, 1956, pp. 26-27.
Communication:	Cianfarra, Jane; "News Via Tertulia", Subtitle: When things happen in Spain, a network of "clubs" in the cafes carries the word. Section 6, June 10, 1956, pp. 66-67.
Theatre:	Guthrie, Tyrone; "Shakespeare Comes to Stratford (Ont.)", Subtitle: Blessed with a spirited citizenry and a felicitous name, this small town set out to do Shakespeare in a big way. The result: a notable contribution to the theatre. Section 6, June 10, 1956, pp. 26-27, 42-47.
Theatre:	Millstein, Gilbert; "Summer Theatre — a 52-week Job", Subtitle: It takes a year of effort, fraught with risk, to transplant Broadway to the sticks for two months — as this Cape Cod operation shows. Section 6, June 24, 1956, pp. 16, 35-37.
Radio:	Millstein, Gilbert; "Helen Trent — Chapter 5,900", Subtitle: The queen of soap operas piles

up a record in longevity by broadcasting the news that a woman can find romance after age 35. Section 6, July 15, 1956, pp. 16-17.

Books:
Theatre: Weinstein, Marybeth; "Out of G.B.S. on His Centenary", Subtitle: The writings of George Bernard Shaw continue to outrage and delight millions. Here is a small treasury of his wit and ideas. Section 6, July 22, 1956, pp. 10-11.

Theatre: Lieberson, Goddard; "The Ten Musicals Most Worth Preserving", Subtitle: The musical comedy is here championed as an authentic American art. And the author goes on to nominate ten examples of the form as deserving of immortality. Section 6, August 5, 1956, pp. 20-21, 26, 29, 31-32.

Film: Hill, Gladwin; "Most Colossal of All", Subtitle: At 75, Cecil B. DeMille is completing the biggest film project of his — or any other's — career. Section 6, August 12, 1956, pp. 16, 18, 20.

Music: Samuels, Gertrude; "Visit With the Exile of Prades", Subtitle: Pablo Casals, cellist and political symbol, lives quietly 40 miles from his native Spain. Section 6, August 12, 1956, pp. 24, 40.

Books:
Television: Lefferts, Barney; "The Return of Frank Merriwell", Subtitle: Having conquered the Harvards, the bullies, and the toadies, that old pillar of rectitude from Yale and Fardale is all set to buck television. Section 6, August 19, 1956, pp. 23, 34.

Books:	Schwartz, Harry; "Poetry From Behind the Iron Curtain", Section 6, August 19, 1956, p. 58.
Television:	Peck, Seymour; "TV Specialities Coming Up", Section 6, September 2, 1956, pp. 26-27.
Theatre:	Maney, Richard; "Fabulous Six Months of a Fabulous Lady", Subtitle: The energy expended getting tickets for "My Fair Lady" may equal that involved in splitting the atom, which many consider a good deal less spectacular. Section 6, September 9, 1956, pp. 27, 30, 32, 34.
Theatre:	Peck, Seymour; "Curtains Going Up", Section 6, September 16, 1956, pp. 28-29.
Radio: Television:	Sarnoff, David; "Electronic Revolution, Present and Future", Subtitle: A pioneer in the nation's fastest-growing major industry tells of the immense progress to date, and predicts even greater things to come. Section 6, September 29, 1956, pp. 14, 36, 38, 42.
Film:	Peck, Seymour; "Hollywood's Search for New Faces", Section 6, October 7, 1956, pp. 28-29.
Theatre:	Peck, Seymour; "New Stars of the Old Vic", Section 6, October 14, 1956, pp. 28-29.
Theatre:	Krutch, Joseph Wood; "The Rediscovery of Eugene O'Neill", Subtitle: Three years after his death, his greatness has again won him the theatre's limelight. Section 6, October 21, 1956, pp. 32-33, 74-75.

Theatre:	Markel, Helen; "Visit With Breathless Ros Russell", Subtitle: About to portray "Auntie Mame", the actress obeys Mame's dictum: "Live, live, live". Section 6, October 28, 1956, pp. 17-20.
Theatre:	Peck, Seymour; "Broadway Goes Song-and-Dance", Section 6, November 4, 1956, pp. 28-29.
Theatre: Music:	Briggs, John; "Onstage: The Prima Donna", Section 6, November 11, 1956, pp. 16, 19-20.
Theatre:	Houghton, Norris; "Off-Broadway Challenges Broadway", Subtitle: With little money but large dreams, theatres far from Times Square work small miracles. Section 6, November 11, 1956, pp. 30-32, 34, 36.
Theatre:	Millstein, Gilbert; "Greener's Pastures", Subtitle: They're in "Shoestring '57" for the funny girl from Gateshood. Section 6, November 18, 1956, pp. 44, 47.
Theatre:	Peck, Seymour; "A Rockefeller Enters 'Show Biz'", Subtitle: There is little in his family background to mark John D. 3d as a man of the theatre. Here he explains how — and why — he became president of the new Lincoln Center. Section 6, November 18, 1956, pp. 15, 56-62.
Music:	Sheed, Wilfrid; "Les Jazz Fans Hot — and Cool — of Europe", Subtitle: The true Continental cat is more likely to be a brooder than a wide-eyed extrovert. He takes his jazz so seriously that even foot-tapping is frowned upon. Section 6, November 18, 1956, pp. 26, 75-78.

Years 1951-1960 — 141

Television:	_____; "TV World Picture", Section 6, November 18, 1956, p. 30.
Communication:	Guthrie, Tyrone; "Case for an 'Arts Council' Here", Subtitle: A noted director outlines the British system of state subsidy of the arts — and its potential value for America. Section 6, November 25, 1956, pp. 26, 42-49.
Music:	Sheed, Wilfrid; "No Paeans to Pedagogues", Subtitle: U. S. student songs stress sports and ivy; Europe's are heavy on nostalgia. None find anything to hail in studying. Section 6, November 25, 1956, pp. 70-71.
Film:	Carey, Alida L.; "Then and Now", Subtitle: Once the wonder boy of Hollywood, Preston Sturges is making movies again — in Paris. Section 6, December 2, 1956, pp. 94-96.
Television:	Millstein, Gilbert; "'Patterns' of a Television", Subtitle: Rod Serling, author of the play of that name and archetype of the species, is young, ardent, prolific, amenable and no intellectual. Section 6, December 2, 1956, pp. 24, 57-60.
Theatre:	Millstein, Gilbert; "The Long-Running Ed Begley", Section 6, December 9, 1956, pp. 77-78.
Radio:	Morris, John; "Britain's Case for 'Egghead' Radio", Subtitle: Daringly devoted to the best in the arts, the Third Program enters its second decade. Section 6, December 9, 1956, pp. 19-22.
Theatre:	Peck, Seymour; "The New Kazans and Logans", Section 6, December 9, 1956, pp. 26-27.

Theatre:
Film: Peck, Seymour; "Tyrone Guthrie's Three-Ring Circus", Subtitle: The British director has something doing every minute — in theatre, movies, opera. Section 6, December 23, 1956, pp. 16-17, 20.

Television: Gould, Jack; "For TV in 1957: A Viewer's Resolution", Subtitle: Being of that accursed breed denied the right to turn off sets at will, a TV critic takes it upon himself to outline what television should do next year. Section 6, December 30, 1956, p. 9.

Rhetoric: Ward, Barbara; "Western Slogans: A Reappraisal", Subtitle: Recent crises warn that we are living by empty formulas, says Miss Ward. The question is: Can they be recharged with meaning?. Section 6, December 30, 1956, pp. 8, 33-34.

Year 1957

Film: Derier, Caman; "Edge of the City", Section 6, January 20, 1957, p. 71.

Film: Peck, Seymour; "Mayerling Lives Again on TV", Section 6, January 27, 1957, p. 26.

Film: Crowther, Bosley; "Communique From Hollywood and Vine", Subtitle: Are movies an empire falling apart? A critic analyzes Hollywood dilemma. Section 6, February 3, 1957, pp. 24, 25, 26, 28, 30.

Film:	Pryor, Thomas M.; "Rise, Fall and Rise of Sinatra", Subtitle: Bobby-sox idol in the forties, has been in the early fifties, the voice is now more securely on top than ever — as The Actor. Section 6, February 10, 1957, pp. 17, 60, 61.
Television:	Devree, Charlotte; "150,000 etc. Question — The Quiz Mind", Subtitle: As TV rewards go up, here is an analysis of the sort of mental ability that pays off. Section 6, February 17, 1957, pp. 25, 62, 63.
Theatre:	Peck, Seymour; "New Dynasties Among Actors", Section 6, March 24, 1957, pp. 30, 31.
Film:	Lefferts, Barney; "Seventy-eight Miles Off Broadway", Section 6, April 7, 1957, pp. 30, 31.
Film:	_____; "Happy Road", Section 6, April 7, 1957, p. 37.
Theatre:	Peck, Seymour; "A Musical in the Making", Section 6, April 14, 1957, pp. 30, 31.
Rhetoric:	Davis, Kenneth S.; "Darrow: Man of a Thousand Battles", Subtitle: Independent of mind and rugged of character, the brilliant lawyer consistently challenged convention. This week the hundredth anniversary of his birth will be celebrated. Section 6, April 27, 1957, pp. 12, 64, 66, 67.
Film:	Walker, Stanley; "The Western Still Rides High", Subtitle: Despite reports that the stuff is buncombe, the gidayup industry flourishes on all fronts. Section 6, April 27, 1957, pp. 26-28.

Film:	Peck, Seymour; "Join Hollywood and See the World", Section 6, May 5, 1957, pp. 30, 31.
Film:	Nichols, Lewis; "Ed Wynn: Up-and-Coming Actor", Subtitle: Once triumphant as a comedian, the erstwhile perfect fool is, at 70, making a new career via TV and movie drama. Section 6, May 12, 1957, pp. 14, 28, 30.
Television:	Shanley, J. P.; "TV Turns to Mother Goose", Subtitle: In their hunt for material, networks are going to fairy tales, a form of entertainment whose appeal to children of all ages has been amply proved. Section 6, May 19, 1957, pp. 26, 62, 64.
Television:	Siepmann, Charles A.; "The Case for TV in Education", Subtitle: Experiments with teaching by television, says a proponent, indicate that electronics can not only help solve our school crisis but raise the level of education generally. Section 6, June 2, 1957, pp. 13, 42, 44, 47.
Press:	Herling, John; "World's Number One Quiz Program", Subtitle: It's the president's press conference, which gives him an idea of what's on people's minds and gives the people a chance to see and hear him thinking out loud. Section 6, June 9, 1957, pp. 11, 38, 40, 43.
Film:	_____; "Filming Pal Joey", Section 6, June 9, 1957, p. 58.
Theatre:	_____; "The Pajama Game", Section 6, August 4, 1957, pp. 40, 41.

Theatre:	Peck, Seymour; "Broadway's Prologue To a New Season", Section 6, August 25, 1957, pp. 28, 29.
Newspaper:	McIntyre, William A.; "War of the Sexes in Cartoonland", Subtitle: A favorite subject for the cartoons is the U.S. male, pictured as a second-class citizen in a matriarchy: an expert suggests that we enjoy him so because we recognize him. Section 6, September 1, 1957, pp. 18, 44.
Television:	Peck, Seymour; "Special Trend on Television", Section 6, September 15, 1957, pp. 24, 25.
Television:	Gould, Jack; "Free TV — or Pay — As You See", Subtitle: The liveliest controversy in Television today is whether the viewer should foot the bill. A TV critic sums up the arguments for and against. Section 6, October 6, 1957, pp. 11, 97, 98, 99.
Theatre:	Kaufman, George S.; "Musical Comedy — or Musical Serious?", Subtitle: Musicals used to be boy and girl, song and dance, humor and happy ending. But now you can not see the chorus boys through your tears. Where will it all end?. Section 6, November 3, 1957, p. 24.
Film:	_____; "Rising Star", Section 6, November 3, 1957, pp. 78, 79.
Television:	Serling, Rod; "TV in the Can vs. in the Flesh", Subtitle: A prize winning video writer states the case for live television, but does not rule out the possibility of the filmed show as an art form. Section 6, November 24, 1957, pp. 39, 52, 54, 56, 57.

Year 1958

Music: Guthrie, Tyrone; "The 'Grand Opera' Behind Grand Opera", Subtitle: A Met production requires an infinity of planning and contriving, of talent and technique. The results, however, can be something unique on the New York stage. Section 6, January 5, 1958, pp. 13, 24, 26, 28.

Music: Samuels, Gertrude; "Why They Rock and Roll — And Should They", Section 6, January 5, 1958, pp. 16-17, 19-20.

Theatre: Stang, Joanne; "My (New) Fair Lady", Section 6, January 5, 1958, p. 18.

Film: _____; "Dr. Sica's 'The Roof'", Section 6, January 5, 1958, p. 53.

Television: Talese, Gay; "Most Hidden Hidden Persuasion", Subtitle: Now TV faces the challenge of the subliminal, or phantom plug — painless, odorless, noiseless and definitely sneaky. Section 6, January 12, 1958, pp. 22, 29, 60.

Music: Taubman, Howard; "American Opera On the Upbeat", Subtitle: Still in its adolescence, it nevertheless gives promise of an early coming of age. Section 6, January 12, 1958, pp. 34, 36, 42.

Film: Plemmer, Charlotte and Dennis; "Extraordinary, 'Ordinary Guy'", Subtitle: William Holden has portrayed "averageness" into a million-dollar box-office draw. Where

Years 1951-1960 — 147

does the role stop and the man begin?. Section 6, January 19, 1958, pp. 57, 59-60.

Theatre: _____; "Sunrise at Campobello", Section 6, January 19, 1958, p. 42.

Theatre: _____; "Oh Captain", Section 6, January 26, 1958, p. 26.

Film: _____; "Up-and-Coming in Movies", Section 6, January 26, 1958, pp. 28-29.

Television: Millstein, Gilbert; "TV's Comics Went Thataway", Subtitle: Shot down by westerns, burned by overexposure and starved for material, the comedian who stars on a weekly show is now all but extinct. Section 6, February 2, 1958, pp. 14, 15, 58.

Television: Jennings, C. Robert; "Quiz Shows: The Woman Question", Section 6, February 9, 1958, pp. 16, 65, 67.

Theatre: Millstein, Gilbert; "Seesaw Saga of an Actress", Subtitle: Ann Bancroft is riding high on Broadway after ups and downs in the Bronx and Hollywood. Section 6, February 9, 1958, pp. 22, 24.

Propaganda: Salisbury, Harrison E.; "To Counter Russian Propaganda", Subtitle: The launching of our own "moon" has by no means halted the march of Soviet propaganda. How can we recapture lost ground?. Section 6, February 9, 1958, pp. 14, 62, 64.

Film: _____; "Tribute to a Top Director", Section 6, February 9, 1958, p. 50.

Theatre: _____; "Onward and Upward Off Broadway", Section 6, February 16, 1958, pp. 24-25.

Theatre: Clurman, Harold; "An Appeal for a 'Regal' Theatre", Subtitle: How can we restore our theatre's glamour? A Broadway veteran says it is first necessary to treat playgoing as something rare and treasured — a festivity. Section 6, February 23, 1958, pp. 26, 33, 36.

Theatre: Beavan, John; "London Queues Up for Eliza", Subtitle: Now it's England's turn to line up for "My Fair Lady," and the 295-year-old Drury Lane has never known such excitement. Section 6, Part I, March 9, 1958, pp. 22, 66-67.

Newspaper: McLean, Robert; "Ochs and Journalism: An Appraisal", Subtitle: On the hundredth anniversary of the birth of Adolph S. Ochs, his contribution to the Times is described and his influence on newspaper-making essayed. Section 6, Part I, March 9, 1958, pp. 17, 76-77.

Film: _____; "Danny Kaye In the Circus", Section 6, Part I, March 9, 1958, pp. 30-31.

Newspaper: _____; "The Ochs Formula for News", Section 6, Part I, March 9, 1958, pp. 18-19.

Newspaper: Middleton, Drew; "A Correspondent Defines His Job", Subtitle: The issue of sending reporters to China raises the question of what the newsman's function is. This is one man's answer. Section 6, March 16, 1958, pp. 98-99.

Years 1951-1960 — 149

Advertising:	Moses, Robert; "Salvo in the Billboard Battle", Subtitle: Mr. Moses holds that advertising on the highways is not only unesthetic but dangerous. Here he states his case and evaluates the opposition's. Section 6, March 16, 1958, pp. 14-15, 102-103.
Film:	_____; "The Long, Hot Summer", Section 6, March 16, 1958, p. 48.
Television:	Wishengrad, Morton; "School for Playwrights — TV", Subtitle: The man who writes TV dramas dreams of escape — and of fulfillment on the stages of Broadway. Yet television provides valuable training toward this goal. Section 6, March 23, 1958, pp. 64, 67-68, 70, 72.
Film:	_____; "The Young Lions", Section 6, March 23, 1958, p. 99.
Film:	_____; "Wide-Screen Windjammer", Section 6, March 30, 1958, p. 44.
Film:	_____; "French Films Go Literary", Section 6, April 6, 1958, pp. 58-59.
Theatre:	Funke, Lewis; "Eatingest Season on the Realto", Subtitle: No actor starves today — on the stage anyway. Current plays have casts consuming everything from olives to orchids. Section 6, April 13, 1958, pp. 50, 52, 54.
Television:	_____; "Teaching by TV", Section 6, April 13, 1958, p. 90.
Television:	Ager, Cecilia; "Desilu, or From Gags to Riches", Subtitle: The Lucy — and Desi —

everybody loved now rule an entertainment empire. Section 6, April 20, 1958, pp. 32, 34, 37-38, 40.

Music: Taubman, Howard; "American Opera's New Tempo", Section 6, April 20, 1958, pp. 16-17.

Film: _____; "A Movie Team Reunited", Section 6, April 20, 1958, p. 93.

Music: _____; "Global Report on Rock 'n Roll", Subtitle: The craze of America's teenagers has met a mixed reception abroad. Eleven correspondents examine the controversy heard "round the world". Section 6, April 20, 1958, pp. 24-25, 56, 58, 61-62.

Propaganda: Goodheart, Arthur L.; "The Power of Slogans in the Missile Age", Subtitle: In the war of ideas, catch phrases — some true, many false — are mighty weapons, too. Section 6, Part I, April 27, 1958, pp. 13, 88-89.

Theatre: _____; "The Lunt Story (cont.)", Section 6, Part I, April 27, 1958, pp. 22-23.

Music: Millstein, Gilbert; "At 70, Berlin Still Says It With Music", Subtitle: "I've always thought of myself as a songwriter," he declares. "What else would I want to be?". Section 6, May 11, 1958, pp. 26, 56-69.

Advertising: Packard, Vance; "Resurvey of 'Hidden Persuaders'", Subtitle: A critic of huckster methods shifts his concern to consumers; it is time, he says, to re-examine our materialistic set of values. Section 6, May 11, 1958, pp. 10, 19-20.

Music:
Theatre: Franklin, Rebecca; "Tenting Tonight — With Songs and Dances", Subtitle: Musical tents are bustin' out all over. This season, as they mark their tenth anniversary, they expect to attract 3,000,000 to see shows under canvas. Section 6, June 8, 1958, pp. 26-27, 29-30.

Music: Brubeck, Dave; "The Beat Heard 'Round the World", Subtitle: Jazz, says a well-known music man, is an American export with an international appeal, making friends wherever it goes. Section 6, June 15, 1958, pp. 14, 31-32.

Rhetoric:
Semantics: Pyles, Thomas; "Subliminal Words Are Never Finalized", Subtitle: Man here gives a rundown on how the knowledgeable and the media-conditioned latch on to those voguish locutions that come and (usually) go, vocabularywise. Section 6, June 15, 1958, pp. 16, 55, 58.

Music: Chasins, Abram; "Will Success Spoil Van Cliburn?", Subtitle: The problem for this young Texan pianist will be to mature as an artist and as a man — something not easily done as a celebrity. Section 6, June 25, 1958, pp. 16, 46-47.

Books: Mauriac, Claude; "Malraux: Again From Letters to Action", Subtitle: Politics once more takes the place of the pen in the eventful life of this renowned author. At de Gaulle's side, he seeks a solution to the French crisis. Section 6, July 6, 1958, pp. 9, 16-17.

Theatre: Peck, Seymour; "The Three Stratfords of W. Shakespeare", Section 6, July 13, 1958, pp. 24-25.

Rhetoric:
Semantics: Evans, Bergen; "Fell Swoop on a Fine Cliche Kettle", Subtitle: Man bites cliches — those once vivid and meaningful figures of speech which have been devalued through too common currency. Section 6, July 27, 1958, pp. 13, 16.

Music: _____; "Hits from the World's Tin Pan Alleys", Subtitle: Production quotas inspire some lyricists but, in the main, love is still triumphant. Section 6, July 27, 1958, pp. 11, 53-54.

Film: Stang, Joanne; "Stevens Relives Anne Frank's Story", Subtitle: Director George Stevens' current project is filming one of the stirring testaments of our time. As always, it is more than "making a picture: it is a mission". Section 6, August 3, 1958, pp. 14, 50-51.

Music: Schonberg, Harold; "The Other Voice of Marian Anderson", Subtitle: The singer has become a symbol of American goodwill. Now she will be a U.N. delegate. Section 6, August 10, 1958, pp. 17, 38-39.

Television: Heffner, Richard D.; "TV as Teacher: Of Adults, Too", Subtitle: Educational television in our schools has made bold strides. Now we need to make greater use of it in the home to nourish the cultural revolution of our times. Section 6, August 17, 1958, pp. 19, 74.

Theatre:	Clurman, Harold; "Defense of the Artist as 'Neurotic'", Subtitle: The idea that creative people have to be neurotic is vigorously denied by a theatre man, who says that artist's behavior — as artist — is always healthy. Section 6, August 24, 1958, pp. 17, 42-44.
Music:	Millstein, Gilbert; "Jazz Makes It Up the River", Subtitle: The long voyage from New Orleans barrelhouse to public respectability ends in a triumph. Section 6, August 24, 1958, pp. 14, 50-54.
Rhetoric: Semantics:	Krutch, Joseph Wood; "Great Cliche Debate (Cont.)", Subtitle: In reply to Bergen Evans, who denounced cliches, Mr. Krutch argues there are times when the cliche is le mot juste. Section 6, August 31, 1958, pp. 13, 32.
Film:	Crowther, Bosley; "End of a Hollywood Legend", Subtitle: One measure of changing filmland is the producer — once a "genius" or a relative with beret, blonde and convertible attached, today a business man in a quiet suit. Section 6, September 7, 1958, pp. 51, 61-64.
Film:	Peck, Seymour; "It Must Be More Than Sex", Subtitle: What makes a pretty girl a movie star? Sex appeal may provide a start, but other qualities are needed to make her name and fame endure. Section 6, September 14, 1958, pp. 34-38.
Theatre:	Taubman, Howard; "Everyman as Clown", Subtitle: East is East and West is West more than ever today, but the art of Russia's Oleg

Popov is a meeting ground for all. Section 6, September 14, 1958, pp. 80-81.

Television: Barclay, Dorothy; "A Decade Since 'Howdy-Doody'", Section 6, September 21, 1958, p. 63.

Theatre:
Television: Peck, Seymour; "Coming Up on TV: A Broadway Anthology", Section 6, September 21, 1958, pp. 16-17.

Books: Pritchett, V. S.; "'Our Mr. Eliot' Grows Younger", Subtitle: At 70, Nobel Prize poet T. S. Eliot insists that he feels neither older — nor wiser. Here is a visit with the greatest living poet writing in English. Section 6, September 21, 1958, pp. 15, 72-73.

Theatre: Schumach, Murray; "Why They Wait for Godot", Subtitle: Now Brussels is witnessing a play that has angered many, delighted others and puzzled all. A reporter probes its appeal and meaning. Section 6, September 21, 1958, pp. 36-41.

Television: Gould, Jack; "Rise and Fall of the Quiz Empire", Subtitle: Even before investigations into the quiz shows began, there was a strong feeling they were reaching the end of their vogue. What about their future now?. Section 6, September 28, 1958, pp. 12-13, 64-65.

Theatre: Schumach, Murray; "Again the Angels Flutter Over Broadway", Subtitle: Checkbooks in hand, they rush in where even fools fear to tread, hoping to back the season's biggest smash. But how man meets hit is an act of faith, not of reason. Section 6, September 28, 1958, pp. 28-35.

Film: Millstein, Gilbert; "The World of France Nuyen", Subtitle: Publicly, it is a star part in "The World of Suzie Wong"; privately, a parlay of physical diet and mental muscle-building. Section 6, October 5, 1958, pp. 12, 75-77.

Photography: _____; "Masters of Portraiture", Section 6, October 5, 1958, pp. 78-79.

Film: Stang, Joanne; "Film Fan to Film Maker", Section 6, October 12, 1958, pp. 34-38.

Rhetoric: Douglas, Paul H.; "Is Campaign Oratory A Waste of Breath?", Subtitle: Not in the view of Senator Douglas, for "personal appearances help dramatize issues". Section 6, October 19, 1958, pp. 26, 72-73.

Rhetoric: Mitgang, Herbert; "Again — Lincoln v. Douglas", Section 6, October 19, 1958, pp. 26-27.

Theatre:
Film: Peck, Seymour; "'Porgy and Bess' Is a Movie Now", Section 6, October 19, 1958, pp. 34-35.

Theatre: Skinner, Cornelia Otis; "Why First Nights Seem Like Last Nights", Subtitle: The fear of everything, including fear itself, bedevils an actor in a new play — and even experience, says a lady Thespian with plenty of same, is no tranquilizer. Section 6, October 19, 1958, pp. 25, 88-90.

Theatre:	Millstein, Gilbert; "Curious Rites of First-Night Parties", Subtitle: Their ostensible purpose is celebration of a new play, their true function to provide communion — even of spite — in an hour of extremity. Section 6, November 16, 1958, pp. 34-38.
Theatre:	Guthrie, Tyrone; "Ten Best for a Repertory Theatre", Subtitle: The possibility that New York may again boast such an enterprise inspires six theatre personages to ponder the question: what plays should its repertory include?. Section 6, November 19, 1958, pp. 18, 73-76.
Theatre:	Stang, Joanne; "R. & H. Brand on a Musical", Subtitle: For most men, putting on a show is more madness than method. Rodgers and Hammerstein make it look easy and effortless — just the way their shows so often look to the public. Section 6, November 23, 1958, pp. 16-17, 86-87.
Books:	Bracker, Milton; "The 'Quietly Overwhelming' Robert Frost", Subtitle: At 84, the new poetry consultant to the Library of Congress looks like the symbol of a poet. And he can move his hearers to an "admiration bordering on awe". Section 6, November 30, 1958, pp. 15, 57-62.
Radio:	Clarke, Arthur C.; "Messages From The Invisible Universes", Subtitle: Radio waves, reaching the earth from vast distances, are clues to a greater cosmos. Section 6, November 30, 1958, pp. 29-36.
Television:	Shanley, John P.; "Video Goofs: Largely Live", Subtitle: Mishaps on TV (or radio) are fun for

the fans, but awful for everybody else. Section 6, November 30, 1958, pp. 42-44.

Magazine: Hawkins, Robert F.; "Roman Pipe Dreams", Subtitle: Through "fumetti," Italian readers find romance in stories told in photographs. Section 6, December 7, 1958, pp. 126-127.

Theatre: Hayes, Helen; "Helen Hayes Relives Her Roles", Subtitle: In a new hit, the theatre's first lady recalls four decades on stage — the successes, the plays that failed, and some that she failed. Section 6, December 7, 1958, pp. 40-48.

Rhetoric:
Satire: _____; "State of the Nation's Humor", Subtitle: A panel of experts ponders the question of whether America's sense of comedy is being straitjacketed by conformity. Section 6, December 7, 1958, pp. 26, 114.

Year 1959

Theatre: Peck, Seymour; "The Broadway Magnet Draws Them Back", Section 6, January 11, 1959, pp. 26, 27.

Television: Millstein, Gilbert; "Genevieve Moves to the Beeg Stedge", Subtitle: Going from Jack Parr to Broadway star, Paris' songstress breaks precedent in broken English. Section 6, January 18, 1959, pp. 22, 24, 26, 28, 30.

Television: Wallace, Mike; "TV in Russia A Really Hard Sell", Subtitle: In its way it is the most commercial in the world, incessantly plugging one product — the Soviet System. Here is a report on what it offers and how it is run. Section 6, January 18, 1959, pp. 12, 17, 19, 20.

Theatre: _____; "Two for the Heehaw", Section 6, January 18, 1959, p. 62.

Books: Beavan, John; "Maugham: A Free Man at Eighty-Five", Subtitle: He has renounced writing for the public, and his birthday today finds him eager to pursue another passion: travel. Section 6, January 25, 1959, pp. 14, 34, 35, 37.

Film: Pryor, Thomas M.; "A Defiant One Becomes a Star", Subtitle: Out of poverty, Sidney Poitier rose to top rank in Hollywood. Section 6, January 25, 1959, p. 27.

Television: Mitgang, Herbert; "Anyway, onward with More Sahl", Subtitle: A nonstop talker from out of the West finds that iconoclasm with comedy pays. Section 6, February 8, 1959, pp. 32, 34, 37.

Theatre: _____; "Africa Dances on Broadway", Section 6, February 8, 1959, p. 61.

Theatre: Millstein, Gilbert; "New Girl in Town — and How", Subtitle: She is Gwen Verdon, the redhead who in Redhead achieves a peak reached by few musical comedy performers. Section 6, February 15, 1959, pp. 16, 17.

Film: Peck, Seymour; "Marilyn a la Mack Sennett", Section 6, February 22, 1959, pp. 16, 17.

Film:	_____; "Compulsion", Section 6, March 1, 1959, p. 26.
Theatre:	Maney, Richard; "Why Can't They Tell It's a Turkey?", Subtitle: Every season Broadway sees flops arrive in flocks. A theatreman ponders: How come?. Section 6, March 8, 1959, pp. 26, 74, 75.
Film:	_____; "Rogue's Progress", Section 6, March 15, 1959, p. 40.
Theatre:	Millstein, Gilbert; "Portrait of Miss Page, On and Off Stage", Subtitle: On these days she is Adriadne del Lago, an awesome spectacle of decay. Off, she has her problems, but prefers cookies to hashish. Section 6, March 19, 1959, pp. 15, 51, 52, 53.
Film:	Peck, Seymour; "Big Stars Go Western", Section 6, April 5, 1959, pp. 30, 31.
Film:	_____; "Mr. Smith sets the Stage", Section 6, April 5, 1959, p. 102.
Books:	Carson, Lettie Gay; "Books Travel to the Crossroads", Subtitle: Cooperation among upstate local libraries promises to end the rural book famine. Section 6, April 12, 1959, pp. 52, 61, 63, 65, 66.
Newspaper:	Millstein, Gilbert; "One As Twain", Section 6, April 19, 1959, p. 24.
Newspaper:	_____; "O'Neill's Sunnyside", Section 6, April 19, 1959, p. 70.

Newspaper:	Weston, Marybeth; "Sunnyside Revisited", Section 6, April 26, 1959, pp. 44, 47, 49.
Theatre:	Guthrie, Tyrone; "Should Gilbert Be Cut and Sullivan Swing?", Subtitle: British Savoyards are petitioning Parliament to prevent the authors works from becoming property. Otherwise, they say, the opera will be emasculated and cheapened. Section 6, May 3, 1959, pp. 56, 61, 62, 64, 66.
Rhetoric:	Millstein, Gilbert; "Man, It's like Satire", Subtitle: Using the argot of hipsters and jazz musicians, Lenny Bruce blows sharp social comment. Section 6, May 3, 1959, pp. 28, 30.
Film:	_____; "Spartacus", Section 6, May 3, 1959, p. 110.
Film:	_____; "Very Early Birds Look at 60", Section 6, May 10, 1959, pp. 8, 9.
Books:	Magenknecht, Edward; "Remarked by Twain", Subtitle: He was for more than a phynnyphellow and his observations on mankind have a universal pertinence. Section 6, May 17, 1959, pp. 88, 90.
Television:	Cotler, Gordon; "For the Love of Mike — and Elaine", Section 6, May 24, 1959, pp. 71, 72.
Rhetoric:	Hechinger, Grace and Fred M.; "Commencement Day at Old Cliche U", Section 6, June 7, 1959, pp. 70, 71.
Television:	Mitgang, Herbert; "Da, Nyet, Spasebo", Subtitle: A quarter-million Americans are studying

Russian in classrooms and over TV. Section 6, June 7, 1959, pp. 36, 37.

Film: _____; "Fantasies from Sweden", Section 6, June 14, 1959, p. 51.

Music: Wilson, John S.; "How No Talent Singers Get Talent", Subtitle: Some of today's pop record stars need little or no talent to be successful, they are the creation of the recording engineers' ingenuity. Section 6, June 21, 1959, pp. 16, 52.

Television: Gould, Jack; "Miraculous Ribbon of TV", Subtitle: A way of pre-recording programs on tape that makes them indistinguishable from live shows is working a revolution, technical and artistic, in the industry. Section 6, June 28, 1959, pp. 14, 18.

Rhetoric: Wechsberg, Joseph; "Is French Knochkoute", Subtitle: Gangster, grill room, groggy, business man, best-seller, party, popline, weekend, voila la nouvelle tongue francaise. Section 6, June 28, 1959, pp. 11, 44.

Poems: _____; "Favorite Poems — The People's Choice", Section 6, July 12, 1959, pp. 18, 19.

Film: _____; "Man In Havana in Havana", Section 6, July 19, 1959, p. 43.

Television: Brown, Nona B.; "When the President Goes on TV", Section 6, August 16, 1959, pp. 14, 15.

Film: _____; "Who Slew Sapphire?", Section 6, August 16, 1959, p. 48.

Film:	_____; "Filming Fugitive Kind", Section 6, August 23, 1959, pp. 96, 97.
Television:	_____; "Hollywood's Cameras Grind — for TV", Section 6, August 23, 1959, pp. 24, 25.
Film:	_____; "Angry Young Man", Section 6, September 6, 1959, p. 35.
Newspaper:	Krutch, Jos. Wood; "The Greatest Talker", Subtitle: Samuel Johnson, born 250 years ago, lived for conversation; here are some Johnsonian jewels. Section 6, September 13, 1959, pp. 82, 84, 86.
Literature:	Reynolds, Horace; "A Proverb in the Hand", Subtitle: Is often worth a thousand words. Herewith an examination of a much used but seldom analyzed form of homely literature. Section 6, September 13, 1959, p. 74.
Music:	Scheider, P. S.; "Formidable M. Montand", Subtitle: While singing the French music hall idol burns up more energy than an athlete. New York will soon see. Section 6, September 13, 1959, pp. 76, 78.
Radio:	Wilson, John S.; "Who is Conover? Only We Ask", Subtitle: We ask because, as the Voice of America's voice of jazz and pop music, he is heard daily by thirty million people in eighty countries. Section 6, September 13, 1959, pp. 64, 65, 68.
Film:	_____; "They Wait on the Beach", Section 6, September 13, 1959, p. 94.

Film:	Ager, Cecilia; "Then and Now", Subtitle: Hoot Gibson, who rode high in Westerns years ago, rides again on the screen in the Horse Soldiers. Section 6, September 20, 1959, pp. 62, 65.
Television:	_____; "H. S. T. on TV", Section 6, September 20, 1959, p. 44.
Film:	Peck, Seymour; "Nostalgia and O'Neil", Section 6, October 4, 1959, pp. 24, 25.
Television:	_____; "Ingrid Bergman on TV", Section 6, October 4, 1959, pp. 76, 77.
Film:	Krutch, Jos. Wood; "Ten American Plays That Will Endure", Section 6, October 11, 1959, pp. 34, 35.
Books:	Schonberg, Harold C.; "At 65, Our Rebel Poet Still Rebels", Subtitle: E. E. Cummings lives, and today precisely as he pleases, just as he has always done. His credo: to be an individual. Section 6, October 11, 1959, pp. 37, 66, 67, 68.
Film:	_____; "Ivan the Terrible", Section 6, October 11, 1959, p. 27.
Film:	_____; "The 400 Blows", Section 6, October 18, 1959, p. 33.
Television:	Gould, Jack; "Quiz for TV: How Much Fakery", Subtitle: A critic considers the revelations concerning quiz shows and their implications for the industry in general. Section 6, October 25, 1959, pp. 13, 73, 74.
Newspaper:	Harrison, Emma; "Comics on Crusade", Subtitle: Good advice is also found in comic

books — a page of it a month in 10,000,000 copies. Section 6, November 1, 1959, pp. 68, 69, 71.

Film: Peck, Seymour; "That $15,000,000 Chariot Race", Section 6, November 8, 1959, pp. 26, 27.

Television: Frankel, Charles; "Is It Just TV or Most of US?", Subtitle: Rigged quiz shows reflect a distortion of values, it is held — a market-place outlook that emphasizes success regardless of how achieved. Section 6, November 15, 1959, pp. 15, 105.

Newspaper: Morgenthau, Hans S.; "Reaction to the Van Doren Reaction", Section 6, November 22, 1959, pp. 17, 106.

Film: _____; "Black Orpheus", Section 6, November 22, 1959, p. 50.

Books: Baedecker, Arthur J.; "A Tour of Baedecker", Section 6, November 29, 1959, pp. 92, 94.

Television: Barclay, Dorothy; "Television and a Child's Values", Section 6, November 29, 1959, p. 109.

Film: Peck, Seymour; "And Still They Are Stars", Section 6, December 6, 1959, pp. 43, 42.

Television: Gould, Jack; "Forgotten Clues to the Television Crisis", Subtitle: The airwaves are public and the broadcasters who use them have a duty to the public which the federal communications commission can and should require them to perform. Section 6, December 13, 1959, pp. 9, 88, 89, 92.

Film: _____; "Suddenly Last Summer", Section 6, December 13, 1959, pp. 72, 73.

Film: Wiskari, Wener; "Another Bergman Gains Renown", Subtitle: Unlike Ingrid, Ingmar Bergman works behind the cameras, the demoniacally creative director of bold searching films. Section 6, December 20, 1959, pp. 20, 21, 48, 49, 50.

Film: _____; "The Story on Page One", Section 6, December 27, 1959, p. 32.

Year 1960

Film: Peck, Seymour; "Hollywood's Safari Around The World", Section 6, January 10, 1960, pp. 26, 37.

Television: _____; "The Tempest on TV", Section 6, January 17, 1960, pp. 50, 51.

Press: Wallace, Carroll; "Press Conferences: Five Men and Five Methods", Section 6, February 21, 1960, pp. 18, 19, 66, 68, 70.

Film: _____; "Immortal Can-Can", Section 6, February 21, 1960, p. 18.

Film: Colbert, Claudette; Gish, Lillian; Laurence, Arthur; Pickford, Mary; and Wyler, William; "Nominations For The Late, Late", Section 6, February 28, 1960, pp. 24, 25, 59.

Television: Walker, Stanley; "Let The Indian Be the Hero", Subtitle: For the stereotype of the first

American Indian as a skulking, scalping, rogue, a flat ugh". Section 6, April 24, 1960, pp. 50, 52, 55.

Television: Barclay, Dorothy; "On the Families' Side of the Set", Section 6, June 5, 1960, p. 63.

Film: Stang, Joanne; "Making Music Silent Style", Section 6, October 23, 1960, pp. 83, 84, 86.

Television: Gould, Jack; "Survey of a Much Surveyed Moderator", Subtitle: At thirty-nine, David Susskind is not only a major TV producer but a major TV personality. What is his impact on the industry and on the public?. Section 6, October 30, 1960, pp. 16, 77, 78.

Advertising: _____; "Persuasive Posters", Section 6, October 30, 1960, pp. 86, 87.

Advertising: Schwab, Armand; "Rising Fortunes", Subtitle: Fortune cookies are not Chinese but who cares? They sell. Section 6, November 27, 1960, pp. 84, 86, 88.

Television: _____; "An Age of Kings", Section 6, November 27, 1960, pp. 67, 68.

Television:
Radio: Meehan, Thomas; "The Soaps Fade But Do Not Die", Subtitle: The daytime radio serial is no more but anguish need not despair. The soap opera survives with some differences but lots of heart on TV. Section 6, December 4, 1960, pp. 27, 28, 111.

Censorship: Morris, James; "Reflections on the Chatterly Case", Subtitle: The exoneration of Lawrence's novel inspires some thoughts about Britain as a nation. Section 6, December 4, 1960, pp. 24, 25, 123, 126.

Film: _____; "Term Paper on Film", Section 6, December 4, 1960, p. 34.

Year 1961

Books: Tolchin, Martin; "Spare the Book Help the Child", Section 6, January 15, 1961, p. 57.

Communication: Schwartz, Emanuel K.; "The Family in an Age of Violence", Section 6, January 22, 1961, p. 61.

Theatre: Kronenberger, Louis; "Why Broadway Is Way-Off-Broadway", Section 6, February 5, 1961, pp. 18, 43, 46.

Magazine: _____; "The Eichman Case: More Debate", Section 6, February 5, 1961, pp. 19, 82.

Film: Schumach, Murray; "The Censor as Movie Director", Subtitle: His influence may grow as a result of rising protests against Hollywood's adult films. Section 6, February 12, 1961, pp. 15, 36, 38.

Public Relations: Cater, Douglass; "How a President Helps Form Public Opinion", Section 6, February 26, 1961, pp. 12, 32, 34, 37, 40.

Theatre: Keating, John; "The Broadway Magnet Draws Them Back", Subtitle: With so many film celebrities working in shows here the west forties are looking like Hollywood and Vine. Why the eastward trek?. Section 6, February 26, 1961, pp. 20, 28.

Theatre: Clurman, Harold; "Plays I'd Like to See", Section 6, March 12, 1961, pp. 34, 35, 78, 80.

Press: Lewis, Flora; "Israel on the Eve of Eichmann's Trial", Subtitle: There is Tenseness but not much more. Most Israelis are too preoccupied with the present. Section 6, April 9, 1961, pp. 12, 101, 103.

Communication: Markel, Lester; "What We Don't Know Will Hurt Us", Subtitle: Kennedy administration faces the huge task of rallying the force of public opinion — of arousing the citizen out of apathy and of casting light in areas of ignorance. Section 6, April 9, 1961, pp. 9, 116, 118.

Television: Barclay, Dorothy; "Monitoring the Home Screen", Section 6, June 11, 1961, p. 56.

Communication: Golman, Eric F.; "Progress By Moderation and Agitation", Subtitle: Though Gradualism has achieved great gains in the U.S. the freedom riders can argue from history that direct action has worked too — when the time was right. Section 6, June 18, 1961, pp. 5, 12.

Theatre: _____; "Broadway Sings a New Season", Section 6, September 3, 1961, pp. 14, 15.

Theatre: Morehouse, Ward; "Moments of Magic on Broadway", Section 6, September 17, 1961, pp. 32, 33.

Press: Raper, H. R. Theva; "Eichmann Is Not Unique", Subtitle: A historian examines the forces that produced Adolf Eichmann — and the many like him. Could such a man, he asks, rise again?. Section 6, September 17, 1961, pp. 13, 109.

Advertising: Topping, Audrey; "Soft Sell in Moscow", Section 6, September 24, 1961, pp. 78, 79.

Theatre:	Funke, Lewis; "John Booth: The Actor's Method His Life", Subtitle: Various players display various modes of acting, but all develop their roles from one primary source — their remembrance of things and people, past. Section 6, October 1, 1961, pp. 34, 35, 40, 47, 49.
Books:	Asimov, Isaac; "Fact Catches Up With Fiction", Subtitle: Yesterday's fantasies of space flight, nuclear bombs and so on are today's realities. Where do the authors go from here?. Section 6, November 19, 1961, pp. 34, 44.
Film:	Millstein, Gilbert; "Talk With Carroll Baker, Ex-Baby Doll", Subtitle: She thinks of herself as a serious motion picture actress, an unusual type in American film. As such, she has refused to play baby dolls, year in and year out. Section 6, December 17, 1961, pp. 18, 23, 24, 26.

Year 1962

Television:	Gould, Jack; "Reappraisal of the TV Picture", Subtitle: A critic's look at the ledger: credits and debits. Section 6, January 14, 1962, pp. 14, 15, 82, 83.
Television:	Kendall, Elaine; "If Perry Mason Lost A Case — He'd Better Once In A While, Or Look Out, People Will Revolt And Demand Quality Programming", Subtitle: Rx for TV. Section 6, January 21, 1962, pp. 12, 27, 29, 30.
Film:	Peck, Seymour; "Not Dolls, But Actors", Section 6, January 21, 1962, pp. 14, 15.

Newspaper:	Worsthorne, Pergrine; "Britain Debates Tony Snowdon", Subtitle: Princess Margaret's husband, entering the highly competitive field of London Journalism, provokes a storm over the proper role for a non-royal member of royalty. Section 6, February 11, 1962, pp. 26, 27, 80.
Film:	Peck, Seymour; "The Director Is The Star", Section 6, February 18, 1962, pp. 24, 25.
Film:	Fox, Frederic; "Nellie Forbush In Rhodesia", Subtitle: Very much lovely was one boy's reaction for South Pacific. Section 6, March 11, 1962, p. 109.
Film:	Archer, Eugene; "Director of Enigmas", Subtitle: France's M. Resnais won renown with far-out films. Section 6, March 18, 1962, pp. 54, 55, 100, 102, 104.
Film:	Peck, Seymour; "The Play's The Thing — For the Movies", Section 6, March 25, 1962, pp. 38, 39.
Television:	Sandek, Robert; "Must It Be 'kookie', and 'Ka-Poo'?", Subtitle: Children's television is overwhelmingly devoted to passive entertainment. Herewith some suggestions for programs that could stimulate young minds too. Section 6, March 25, 1962, pp. 52, 53, 54, 56.
Theatre:	Lewis, Flora; "Thorton Wilder at Sixty-Five Looks Ahead — and Back", Subtitle: An American writer who has reported from Europe for several years. Stage successes past and present. Section 6, April 15, 1962, pp. 28, 29, 54, 46, 48.

Film:	Foreman, Carl; and Guthrie, Tyrone; "For the Movies — For the Theatre", Section 6, April 29, 1962, pp. 10, 11, 46, 48, 50, 53.
Television:	Keats, John; "Rx for an MD on TV", Subtitle: Combine blood, sweat, tears and violence; and add a problem patient, one or two nurses, and you've got today's medicine show. Section 6, May 27, 1962, pp. 33, 34, 36, 38.
Film:	Peck, Seymour; "Bringing Life To The Movies", Section 6, July 15, 1962, pp. 16, 17.
Newspaper:	Moses, Robert; "Moses Meets The Press Head On", Subtitle: Drawing upon his years of experience, one of our town's best known public servants describes the oft-tangled relations of his colleagues and their journalistic chronicles. Section 6, August 5, 1962, pp. 18, 23, 24, 26, 28.
Television:	Minow, Newton N.; "ETV Takes A Giant Step", Subtitle: WNDT's debut in New York will bring educational television to a vast new audience. Section 6, September 16, 1962, pp. 32, 33, 37, 39, 40.
Film:	Even, Edward T.; "Eh-wa-au-wau-aoooow!", Subtitle: Tarzan's bloodcurdling cry still carries although it is fifty years since fiction's number one nature boy first swung through the trees. Section 6, September 23, 1962, pp. 55, 57, 60, 62.
Television:	Hoggart, Richard; "Not So Popular As Gunsmoke But —", Section 6, November 4, 1962, pp. 22, 102, 114, 115.

Year 1963

Television:	Lipsyte, Robert M.; "TV Goes C-C", Section 6, April 7, 1963, pp. 15, 159, 160.
Film:	Everson, William; "The 60-years Saga of the Horse Opera", Section 6, April 14, 1963, pp. 74, 75.
Film:	_____; "This Sporting Life", Section 6, April 14, 1963, pp. 126, 127.
Film:	Alpert, Hollis; "So Deeply Obscure, So widely Discussed", Section 6, April 21, 1963, pp. 68, 69, 71, 73, 75, 76.
Theatre:	Lerner, Alan Jay; "Oh, What A Beautiful Musical", Section 6, May 12, 1963, pp. 30, 31, 84, 85.
Film:	_____; "Act One in Action", Section 6, May 19, 1963, pp. 62, 64.
Music:	_____; "Words and Music by the Top", Section 6, June 9, 1963, pp. 30, 31.
Film:	Alpert, Hollis; "Now the Earlier, Earlier Show", Section 6, August 11, 1963, pp. 22, 23, 38, 39.
Television:	Smith, Osmond; "TV's Unending Numbers Game", Subtitle: The influence of voting upsets critics and in turn, makes broadcasters uneasy. Section 6, August 18, 1963, pp. 40, 56, 58, 60.

Film:	_____; "The Music Room", Section 6, August 18, 1963, p. 54.
Television:	Even, Edward T.; "The Mummy Case to Ben Casey", Section 6, August 25, 1963, pp. 42, 44, 46, 48.
Film:	Peck, Seymour; "Enry Iggins in 'Ollywood", Section 6, September 1, 1963, pp. 20, 21.
Film:	Peck, Seymour; "At Lincoln Center, The Art of the Film", Section 6, September 8, 1963, pp. 76, 77.
Theatre:	Schumach, Murray; "A Pox on Broadway", Subtitle: Rudolph Friml, now 83, speaks out on the song writing of today and yesterday. Section 6, September 15, 1963, pp. 54, 57, 59, 62.
Film:	_____; "Gone Are The Days", Section 6, September 15, 1963, p. 64.
Film:	_____; "Tom Jones Foundling", Section 6, September 29, 1963, pp. 104, 105.
Public Relations:	_____; "The Jefferson Story", Section 6, October 27, 1963, pp. 100, 101.
Film:	Hano, Arnold; "The G.A.P. Loves the Hillbillies", Subtitle: Folks who look down their noses at TV's number one show have it all wrong. In truth, it mocks pretension, a spectacle the Great American Public has always enjoyed. Section 6, November 17, 1963, pp. 30, 120, 122.
Film:	_____; "Movies (Non-Escape)", Section 6, November 17, 1963, pp. 86, 88.

Year 1964

Film: Clurman, Harold; "There's A Method In British Acting", Subtitle: English Actors, They Play Classic and Modern Roles, American Actors, They Play Modern Roles. Section 6, January 12, 1964, pp. 18, 19, 62, 64, 66.

Film: Losey, Joseph; "The Servant", Section 6, February 9, 1964, pp. 68, 69.

Film: Peck, Seymour; "Hollywood Laughs It Up", Section 6, February 23, 1964, pp. 16, 17.

Photography: Falk, Sam; "One Photographer's New York", Section 6, March 1, 1964, pp. 36, 37.

Telephone: Jacobs, Hayes B.; "Bell Grows Two Billion Dollars Bigger", Section 6, March 1, 1964, pp. 29, 44, 46, 49, 51, 54.

Film: _____; "Burton's Beckett", Subtitle: The martyred man of God, Thomas Beckett, whom Laurence Olivier played in 1960, will be acted in the movies by a younger British actor who has displayed some of Olivier's luster, Richard Burton. Section 6, March 1, 1964, p. 92.

Film: _____; "Pictures Presidents", Subtitle: The presidency is in the limelight these days in a ocmmunity not usually known for its concern with politics. Hollywood presidents as fictional characters are leading figures in two current hits, Seven Days in May and in Strange Love

The Presidency. Section 6, March 8, 1964, p. 50.

Film: Shabad, Theodore; "A Thaw In Soviet Movies", Subtitle: Two important soviet films, The Living and the Dead, a story of the confused retreat of the red army before the Germans' onslaught in 1914 and Stillness, an account of the effect of Stalinist purges on Soviet family. Section 6, March 22, 1964, pp. 26, 27.

Film: Everson, William K.; "Continued Next Week", Subtitle: The girl was all tied up in heavy rope egad! A couple of swarthy cads had pushed her right to the edge of the cliff. It looked like the end! But it wasn't. The stamping cheering audience knew it wasn't even before continued next week flashed on the screen. Section 6, March 29, 1964, p. 16.

Communication: Lipset, Seymour Martin; "A Private Opinion on the Polls", Subtitle: Why do they go wrong in their predictions? The answer involves not only how samplings are made but how results are interpreted. Section 6, August 30, 1964, pp. 14, 62.

Photography: _____; "To Force the Sun to Paint Pictures", Section 6, August 30, 1964, pp. 22, 23.

Film: Peck, Seymour; "Based On the Best Seller By ...", Section 6, September 13, 1964, pp. 44, 45.

Radio: Whitman, Arthur; "K7UGA Will Get the Ham Vote", Subtitle: The U. S. has 266,000 amateur radio operators and these days it seems as if they all want time to tune in the candidate from

Film: Peck, Seymour; "Getting Into The Act", Section 6, September 20, 1964, pp. 80, 82.

Film: Peck, Seymour; "They Think She's Got It For the Movies", Section 6, October 11, 1964, pp. 122, 123.

Film: Mosley, Leonard; "Mr. Kiss Kiss Bangbang", Section 6, November 22, 1964, pp. 38, 70, 72, 74, 76.

Rhetoric: Sher, Dick; "Toward A Universal Non-Language", Section 6, November 22, 1964, pp. 62, 64, 66, 68.

Film: Peck, Seymour; "The Autumn of John Ford", Subtitle: Ford's art has ranged far and wide. Four movies brought him academy awards, The Informer, The Grapes of Wrath, How Green Was My Valley, and The Quiet Man; none was a western. Section 6, November 29, 1964, pp. 124, 126, 129.

Year 1965

Film: Goodman, Ezra; "Low-Budget Movies With Pow", Subtitle: Most fans never heard of director Sam Fuller, but to some film buffs he has real class. Section 6, February 28, 1965, pp. 42, 43, 45, 46, 48, 50.

Film: Colling, Larry; and Laprese, Dominique; "The Name is Moreau (Not Bardot)", Subtitle: Her private life has tended to parallel that of the spiritually hungry, but coldly independent women she has portrayed. Section 6, March 21, 1965, pp. 46, 47, 70, 72, 74.

Theatre:
Propaganda: Hughes, Richard; "Chinese Opera Walks the Party Line", Subtitle: Incongruous: some of the difficulties of adapting Peking opera to the Peking line were discussed in a frank critique in a red chinese journal: the slightest change in has a compact and complex artistic structure; it disturbs the harmony of stage setting and classical style when one sees an actor, unbearded and with unpainted face dressed in a uniform of a modern soldier step on the stage with the stately steps of a legendary general; or sees a girl worker like yang kuei-fei, the very gesture which adjusts long hair is incongruous with short hair. Section 6, March 21, 1965, pp. 62, 64, 67, 69.

Books: Kirsch, Robert; "The Case of the Busy Copyright", Section 6, March 21, 1965, pp. 89, 92, 94, 97.

Communication: Meehan, Thomas; "Not Good Taste, Not Bad Taste — It's Camp", Subtitle: Camp, n. third stream of taste — adj., too much, not to be believed or camp can be defined as something that's so bad — in the beholder's eye, of course — that it appears to be good. Items currently rated as being camp are further defined into subdivisions such as middle camp. Low camp intentional and unintentional camp — some examples of which, along with others are shown here. Section 6, March 21, 1965, pp. 30, 31, 113, 114, 115.

Advertising:	_____; "Roar of an Underdog", Subtitle: Leslie Bricusse and Anthony Newley the British team that wrote Stop The World, I Want To Get Off, are bringing in a musical with an even zanier title "The Roar of the Grease Paint — The Smell of the Crowd". As is his custom Neeley is also serving the new show as director and actor. It opens here May 16. Section 6, March 21, 1965, pp. 98, 100.
Public Relations:	Crankshaw, Edward; "Russia Discovers the Customer Is Always Right", Section 6, March 28, 1965, pp. 26, 27, 98, 100.
Television:	Lear, Martha Weinman; "Winging it with Jonathan Winters", Subtitle: Jonathan Winters, perhaps today's number one free-winging (or improvisational) comic, demonstrates the stupefying range of facial expressions he can summon at the drop of a hat, wise crack or — for that matter cure. Section 6, March 28, 1965, pp. 36, 37, 52, 56, 58.
Television:	Litwak, Leo E.; "Visit to the Town of the Mind", Subtitle: There are no discernible Negroes, no obvious Jews, no bigotry. The problems in Peyton Place: murder, adultery, lonely widows, illegitimacy are perhaps manageable. Section 6, April 4, 1965, pp. 46, 47, 50, 52, 54, 56, 59, 60, 64.
Rhetoric:	Wicker, Tom; "The Son of the Kingfish", Section 6, April 4, 1965, pp. 76, 77, 89, 90, 92, 100.
Television:	Blum, Sam; "And Now A Message About Commercials", Subtitle: Do you ever see

	nothing but spots before your eyes when watching TV? Do your nerves jangle from the hard sell and stepped-up audio? Then read why some people think even the worst of TV advertising is really art. Section 6, April 11, 1965, pp. 26, 27, 108, 110, 112, 114, 116, 117.
Television:	Keating, Kenneth B.; "Not Bonanza Not Peyton Place, But the U.S. Senate", Section 6, April 25, 1965, pp. 66, 67, 72.
Film:	Peck, Seymour; "The Collector", Subtitle: William Wyler, a top Hollywood director for more than 30 years, shares the limelight with some promising newcomers in his latest movie, The Collector. A young Englishman, John Fowles, wrote the novel (is his first) on which the film is based. In telling a suspenseful and touching story of a youth who kidnaps a girl, hoping she will come to love him. Section 6, April 25, 1965, p. 39.
Film:	Alpert, Hollis; "The David Lean Receipe: A Whack in the Guts", Subtitle: The world's most wanted movie director, England's F. David Lean owes his eminence to high professionalism and a talent for stirring the emotions. He now faces what may be his biggest challenge — filming Pasternak's Dr. Zhivago. Section 6, May 23, 1965, pp. 32, 33, 94, 96, 98, 110.
Newspaper:	Lewis, Anthony; "British Verdict on Trial-by-Press", Subtitle: To protect the accused's right to a fair trial, British papers unlike our own, may only print what is brought out in court. But the readers still get their thrills. Section 6, June 20, 1965, pp. 14, 15, 46, 47.

Years 1961-1970 — 181

Magazine:	Lasch, Christopher; "The Magazines of Dissent Thrive on Unpopularity", Subtitle: Protest journalism, right to left, through the years — if they served no other purpose, they would still be valuable for the powerful enemies they have made. Section 6, July 18, 1965, pp. 10, 11, 33, 34, 35.
Film:	Carthew, Anthony; "The Knack of Being Richard Lester", Section 6, August 8, 1965, pp. 15, 17, 51, 52, 53.
Propaganda:	Markel, Lester; "Public Opinion and the War in Vietnam", Subtitle: At home and abroad debate goes on over our foreign policy. Here, an examination of what is behind it and what is to be done about it. Section 6, August 8, 1965, pp. 9, 68, 72.
Film:	Alpert, Hollis; "Saga of Greta Lovisa Gustafsson", Subtitle: Garbo's was a face that mesmerized a generation of movie goers — and still startles passers-by on the streets of New York. Now the woman behind the face is 60. Section 6, September 5, 1965, pp. 26, 27, 56, 57, 58.
Television:	Peck, Seymour; "TV Sweepstakes", Subtitle: A Week from tomorrow the great TV race begins. Section 6, September 5, 1965, pp. 28, 29.
Film:	Davis, Melton S.; "The Hamlet Who Wants to Play Clown", Subtitle: The earnest image of Gassman the stage tragedian has been giving way to that of Gassman the movie idol and comedian. Section 6, September 19, 1965, pp. 46, 47, 92, 94, 96, 98, 100, 102, 104.

Film:	Levy, Alan; "Voice of the Underground Cinema", Section 6, September 19, 1965, pp. 70, 72, 74, 76.
Television:	Wolfe, Bernard; "The Man Called Illya", Subtitle: The proletarian half of an east-west spy spoof called the Man from Uncle is represented by Illya Kurryakin, an enigmatic gymastic Russian in a turtleneck sweater who is otherwise known as David McCallum. Section 6, October 24, 1965, pp. 56, 57, 107, 109, 112, 117.
Film:	_____; "Damsel in (Mental) Distress", Subtitle: Movie: Juliet of the Spirits by Federico Fellini. Section 6, October 24, 1965, p. 194.
Books:	Ellman, Richard; "Odyssey of a Unique Book", Subtitle: Ulysses for all its fame and influence has never been a best seller, but is a steady one. Since the book's American publication in 1934, Random house has sold some 440,000 copies — 379,000 of them in the modern library edition which first appeared in 1940. Section 6, November 14, 1965, pp. 56, 57, 98, 94, 96, 102, 104, 106.
Books:	Meehan, Thomas; "Public Writer No. 1?", Subtitle: Who needs Saul Bellow. Section 6, December 11, 1965, pp. 44, 45, 130, 132, 124, 134, 136.
Film:	Slenter, Israel; "The Man Who Made Apathy Irresistible", Subtitle: Latin lover — new Marcello Mastronianni — played it so languidly that he has become the screen's reigning Lothario as the roster of his leading ladies

	suggests. Section 6, December 12, 1965, pp. 54, 55, 58, 60, 62, 65, 67, 70.
Television:	Walthan, John; "Soap Opera — Japanese Style", Subtitle: There is Kabuki. There is Noh and there is the less well-known Shimpa. Section 6, December 19, 1965, pp. 12, 13, 60, 62, 64, 67, 68.
Television:	Hano, Arnold; "TV's Top Most — This Is America?", Section 6, December 26, 1965, pp. 10, 11, 18, 22, 23.

Year 1966

Film:	Alpert, Hollis; "Offbeat Director in Outer Space", Subtitle: Is it strangelove? Is it Buck Rogers? Is it the future?. Section 6, January 16, 1966, pp. 14, 15, 40, 41, 43, 46.
Television:	Karp, David; "TV Shows Are Not Supposed to be Good", Subtitle: TV shows are supposed to make money. Section 6, January 23, 1966, pp. 6, 7, 40, 42, 44, 45.
Theatre:	Esslin, Martin; "The Theatre of Cruelty", Subtitle: Kitchen sink, angry young men, theatre of absurd, theatre of revolt. Section 6, March 6, 1966, pp. 22, 23, 71, 72, 73, 74, 75, 76, 77.
Books:	Smith, Godfrey; "Astonishing Story! About A Science Fiction Writer!", Section 6, March 6, 1966, pp. 28, 29, 75, 76, 77.

Theatre:	Kleen, Howard; "Caesar Means Emperor of Bassos", Section 6, March 20, 1966, pp. 44, 47, 49, 50, 52, 54.
Television:	Plums, Barbara; "Lights! Camera... Model Rooms", Section 6, March 20, 1966, pp. 106, 107.
Film:	Markfield, Wallace; "The Dark Geography of W. C. Fields", Section 6, April 24, 1966, pp. 32, 33, 110, 112, 114, 116, 119.
Communication:	Mayer, Martin; "The Man From Xerox Multiplies His Role", Section 6, April 24, 1966, pp. 44, 45, 47, 49, 50, 52, 54, 57, 59, 60.
Theatre:	Weightman, John; "Ionesco: The Absurd and Beyond", Section 6, May 1, 1966, pp. 24, 25, 113, 114, 115, 116, 117.
Television:	LeShan, Eda J.; "At War With Batman", Subtitle: When Batman becomes Batboy. Section 6, May 15, 1966, pp. 112, 114, 115, 117.
Music:	Cleave, Maureen; "Old Beatles — A Study in Paradox", Subtitle: Now an institution, they make fewer figures than any other public figure. They are even sometimes conventional. Section 6, July 3, 1966, pp. 10, 11, 30, 31, 32.
Film:	Behrman, S. N.; "You Can't Release Dante's Inferno in the Summertime", Subtitle: In Hollywood's Golden Era a producer could say anything and did. Section 6, July 17, 1966, pp. 6, 7, 30, 32, 33.

Years 1961-1970 — 185

Communication:	Homan, William H.; "Good Case of the Poll Sniffles", Section 6, August 21, 1966, pp. 34, 35, 59, 60, 62, 67, 69.
Books:	Smith, Godfrey; "An Outline of H. G. Wells", Subtitle: The fantastically prolific Englishman helped shape the 20th century intelligentsia. Section 6, August 21, 1966, pp. 30, 31, 39, 40, 42, 44.
Film:	Stewart, Robert Sussman; "The Vision of Franco: Zefferelli Direction", Subtitle: Renaissance man at the Met. Section 6, September 4, 1966, pp. 10, 11, 14, 16, 18.
Theatre:	Kostelanetz, Richard; "The Artist as Playwright and Engineer", Subtitle: The stage becomes a canvas for one of today's innovating painters whose views on art are nothing if not Catholic. Section 6, October 9, 1966, pp. 32, 33, 109, 110, 114, 119, 120, 122, 124.
Film:	Barthel, Joan; "Biggest Money Making Movie of All — How Come?", Section 6, November 20, 1966, pp. 45, 46, 47, 60, 64, 66, 69, 72, 74, 76, 78, 80, 82, 84, 86.
Books:	Carry, Joan; "An American Novelist Who Sometimes Teaches", Section 6, November 20, 1966, pp. 54, 55, 170.
Advertising:	Navasky, Victor S.; "Advertising is, A Science, An Art, A Business", Section 6, November 20, 1966, pp. 52, 53, 162, 164, 166, 167, 169, 170, 172, 174, 176, 177.

Year 1967

Television: Honan, William H.; "Dr. Jonathan Miller Operates on Alice", Subtitle: Show biz's well-known young physician-intellectual directs an outrageous version of Alice in Wonderland for the BBC, and questions are raised in Parliament. Section 6, January 22, 1967, pp. 24, 25, 26, 27, 78, 79.

Communication: Kostelanetz, Richard; "Understanding McLuhan", Subtitle: A typical reader's scorecard for Media might show about one-half brilliant insights, one-fourth suggestive hypothesis; one-fourth nonsense. Section 6, January 29, 1967, pp. 18, 19, 37, 40, 42, 44, 47.

Television: Markel, Lester; "A Program for Public-TV", Subtitle: The needs, the remedies. Section 6, March 12, 1967, pp. 25, 126, 127, 128, 129, 130.

Film: Flatley, Guy; "And For Best Director", Section 6, March 19, 1967, p. 174.

Television: Agel, Jerome B.; "Who Will Finance Public TV?", Section 6, April 2, 1967, pp. 22, 133.

Television: Blum, Sam; "The Great TV Commercial War", Subtitle: It's not just the ad agencies that are responsible for those TV interruptions; it's also companies like Schwerin that claim to measure a commercial effectiveness beforehand. Section 6, April 9, 1967, pp. 32, 33, 76, 85, 86, 88, 91, 92, 94, 96.

Film:	Canby, Vincent; "Czar of the Movie Business", Subtitle: I don't remember seeing any really bad movies recently: says Valenti. Section 6, April 23, 1967, pp. 38, 39, 42, 44, 47, 49, 52, 57, 59.
Television:	Maxwell, Robert J.; "Getting Excited", Section 6, April 23, 1967, p. 22.
Television:	Swados, Harvey; "Fred Friendly and Friendlyvision", Subtitle: In the course of his TV career, he has left an imprint on our history, holding open a door to the future. Section 6, April 23, 1967, pp. 30, 31, 101, 104, 109, 114, 116, 117, 119, 121.
Television:	Barthel, Joan; "After 19 TV Years Only Ed Sullivan Survives", Subtitle: Says Mrs. Sullivan, Ed makes nice money. Section 6, April 30, 1967, pp. 24, 25, 100, 102, 104, 109, 110, 111.
Newspaper:	Raskin, A. H.; "What's Wrong With American Newspapers?", Section 6, June 11, 1967, pp. 28, 77, 78, 80, 81, 82, 83, 84.
Theatre:	Wolfe, Bernard; "The Ten Percenters of Hollywood", Section 6, June 18, 1967, pp. 26, 27, 28, 30, 32.
Theatre:	Kerr, Walter; "The Theatre is The Victim of a Plot", Section 6, June 25, 1967, pp. 10, 11, 13, 15, 16, 18.
Newspaper:	Schlesinger, Arthur; Milgrary, Joseph B.; "Inside Stories", Section 6, June 25, 1967, p. 2.

Television: Blum, Sam; "Who Decides What Gets on TV — and Why?", Section 6, September 3, 1967, pp. 1, 8, 9, 19, 20, 21, 23, 24, 26.

Television: Schultz, Bert; "A Mother's Lobby?", Section 6, October 8, 1967, p. 41.

Radio: Honan, William H.; "The New Sound of Radio", Subtitle: All-News, All-Music, All Ghetto Radio is a Success. Section 6, December 3, 1967, pp. 56, 57, 58, 60, 62, 64, 66, 69, 70, 72, 74, 76.

Film: Kurland, Alan E.; "Living Legend", Section 6, December 10, 1967, p. 39.

Television: Edson, Lee; "Lone Inventor With A Genie Complex", Subtitle: Hottest thing since color TV — EVR. Section 6, December 17, 1967, pp. 28, 29, 80, 82, 84, 86, 87.

Year 1968

Television: _____; "To the Editor", Section 6, January 7, 1968, p. 110.

Television: _____; "To the Editor", Section 6, January 7, 1968, p. 111.

Film: Levine, M.; "Green Berets and Greenbacks to the Editor", Section 6, January 14, 1968, p. 4.

Music: Shifin, Arthur; Flushing, L. I.; "P. S. on LP's to the Editor", Section 6, January 14, 1968, p. 19.

Communication: Kramer, Hilton; "Postermania", Subtitle: The poster producers and the poster consumers have, between them introduced a genuinely new popular art. Section 6, February 11, 1968, pp. 28, 29, 30, 31.

Film: Shenker, Israel; "Good Grief — It's Candy on Film!", Section 6, February 11, 1968, pp. 50, 51, 53, 56, 58, 60.

Film: Toland, John; "Sad Ballad of the Real Bonnie and Clyde", Section 6, February 18, 1968, pp. 26, 27, 28, 29, 82, 83, 84, 85, 86.

Film: Toland, John; "The Talk in the Big House", Section 6, February 25, 1968, p. 92.

Film: Kavanaugh, James V.; "Heroes to the Common Herd?", Section 6, March 3, 1968, pp. 19, 22.

Film: Kerr, Walter; "The Movies Are Better Than the Theatre", Section 6, March 3, 1968, pp. 37, 39, 41, 42, 44, 46, 48, 50.

Television: Schecter, Leonard; "Why It's Better to Watch the Game on TV", Section 6, March 3, 1968, pp. 32, 33.

Advertising: Lear, Martha Weinman; "What Do These Women Want? The Second Feminist Wave", Section 6, March 10, 1968, pp. 24, 25, 50, 53, 55, 56, 58, 60, 62.

Film: Shanefield, Daniel; "Public Servants, Public Enemies", Section 6, March 10, 1968, pp. 16, 21.

Film: Canby, Vincent; "D.Z. The Last Tycoon", Section 6, March 17, 1968, pp. 32, 33, 72, 74, 75, 77, 80, 82, 83.

Newspaper:	Van Voorst, L. Bruce; "Press Lord Axel Springer Is A German Problem", Section 6, March 17, 1968, pp. 35, 55, 57, 62, 64, 65, 67, 70.
Film:	Murphy, Eugene; "Thugs With Romance", Section 6, March 24, 1968, p. 14.
Advertising:	Lingemen, Richard R.; "Commercials Are ... Better Than Ever?", Section 6, April 7, 1968, pp. 6, 12, 14, 16.
Film:	Fisher, Nancy; "Bonnies and Clydes", Section 6, April 21, 1968, pp. 21, 142.
Newspaper:	Springer, Axel; "Springer on Springer", Section 6, May 12, 1968, p. 100.
Advertising:	Cunningham, Frederic; "Segregated Advertising", Section 6, May 19, 1968, p. 120.
Television:	Smith, Ralph Lee; "Deadlier Than a Western The Battle Over Cable TV", Subtitle: Cable TV has the power to revolutionize television land. Whether it will depends on the outcome of the struggle for control going on just off-camera. Section 6, May 26, 1968, pp. 34, 35, 37, 39, 40, 42, 44, 46, 49.
Film:	Swados, Harvey; "How Revolution Came to Cannes", Section 6, June 9, 1968, pp. 128, 129, 130, 131.
Television:	Leonard, John; "Since the Kiddies are Hooked — Why Not Use TV for a Head Start Program", Section 6, July 14, 1968, pp. 5, 24, 26, 29, 31, 32, 34, 36.

Television:	Buck, Louise; Miller, M. B.; Mrs. Bance; Wellworth, George; Jackson, Elease D.; Chasen, Barbara G.; "TV and the Kiddies", Section 6, August 18, 1968, pp. 2, 4, 10.
Television:	Barthel, Joan; "The World Has Turned More than 3,200 Times... and a Million People", Subtitle: Soap opera has come a long way since its radio days and all indications are that it is going an even longer way from here; as plot lines thicken and ratings soar. Section 6, September 8, 1968, pp. 66, 67, 142, 144, 147, 152, 154.
Newspaper:	Levy, Alan; "The Short, Happy Life of Prague's Free Press", Section 6, September 8, 1968, pp. 34, 35, 122, 124, 126, 127, 129, 130, 132.
Television:	Barthel, Joan; "Hilarious, Brash, Flat, Peppery, Repetitious, Topical and in Borderline Taste", Section 6, October 6, 1968, pp. 33, 140, 142, 144, 146, 147, 149, 150, 154, 155.
Television:	Velk, Thomas; "Sock It To Whom?", Section 6, October 27, 1968, p. 14.
Books:	Leonard, John; "The Return of Andy Warhol", Subtitle: Ultra violet and ingrid superstar and the whole gang at the factory are wild about his new novel "a". Section 6, November 10, 1968, pp. 32, 33, 142, 144, 145, 147, 150, 151.
Television:	Frieland, Samuel; Gaugham, Norbert F.; "Dating the Socker", Section 6, November 17, 1968, p. 122.

Television:	Blum, Sam; "De-escalating the Violence on Television", Section 6, December 8, 1968, pp. 127, 129, 132, 137, 139, 140.
Film:	Leonard, John; "The Making of a Movie Revolutionary", Section 6, December 8, 1968, pp. 56, 57, 59, 62, 64, 66, 72, 74, 76, 79, 80.

Year 1969

Film:	Schickel, Richard; "The Movies are now High Art", Section 6, January 5, 1969, pp. 32, 33, 34, 36, 38, 40, 43, 44.
Film:	_____; "Che! 20th Century", Section 6, January 12, 1969, p. 22.
Film:	Levy, Alan; "A Promised Land Across the Barbed Where the Meadow Ends", Subtitle: Czech movie that includes filming of the question (where did you see this man) took a whole day, the answer (at the window) took still another. Section 6, February 9, 1969, pp. 28, 29, 54, 55, 56, 62, 77, 78.
Newspaper:	Sale, Kirk J.; "The Amsterdam News", Subtitle: Black is beautiful-ugly, comfortable-sensational, moderate-militant. Section 6, February 9, 1969, pp. 30, 31, 37, 39, 40, 42, 44, 46, 49, 52.
Film:	_____; "Zanuck Rebuttal to Leonard", Section 6, February 9, 1969, p. 101.
Film:	Murray, William; "The Return of Busby Berkeley", Subtitle: Tonite on the late great show a genuine 1930 film musical spectacular

	directed by Busby Berkeley groovy. Section 6, March 2, 1969, pp. 26, 27, 46, 47, 48, 51, 53, 54, 56, 58.
Film:	_____; "Cutting Edge", Section 6, April 20, 1969, p. 126.
Music:	Braudy, Susan; "As Arlo Guthrie Sees It ... Kids are Groovy, Adults Aren't", Section 6, April 27, 1969, pp. 56, 57, 59, 60, 62, 63, 66, 69, 70, 72, 74, 76, 79, 80.
Theatre:	Lester, Elenore; "Professor of the Dionysiac Theatre", Subtitle: Busy scouting new territory for the avantgarde, Richard Schichner — teacher, stripper, critic, producer and middle class dropout — feels that the safest place to be in a revolution is with the revolution. Section 6, April 27, 1969, pp. 32, 33, 131, 132, 133, 134, 135, 136.
Film:	Gramant, Sanchi De; "Life Style of Homo Cinematicus", Subtitle: Charter member of a brand new species Francois Truffaut cares for only life at 24 frames a second. Section 6, June 15, 1969, pp. 12, 13, 34, 36, 38, 40, 42, 44, 47.
Film:	Meehan, Thomas; "If You're Still Curious", Subtitle: Here are advance reviews of three important upcoming movies' rating. Section 6, June 29, 1969, pp. 12, 13.
Film:	McDermott, John F.; "The Violent Bugs Bunny", Section 6, September 28, 1969, pp. 95, 96, 100, 102, 105, 107.
Television:	Sarson, Evelyn; "Miniature Consumers", Section 6, October 26, 1969, pp. 58, 60.

Television: _____; "Viewing Violence", Section 6, November 9, 1969, p. 4.

Television: Burgess, Anthony; "Seen Any Good Galsworthy Lately?", Section 6, November 16, 1969, pp. 57, 59, 60, 62, 64.

Television: Culhane, John; "The Men Behind Dastardly and Muttley", Section 6, November 23, 1969, pp. 50, 51, 102, 104, 107, 109, 110, 112, 114, 119, 120, 122, 129, 130.

Television: Hellman, Peter; "What Makes David Frost Talk", Subtitle: He's no singer, no comedian, no sex symbol. Section 6, December 7, 1969, pp. 54, 55, 67, 69, 72, 74, 77, 79.

Newspaper: Rovere, Richard H.; "The Sixties: This Slum of a Decade", Section 6, December 14, 1969, pp. 25, 26, 27, 66, 71, 76, 73, 78.

Film: Weinraub, Bernard; "Director Arthur Penn takes on General Custer", Section 6, December 21, 1969, pp. 10, 11, 38, 40, 46, 43, 50.

Newspaper: Bergman, Lewis; "Reading Tea Leaves — What Will Happen in 1970", Section 6, December 28, 1969, pp. 8, 9, 10, 12.

Year 1970

Television: Gans, Herbert J.; "How Well Does TV Present the News", Subtitle: Insofar as there is bias in TV newscasts, news magazines and newspapers it stems far less from their own prejudices than from the nature of modern journalism. Section

Years 1961-1970 — 195

	6, January 11, 1970, pp. 30, 32, 35, 58, 40, 43, 45.
Theatre:	Kerr, Walter; "What Simon Says", Section 6, March 22, 1970, pp. 6, 12, 14, 16.
Press:	Hodierne, Robert; "How the GIs in Vietnam Don't Learn About the War", Subtitle: The military's hand on giving out news limits a soldier's view of his own war to little more than what he can see down the sights of his rifle. Section 6, April 25, 1970, pp. 28, 29, 133, 135, 140.
Television:	Bendimer, Robert; "Great Expectations A Quarter of a Century", Section 6, May 3, 1970, pp. 36, 39, 42, 46, 50, 54.
Television:	Culhane, John; "Report Card on Sesame Street", Section 6, May 24, 1970, pp. 34, 35, 50, 54, 57, 60, 62, 65, 70, 71.
Film:	Seligson, Marcia; "Hollywood's Hottest Writer — Buck Henry", Subtitle: Some movies still use scripts, and it's like Henry writes most of them Catch-22, The Graduate, The Owl and the Pussycat and more, more, more. Section 6, July 19, 1970, pp. 10, 11, 13, 14, 18, 20, 22, 25.
Magazine:	Buckley, Tom; "With The National Geographic On Its Endless Cloudless Voyage", Subtitle: The 1960's were tough on most magazines but this parlor-table classic circulation is now near seven million. Section 6, September 6, 1970, pp. 10, 11, 13, 14, 18, 20, 22, 25.
Newspaper:	Sterba, James P.; "Scraps of Paper From Vietnam", Subtitle: Excerpts from orders,

articles, documents, messages, plus what men said, add up to one reporter's vivid impression of the war. Section 6, October 18, 1970, pp. 28, 29, 114, 120.

Television: Barthel, Joan; "How to Merchandise An Actor on Television", Section 6, October 25, 1970, pp. 14, 16, 22, 24, 28.

Television: Cotler, Gordon; "The Question About Quiz Shows", Subtitle: After reaching Dizzy Heights of popularity, they have dropped somewhat as westerns took the TV spotlight. What now, of their future?. Section 6, December 1, 1970, pp. 90, 93, 94, 96, 98.

Film: Pryor, Thomas M.; "Their Past Recaptured", Subtitle: Hollywood's stars see some of their oldest movies brought back on television. How do they react to the experience?. Section 6, December 8, 1970, pp. 96, 97.

Television: _____; "Chelsea's Own TV", Section 6, December 15, 1970, pp. 70, 71.

Newspaper: Jorden, William J.; "Fit to Print — Moscow's Formula", Subtitle: The year's biggest stories the Soviet press shed light on what and how the Russian people learn about world events. Section 6, December 29, 1970, pp. 10, 35.

Year 1971

Rhetoric: Maliver, Bruce L.; "Encounter Groupers Up Against The Wall", Subtitle: Not everyone is ready for group encountering says a psychologist. It's a contact sport that can leave bruises. Section 6, January 3, 1971, pp. 4, 5, 37, 38, 39, 40, 41, 43.

Film: Davis, Melton S.; "Agent Provocateur of Films", Section 6, March 21, 1971, pp. 32, 33, 34, 37, 39, 40, 42, 44, 46, 47.

Censorship: Kristol, Irving; "Pornography, Obscenity and The Case for Censorship", Section 6, March 28, 1971, pp. 24, 25, 112, 113, 114, 116.

Theatre: Kerr, Walter; "Musicals That Were Playful, Irresponsibly and Blissfully", Subtitle: A theatergoer makes a plea for more No, No, Nanettes. Section 6, April 11, 1971, pp. 14, 15, 18, 22, 25, 26, 28.

Television: Sherrill, Robert; "The Happy Ending (Maybe) or The Selling of the Pentagon", Section 6, May 16, 1971, pp. 25, 26, 27, 78, 80, 87, 90, 92, 93, 94.

Newspaper: Collier, Bernard Law; "The Joe Alsop Story", Section 6, May 23, 1971, pp. 22, 23, 64, 68, 69, 70, 71, 72, 73, 74, 75.

Television: Greenfield, Jeff; "A Member of the First TV Generation Looks Back", Section 6, July 4, 1971, pp. 8, 9, 10, 11.

Books: Lathaw, Rarou; "The Lardners: A Writing Dynasty", Section 6, August 22, 1971, pp. 10, 11, 42, 44, 45, 51.

Communication: Luce, Gay; and Peper, Erik; "Mind Over Body, Mind Over Mind", Subtitle: Such is the twin promise of "biofeedback," a process that some scientists say can teach us to control the body's internal working, to relieve illnesses like ulcers or hypertension and, perhaps, to catch a glimpse of nirvana too. Section 6, September 12, 1971, pp. 34, 35, 132, 134, 136, 138, 139.

Communication: Johnson, Sheila K.; "The Christmas Card Syndrome", Section 6, December 5, 1971, pp. 38, 39, 147, 148, 149, 151, 154, 158, 163.

Film: Wienrauf, Bernard; "If You Don't Show Violence the Way It Is, Says Roman Palanski, I Think That's Immoral and Harmful. If You Upset People Then That's Obscenity", Section 6, December 12, 1971, pp. 36, 37, 64, 68, 69, 70, 72, 74, 76, 79, 80.

Rhetoric: Safire, William; "It's Time For A Change Political Slogans", Section 6, December 26, 1971, pp. 8, 9.

Year 1972

Theatre: Gruen, John; "Do you mind critics calling you cheap, overinflated, megalomaniacal? 'I don't read Reviews very much,' Answers Tom O'Horgan", Section 6, January 2, 1972, pp. 14, 15, 16, 18, 19, 20.

Television: Halberstam, Michael J.; "An M.D. Reviews Dr. Welby of TV", Section 6, January 16, 1972, pp. 12, 30, 32, 34, 35, 37.

Newspaper: Schlesinger, Arthur; "The Secrecy Dilemma", Subtitle: The recent publication of secret documents has produced a collision between two equally venerated principles — disclosure and confidentiality. Section 6, February 6, 1972, pp. 12, 13, 38, 41, 43, 44, 46, 50.

Theatre: Greenfeld, Josh; "Writing Plays is absolutely senseless, Arthur Miller says, But I love it. I just love it", Section 6, February 13, 1972, pp. 16, 17, 34, 35, 36, 37, 38, 39.

Television: Hechenger, Grace; and Fred; "Why Daddy Rushed Home to Watch Batman", Section 6, February 20, 1972, pp. 52, 53, 58.

Books: Botsford, Keith; "Jean Genet — Thief, male prostitute, Pimp... But he writes like an Angel", Section 6, February 27, 1972, pp. 16, 17, 61, 62, 63, 64, 65, 70.

Television: Hano, Arnold; "Can Archie Bunker Give Bigotry A Bad Name", Section 6, March 12, 1972, pp. 119, 124, 125, 126, 129, 32, 33.

Radio: Kamm, Henry; "Listening in on Radio Free Europe — The Station that Fulbright Wants to Shut Down", Section 6, March 26, 1972, pp. 36, 37, 112.

Film: Schickel, Richard; "Hail Chaplin — The Early Chaplin", Section 6, April 2, 1972, pp. 12, 13, 47, 48, 49.

Television: _____; "Pow! Comic Strips Take on the Candidates", Section 6, April 16, 1972, pp. 48, 49.

Television: Burgess, Anthony; "Said Mr. Cooper to His Wife: 'You Know, I Could Write Something Better Than That'", Section 6, May 7, 1972, pp. 108, 112, 114, 115.

Television: Conaway, James; "They Tried It", Section 6, May 21, 1972, pp. 48, 50, 52, 54.

Television: Hennessee, Judith Adler; and Nicholson, John; "Now Say: TV Commercials Insult Women", Section 6, May 28, 1972, pp. 12, 13, 48, 49.

Newspaper: Lewis, Anthony; "'You Americans do not understand Vietnam,' They kept telling me...", Subtitle: Journal of a correspondent in North Vietnam. Section 6, June 18, 1972, pp. 9, 30, 33, 40, 41, 44, 45.

Television: Javasky, Victor S.; "Can You Top This?", Subtitle: A new television show and other bright ideas for the F.B.I.. Section 6, July 16, 1972, pp. 8, 9, 23, 24, 26, 34, 35, 36, 37.

Newspaper: Sheehan, Susan; "The Anderson Strategy: 'We hit you — pow! Then you issue a denial, and — bam! — we really let you have it'", Section 6, August 13, 1972, pp. 9, 92, 93, 95, 97, 100.

Theatre: Gussow, Mel; "The Badassss success of Melvin Van Peebles", Section 6, August 20, 1972, pp. 14, 15, 86, 91.

Television: Conaway, James; "How to Talk With Barbara Walters about Practically anything", Section 6,

September 10, 1972, pp. 40, 41, 43, 45, 46, 48, 50, 52.

Television: Kasindorf, Martin; "How not, Dick Darling?", Section 6, September 10, 1972, pp. 54, 55, 57, 59, 60, 62, 64.

Radio: Braudy, Susan; "A Radio Station With Real Hair, Sweat and Body Odor", Section 6, September 17, 1972, pp. 10, 11, 56, 61, 63.

Newspaper: Maremaa, Thomas; "Who is this Crumb?", Section 6, October 8, 1972, pp. 12, 13, 64, 66, 68, 70, 73.

Press: Orwell, George; "The Freedom of the Press", Section 6, October 8, 1972, pp. 12, 13, 72, 74, 76.

Film: Conaway, James; "Instead of fighting for a place on it, Sammy Davis Jr. has bought the bus", Section 6, October 15, 1972, pp. 32, 110, 119.

Film: Shickel, Richard; "We're living in a Hitchcock World, all right", Section 6, October 29, 1972, pp. 22, 40, 42, 46, 48, 50, 52, 54.

Theatre: Henahan, Donald; "When the Stage director takes on the Opera", Section 6, November 12, 1972, pp. 44, 46, 48, 50, 52, 57, 58, 60, 62, 64, 66, 69, 70.

Television: Daley, Robert; "Police Report on the TV Cop Shows", Section 6, November 19, 1972, pp. 39, 84, 86, 88, 90, 92, 94, 96, 98, 102, 104, 106.

Theatre: Marowitz, Charles; "Arrabal's Theater of Panic", Section 6, December 3, 1972, pp. 40,

41, 75 77, 80, 82, 89, 91, 92, 96, 101, 103, 105, 106.

Communication: Freeman, David; "A Media Fable", Section 6, December 10, 1972, pp. 22, 25, 27, 30.

Magazine: Kennedy, Mopsy Strange; "Juvenile, puerile, sophomoric, jejeune, nutty — and funny", Section 6, December 10, 1972, pp. 34, 35, 102, 104, 106, 107.

Press: Hume, Brit; "A Chilling effect on the Press", Section 6, December 17, 1972, pp. 13, 78, 79, 81, 82, 83.

Radio: Meehan, Thomas; "Amos 'n' Andy WEAF, 7:00-7:15 — 'ow wah, ow wah'", Section 6, December 31, 1972, pp. 5, 7, 26, 28, 31, 33.

Year 1973

Film: Schickel, Richard; "The basic Woody Allen Joke", Subtitle: "Not only is God dead, but try getting a plumber on weekends". Section 6, January 7, 1973, pp. 10, 11, 33, 37.

Film: Blumenthal, Ralph; "Porno Chic", Subtitle: "Hard-Core" grows fashionable — and very profitable. Section 6, January 21, 1973, pp. 28, 30, 32, 34.

Television: Mayer, Martin; "The Electric Company: Easy Reader and a lot of other hip teachers", Section 6, January 28, 1973, pp. 14, 15, 17, 19, 22, 24, 26, 28, 29.

Press:	Rosenthal, A. M.; "The press needs a Slogan: 'Save the First Amendment'", Section 6, February 11, 1973, pp. 16, 17, 47, 49, 51, 54, 56, 58, 60.
Theatre:	Lear, Martha Weinman; "Clare Boothe Luce, She who is behind 'The Women'", Subtitle: Oh Harry, and Henry, and Ike and Mr. Shaw. Section 6, April 22, 1973, pp. 10, 11, 47, 50, 53, 56.
Television:	Harrington, Stephanie; "What's all this on TV?", Section 6, May 27, 1973, pp. 9, 34, 35, 38, 40, 46, 47.
Theatre:	Kerr, Walter; "Can Broadway Move?", Section 6, June 3, 1973, pp. 22, 23, 26, 28, 30, 32, 34, 36, 37.
Television:	Kasindorf, Martin; "A TV Dynasty", Subtitle: Archie and Maude and Fred and Norman and Alan. Section 6, June 24, 1973, pp. 12, 13, 15, 17, 18, 20, 22.
Film:	Marowitz, Charles; "As normal as Smorgasbord", Subtitle: The Man of "Cries and Whispers". Section 6, July 1, 1973, pp. 12, 14, 16, 18.
Film:	Kasindorf, Martin; "A Kind of X-rated Disney", Subtitle: Cartoon vision and Brownsville reality. Section 6, October 14, 1973, pp. 40, 41, 134, 138, 140, 142.
Television:	Bagdikian, Ben H.; "Out of the can and into the bank", Subtitle: KGGM-TV, Albuquerque, and CBS, New York. Section 6, October 21, 1973, pp. 31, 109, 119.

Television: Roiphe, Anne; "The Waltons", Subtitle: Ma and Pa and John-Boy in mythic America. Section 6, November 18, 1973, pp. 40, 41, 130, 134, 146, 147.

Books: Symons, Julian; "The Case of Raymond Chandler", Section 6, December 23, 1973, pp. 12, 13, 22, 25, 27.

Year 1974

Film: Gelb, Barbara; "Jason Jamie Robards Tyrone", Subtitle: Playing O'Neil, in life and on stage. Section 6, January 20, 1974, pp. 14, 15, 64, 66, 68, 72, 74.

Newspaper: Bagdikian, Ben H.; "The Little Odd Daily of Dubuque", Subtitle: A fine specimen of power — and profit — of the press in Middle America. Section 6, February 3, 1974, pp. 14, 15, 30, 32, 35.

Film: Kasindorf, Martin; "Fonda: A Person of Many Parts", Subtitle: A restless yawing between extremes. Section 6, February 3, 1974, pp. 16, 17, 19, 20, 22, 24, 26, 28.

Television: Johnston, Tracy; "Why 30 million are Mad about Mary", Subtitle: What's a TV star? Someone who is beautiful and sexy, but not threatening. Section 6, April 17, 1974, pp. 30, 31, 96, 98.

Books: Morgan, Ted; "Sharks", Subtitle: ... and then, and then ... The making of a best seller. Section

	6, April 21, 1974, pp. 10, 11, 85, 86, 88, 91, 95, 96.
Newspaper:	Culhane, John; "Leapin' Lizard! What's happening to the Comics?", Section 6, May 5, 1974, pp. 16, 17, 38, 39, 42, 44, 47.
Film:	Buckley, Tom; "The Day of the Locust", Subtitle: Hollywood, by West, by Hollywood. Section 6, June 2, 1974, pp. 10, 13, 50, 52, 55, 56, 58, 68, 70, 72, 73.
Communication:	Brustein, Robert; "News Theater", Subtitle: Media exploit celebrities exploit media exploit celebrities exploit. Section 6, June 16, 1974, pp. 7, 36, 38, 39, 44, 45, 48.
Film:	Lear, Martha Weinman; "Anatomy of a Sex Symbol", Subtitle: Is Redford just another pretty face?. Section 6, July 7, 1974, pp. 8, 9, 31, 33.
Books:	Rosen, Norma; "Who's Afraid of Erica Jong?", Subtitle: How many brave, but irrelevant books must women writers write to prove they can write like men. Section 6, July 28, 1974, pp. 8, 38, 46, 48, 50, 54.
Film:	Harmetz, Aljean; "The dime-store way to make movies — and money", Subtitle: If what AIP peddles is trash, it is trash with an eager market. Section 6, August 4, 1974, pp. 12, 13, 32, 34.
Magazine:	Harrington, Stephanie; "Two Faces of the same Eve", Subtitle: Ms. Versus Cosmo. Section 6, August 11, 1974, pp. 10, 11, 36, 74, 76.

Television: Daley, Robert; "The Man They Love To Hate", Subtitle: Trapped in an elevator with Howard Cosell. Section 6, September 1, 1974, pp. 10, 11, 27, 30, 31.

Books: Cameron, James; "The Case of the Hot Writer", Subtitle: A visit to Cornwall's Cornwell bar from the neurotic insecurity of John Le Carre's unholy underworld. Section 6, September 8, 1974, pp. 18, 19, 86, 88, 90, 92, 94, 95.

Film: Davidson, Bill; "America Discovers a Sacred Monster", Subtitle: Bronson looks as if at any moment he's about to hit someone. Section 6, September 22, 1974, pp. 18, 19, 86, 88, 90, 92, 94, 95.

Press: Harris, Mark; "The Last Article", Subtitle: Freedom from the press: An essay on the daily addiction of news and why, the reader were to take the author's argument to heart, this would be.... Section 6, October 6, 1974, pp. 20, 22, 30, 32, 34.

Newspaper: Wax, Judith; "Dear Ann Landers: Is incest hereditary?", Subtitle: From Shamokin, PA, to the Fiji Islands, 60 million people read her every day, and many ask her questions they'd never ask their doctors. Section 6, October 13, 1974, pp. 32, 33, 112, 114, 116, 117, 119, 122, 124.

Television: Davidson, Bill; "Rhoda Alone, Married", Subtitle: Can Valerie Harper, who is neither Jewish nor from New York, find happiness (and maintain her ratings) playing role of a prototypical Jewish girl once she marries Joe,

	the building-wrecker?. Section 6, October 20, 1974, pp. 34, 35, 120, 124, 128, 129, 132, 134.
Books:	Levy, Alan; "The Box Man Cometh", Subtitle: As soon as they put the box over their same heads, they become no one. Being no one means at the same time that one can be anyone. Kobo Abe, Japan's foremost fiction writer. Section 6, November 17, 1974, pp. 36, 64, 66, 68, 70, 72, 74, 78, 80, 82.
Theatre:	Jowitt, Deborah; "Robbins articulates social conventions through dance structure", Section 6, December 8, 1974, pp. 32, 33, 96, 98, 100, 102, 104, 106, 108, 109.
Television:	Daley, Robert; "We deal With Emotional Facts", Subtitle: TV news: visual newspapers or entertainment shows?. Section 6, December 15, 1974, pp. 18, 19, 48, 54, 56, 58, 60, 62, 70.
Television:	Newstadt, Rick; and Paisner, Richard; "How To Run On TV", Subtitle: If they ask a tough question, give them an answer that they cannot use. Section 6, December 15, 1974, pp. 20, 72, 74.
Film:	Alvarez, A.; "Scenes from an actress's life", Subtitle: To the women in the audience, Liv Ullmann is the woman they would be; to the man, all the women they would like to know. Section 6, December 22, 1974, pp. 12, 13, 36, 37, 40, 42.

Year 1975

Advertising:
Television: Barthel, Joan; "Boston Mothers agaist kidvid", Subtitle: They talk about the economics of easing commercials, but not of fixing teeth, fixing health. Section 6, January 5, 1975, pp. 14, 15, 35, 38, 39, 43.

Film: Marowitz, Charles; "The Honesty of a Suburban superstar", Subtitle: Glenda Jackson. Sometimes she looked plain ugly, sometimes just plain and then, sometimes, the most beautiful creature!. Section 6, January 19, 1975, pp. 12, 13, 50, 53, 64.

Film: Davidson, Bill; "The Entertainer", Subtitle: He is a master of nostalgia. His films "The Sting" and "Butch Cassidy and the Sundance Kid" made fortunes and won awards. Who is he?. Section 6, March 16, 1975, pp. 18, 19, 68, 71, 76.

Television: Astrahan, Anthony; "Life can be beautiful and relevant", Subtitle: There's a chism in the world of the Grand Old Soap Opera. Section 6, March 23, 1975, pp. 12, 13, 54, 56, 58, 61, 62, 64.

Film: Gold, Herbert; "Funny is Money", Subtitle: 2,000 years-old, 48-years-old Mel Brooks; Comedy is not surprise. It's knowing. Section 6, March 30, 1975, pp. 16, 17, 19, 21, 22, 26, 28, 30, 31.

Film: Buckley, Tom; "'Write me,' said the play to Peter Schaffer", Subtitle: Why are there two U's in "Equus"?. Section 6, April 13, 1975, pp. 20, 21, 25, 26, 28, 30, 32, 34, 37, 38, 40.

Television:	McPherson, James; "The new comic of Richard Pryor", Subtitle: "I know what I won't do," says the man behind the face of hundreds of subtle moods. Section 6, April 27, 1975, pp. 20, 22, 26, 32, 34, 40, 42, 43.
Film:	Richler, Mordecai; "O God! O Hollywood!", Subtitle: The apprenticeship of Mordecai Richler. Section 6, May 18, 1975, pp. 18, 20, 22, 24, 28, 30, 35, 36.
Television:	Lanier, Robin; "A Home TV Revolution", Subtitle: A battle is on between two video disc systems. Whichever wins, the home viewers will be able to play everything from ballet to cooking lessons to X-raters. Section 6, May 25, 1975, pp. 9, 43, 50, 52.
Newspaper:	Meehan, Thomas; "Pop-Eyed Professors", Subtitle: To popular culturists, cartoon characters like Wimpy symbolize the effete American intellectual who cravenly chose to ignore the resurgence of barbarism in Post-Weimar Europe. In other words, low brow becomes highbrow. Section 6, June 1, 1975, pp. 32, 34, 36, 39.
Film:	Simon, John; "From fake happy endings to fake unhappy endings", Section 6, June 8, 1975, pp. 18, 20, 22, 24, 26, 28, 32, 35.
Television:	Harrington, Stephanie; "To Tell The Truth, The Price is Right", Subtitle: The audience participates while everyone else on the television give-aways collects. Section 6, August 3, 1975, pp. 10, 11, 19, 21, 23, 26, 27.

Television:	Meehan, Thomas; "Guest Observer", Subtitle: The Children's hour after hour. Section 6, August 10, 1975, p. 4.
Television:	Greenfield, Jeff; "The fight for $60,000 a half minute", Subtitle: How NBC decided what millions will — and won't — see on their TV screens this fall. Section 6, September 7, 1975, pp. 14, 15, 55, 58, 60, 62, 64, 66, 68, 74.
Film:	Davidson, Bill; "The Conquering Antihero", Subtitle: His portrayals of losers and misfits allow Jack Nicholson to say, truthfully, "Another day, another $21,000." But he wants to write and direct. Why can't he leave well enough alone?. Section 6, October 12, 1975, pp. 18, 19, 22, 24, 26, 28, 30, 32, 35, 36.
Communication:	Brustein, Robert; "The retread culture", Subtitle: It makes plays of books and movies of plays and TV serials of movies and cop-out artists of us all. Section 6, October 26, 1975, pp. 38, 40, 42, 44, 46, 48, 50, 52, 54.
Newspaper:	Culhane, John; "The Cartoon Killers Thrive Again", Subtitle: Their politicians are guilty of course, until proven innocent. Section 6, November 9, 1975, pp. 38, 39, 42, 44, 46, 48, 50, 52.
Theatre:	Gussow, Mel; "A Playwright's invention named Papp", Subtitle: Even as he talks, the most powerful and single-minded man in the American theater is changing his mind, and tactics, and schedule. Section 6, November 9, 1975, pp. 18, 19, 78, 81, 84, 85, 92, 94, 96.

Film:	Alvarez, A.; "A visit with Ingmar Bergman", Subtitle: The great Swedish film director is not particularly optimistic about his country's efforts to produce a social paradise. But "the trying itself is beautiful". Section 6, December 7, 1975, pp. 36, 37, 90, 92, 94, 100, 101, 103, 104, 106.
Books:	Simpson, Louis; "The Ghost of Delmore Schwartz", Subtitle: He returns in Saul Bellow's "Humboldt's Gift" to haunt the conscience of an American that "has not been kind to its poets".. Section 6, December 7, 1975, pp. 38, 30, 43, 48, 52, 56.
Television:	Levine, Richard M.; "As The TV World Turns", Subtitle: The making and remaking (and soap opera itself). This week, "One Day at a Time" goes on the tube because "Beacon Hill" bombed. Will "Day" Succeed?. Section 6, December 14, 1975, pp. 20, 21, 88, 92, 96.
Film:	Davidson, Bill; "King of Schlock", Subtitle: Roger Corman, auteur of major minor movies like "The Beast With a Million Eyes," is not the critics darling. But many top directors, actors, and writers learned the ropes working for him. Section 6, December 28, 1975, pp. 12, 13, 29, 31.

Year 1976

Advertising:	Morgan, Ted; "New! Improved! Advertising!", Subtitle: The 60's were the era of the better mousterap — "miracle suds". In the 60's, no idea was too wild. In the "overcommunicated"

present, a hot shop prospers with the credo that "every client has an enemy". Section 6, January 25, 1976, pp. 12, 14, 52, 53, 56, 58.

Film: Flatley, Guy; "Martin Scorsese's Gamble", Subtitle: What makes a young director jeopardize his career by filming a despairing close-up of urban depravity and greed with no jokes and no jaws?. Section 6, February 8, 1976, pp. 34, 37, 39, 41, 43.

Television: Greenfield, Jeff; "The Silver Man Strategy", Subtitle: How Fred Silverman is helping ABC get over its inferiority complex. "Freddie's not out to put 'better' television on the air. Freddie's out to win". Section 6, March 7, 1976, pp. 19, 26, 30, 32, 35, 36.

Film: Maremaa, Thomas; "The sound of movie music", Subtitle: Audiences have changed — they want the music to work on them, to wipe them out. And that's what the new film scores are all about. Section 6, March 28, 1976, pp. 40, 41, 45, 50.

Theatre: Gelb, Barbara; "Producing — and reproducing — A 'Chorus Line'", Subtitle: How Michael Bennet tries simultaneously to direct three companies of the hit musical that may soon become the World's biggest employer of dancers. Section 6, May 2, 1976, pp. 18, 20, 26, 28, 30, 32, 35.

Film: Schary, Dore; "I remember Hughes", Subtitle: A movie maker's memories cast an oblique light on a shadowy, lonely playwright, director, producer. Section 6, May 2, 1976, pp. 42, 43.

Theatre:	Goldner, Nancy; "The Inimitable Balanchine", Subtitle: He has joined music and dance with classical virtuosity to fashion an unparalleled array of dazzling works. Section 6, May 6, 1976, pp. 10, 11, 28, 29, 31, 33, 35.
Theatre:	Brantley, Robin; "'Knock, Knock' 'Who's There?' 'Feiffer' Brantley", Subtitle: Feiffer who? Jules Feiffer who has become a successful Broadway playwright. Maybe now he no longer feels like a character in a Feiffer cartoon. Section 6, May 16, 1976, pp. 44, 46, 48, 50, 54, 56, 59, 60.
Film: Television:	Culhane, John; "The Old Disney Magic", Subtitle: Can a new generation of artists make audiences cry the way they did for Snow White?. Section 6, August 1, 1976, pp. 10, 11, 32, 34, 36.
Television:	Weaver, Paul H.; "Captives of Melodrama", Subtitle: In TV's campaign world, the election year becomes a zany carnival of buncombe. Instead of a window, the tube becomes a screen. Section 6, August 29, 1976, pp. 6, 7, 48, 50, 51, 54, 56, 57.
Television:	Morgan, Ted; "M H2 recycles our garbage", Subtitle: No longer merely a spoof of soap opera, "Mary Hartman, Mary Hartman" begins its second year already enshrined as a cultural signpost. Section 6, October 3, 1976, pp. 40, 42, 44, 46, 48, 50, 54, 56.
Radio:	Bagdikian, Ben H.; "Fires, Sex and Breaks", Subtitle: All-news radio, broadcasting's fastest growing form, appeals to people's need to listen

	for word of trouble — or for reassurance that nothing horrible has happened. Section 6, October 10, 1976, pp. 40, 42, 44, 46, 48, 50, 52, 54.
Film:	Wood, Michael; "A decent man, an indecent subject", Subtitle: Can a documentary film maker be at once passionate and fair?. Section 6, October 17, 1976, pp. 36, 38, 40, 42, 44, 46, 49, 51, 52, 54, 56.
Film:	Singh, Khushwant; "We sell them 'dreams'", Subtitle: India's movie industry makes the worst films in the world — and the Indians love them. Section 6, October 31, 1976, pp. 42, 43, 89, 95, 98.
Books:	Stern, Richard; "Bellow's Gift", Subtitle: "How many American writers have published first-rate imaginative books over a 30 year period? Perhaps three, Henry James, Faulkner and now Bellow". Section 6, November 21, 1976, pp. 42, 44, 46, 48, 50, 52.
Communication: Telephone:	Benjamin, Milton R.; and Read, William H.; "Ma Bell fights for her monopoly", Subtitle: The promise for high profits through high technology has set off a spectacular battle among communications giants, in the M. R. B.-editor of Newsweek and in the marketplace and in congress. Section 6, November 28, 1976, pp. 11, 33, 112, 119, 122.
Theatre:	Jowitt, Deborah; "Call me a Dancer", Subtitle: In theory, there is no superstar in the Alvin Ailey company, but audiences and critics know

better. Section 6, December 5, 1976, pp. 40, 136, 139, 142, 148.

Film: Markfield, Wallace; "The Kong and I", Subtitle: Obsessed for 40 years with the original "King Kong", the author traces the sources of the film's power to the artful artlessness of its maker. Section 6, December 12, 1976, pp. 36, 37, 78, 80, 82, 84, 86, 90.

Books: Gussow, Mel; "Writer Without Roots", Subtitle: U.S. Naipaul is as cynical about emerging Nations as about dying ones. Democracy, colonialism, revolution — his books drama critic and cultural writer. Section 6, December 26, 1976, pp. 8, 9, 19, 22.

Year 1977

Film: Gelb, Barbara; "Great Scott!", Subtitle: Despite George C. Scott's glittering success, his world of playacting is hedged by pain and nourished by alcohol. Section 6, January 23, 1977, pp. 10, 12, 35, 38, 40, 41.

Film: Schwartzman, Paul; "Fellini's Unlovable Cassanova", Subtitle: The chilling version in his most recent film tells us more about the Italian director than about the Italian rake. Section 6, February 6, 1977, pp. 22, 24, 28, 32, 34.

Theatre: Eder, Richard; "Andrei Serban's Theater of Terror and Beauty", Subtitle: He did "Julius Caesar" as a Kabuki that would be Greek to Greeks. Now he's taken on "The Cherry

Orchard". Section 6, February 13, 1977, pp. 42, 43, 46, 50, 55.

Television: Greenfield, Jeff; "The Showdown at ABC News", Subtitle: Behind the personality conflict between Walters and Reasoner lies a serious disagreement over what a TV news show ought to be. Section 6, February 13, 1977, pp. 32, 34, 36.

Censorship: Morgan, Ted; "United States versus the princes of porn", Section 6, March 6, 1977, pp. 16, 17, 26, 28, 30, 33, 34, 36, 37.

Press: Neville, Richard; "Has the first amendment met its match?", Section 6, March 6, 1977, p. 18.

Television: Galbraith, John Kenneth; "It started with Adam (Smith)", Section 6, May 15, 1977, pp. 23, 24, 30, 34, 37.

Newspaper:
Public
Relations: Lukas, J. Anthony; "The White House Press Club", Section 6, May 15, 1977, pp. 22, 64-72.

Television: Reeves, Richard; "Maestro of the Media", Subtitle: The Prime-Time President. Section 6, May 15, 1977, pp. 17-19.

Theatre: Glueck, Grace; "Spoleto U.S.A.", Section 6, May 22, 1977, pp. 20-22, 28, 37.

Film:
Theatre: Gussow, Mel; "The Basic Training of Al Pacino", Subtitle: Already a "bankable" movie superstar, he gives promise of becoming a

modern Prince of Players on stage. Section 6, June 5, 1977, pp. 21-22, 64-71.

Film: Eder, Richard; "A New Visionary in German Films", Subtitle: Weaving man and nature into strange and poetic fables, director Werner Herzog presents a fresh and profound view of the human condition. Section 6, July 10, 1977, pp. 24-34.

Broadcasting: Carmody, Deirdre; "Challenging Media Monopolies", Subtitle: Young lawyers are attacking local newspaper-broadcast complexes and pressing for more public control. Is this "broadcast reform" really in the public interest?. Section 6, July 31, 1977, pp. 21-24.

Film: Lindsey, Robert; "The New Tycoons of Hollywood", Subtitle: The day of the almighty mogul is over. Now moviemaking is in the hands of packagers and budget-watchers who are the hired hands of the conglomerates that own the studios. And what they're after is blockbusters. Section 6, August 7, 1977, pp. 12-23.

Music: Bradshaw, Jon; "The Reggae Way to "Salvation"", Subtitle: Out of Jamaica comes a star singing hellfire, revolution and biblical beginnings. To the "downpressed" of the third world, Bob Marley is a hero. Now he takes on America. Section 6, August 14, 1977, pp. 24-30.

Photography: _____; "A Festival of F-Stops in France", Subtitle: Photograpy by Elliott Erwitt. Section 6, August 14, 1977, pp. 9-10.

Newspaper:	Abrams, Floyd; "The Press, Privacy and the Constitution", Section 6, August 21, 1977, pp. 11-13, 65-71.
Advertising:	Lelyveld, Joseph; "Rafshoon vs Garth", Section 6, August 21, 1977, p. 78.
Newspaper:	Elliott, Osborn; "From City Desk to City Hall: The Odyssey of an Erstwhile Journalist", Section 6, August 28, 1977, pp. 30-38.
Photography:	Quindlen, Anna; "He Was There", Subtitle: A man with a camera and the curious name of Weegee made photo history as he captured the city's night dramas and disasters. Now a major exhibition puts him in the spotlight. Section 6, September 11, 1977, pp. 40-43.
Newspaper:	Lyons, Gene; "The Other Carters", Section 6, September 18, 1977, pp. 14-16, 76-78, 86-100.
Film:	Flatley, Guy; "The Sound That Shook Hollywood", Subtitle: On the 50th anniversary of the talkies, survivors of the silent-film era recall the panic of '27. Section 6, September 25, 1977, pp. 31-37, 80-98.
Film:	Eames, David; "Watching Wiseman Watch", Subtitle: His films do not just depict social institutions. Like complex novels, they explore the human condition. Section 6, October 2, 1977, pp. 96-104, 108.
Theatre:	Gussow, Mel; "Gorey Goes Batty", Subtitle: The master of the morbid has spread his wings, turning "Dracula" into a Broadway thriller. Section 6, October 16, 1977, pp. 40-42, 70-71, 74-78.

Books:	Latham, Aaron; "A Farewell to Machismo", Subtitle: Hemingway, as novelist and public he-man, still haunts our culture. His unpublished works, just given to the Kennedy Library, show him beset by conflicting ideas of masculinity and femininity. This "new" Hemingway may reclaim a lost generation of readers. Section 6, October 16, 1977, pp. 52-55, 80-82, 90-99.
Photography:	Papageorge, Tod; "Winogrand's Theatre of Quick Takes", Subtitle: A photographer's studies of the rituals of public events from press parties to peace demonstrations are exhibited in a show called "Public Relations" opening this week at the Museum of Modern Art. Section 6, October 16, 1977, pp. 57-58, 62-67.
Music:	Rubin, Stephen E.; "Behind the Berman Legend", Subtitle: Piano buffs have a new hero, but critics debate whether Lazar Berman is a romantic throwback or just a pounder. Section 6, October 23, 1977, pp. 33, 101-103, 109-111.
Photography:	Edwards, Owen; "From Rags to Photographic Riches", Section 6, November 6, 1977, pp. 151-154.
Television:	Lelyveld, Joseph; "Off Color", Section 6, November 6, 1977, p. 174.
Photography:	Seiberling, Dorothy; "Portraits at an Exhibition", Section 6, November 20, 1977, pp. 57-59.
Theatre:	Wolff, Ruth; "We Open in Florence", Subtitle: An anxious American playwright flies to Italy for the premiere of her play, "Confessione

Scandalosa" ("The Abdication"), and chronicles her hopes and fears. Section 6, December 4, 1977, pp. 50-52, 56-64, 68, 70, 74, 76.

Theatre: Gelb, Barbara; "A Touch of the Tragic", Subtitle: Director Jose Quintero has been reliving Eugene O'Neill's life — on stage and off. Section 6, December 11, 1977, pp. 43-45, 118-138.

Year 1978

Books: Mossman, Elliot; "The Unpublished Letters of Boris Pasternak", Section 6, January 1, 1978, pp. 9-13, 24-25, 29-29, 32-33.

Music: Epstein, Helen; "The Grand Eccentric of the Concert Hall", Subtitle: Vladimir Horowitz, The "fire-eating virtuoso" who gives his 50th anniversary concert at Carnegie Hall today, behaves like no other artist. But no other artist produces such music. Section 6, January 7, 1978, pp. 12-15, 46-47.

Film: Goodwin, Michael; "Close Encounters with a Rising Star", Section 6, January 15, 1978, pp. 14-18, 20-24, 28-29.

Newspaper: Stone, I. F.; "Izzy on Izzy", Subtitle: I. F. Stone at seventy. Section 6, January 22, 1978, pp. 12-15, 40-45, 54-55.

Photography: Kramer, Hilton; "Exotics in the White Man's World", Section 6, February 5, 1978, pp. 16-18.

Books:	Ross, Mitchell S.; "Prince of the Paperback Literati", Section 6, February 5, 1978, pp. 16-17, 66-69, 72-77, 86.
Books:	Pritchett, V. S.; "The Human Factor in Graham Greene", Subtitle: At 73, the elusive and peripatetic author still likes belonging to the opposition, to be the odd man out, and to make his own flesh creep. Section 6, February 26, 1978, pp. 33-46.
Film:	Truscott, Lucian K.; "Hollywood's Wall Street Connection", Subtitle: What has become known as the "Bagelman affair" is really a story of high finance and the money that fuels the glamour business. Section 6, February 26, 1978, pp. 18-30, 50-52.
Music: Theatre:	Gussow, Mel; "Elizabeth Swados — A Runaway Talent", Subtitle: This 27-year-old composer has written everything from birdcalls to ancient Greek chants. In her upcoming show, "Runaways," she is in total charge and moves from rare bird to popular artist. Section 6, March 5, 1978, pp. 17-20, 22, 52-59.
Theatre:	Eder, Richard; "David Mamet's New Realism", Subtitle: This young playwright uses common speech — charged with a desperate energy — to achieve a unique and moving lyricism. Section 6, March 12, 1978, pp. 40-47.
Music:	Schonberg, Harold C.; "Singing Schubert's Praises", Section 6, March 19, 1978, pp. 40, 45, 49-54, 58-59.

Music: Reinert, Al; "King of Country", Subtitle: For more than two decades, Texas singer and songwriter Willie Nelson has been a favorite of country-music fans. Now he's become a superstar with the rock-and-roll crowd. Has he changed? No, but country has. Section 6, March 26, 1978, pp. 20-28, 33, 50-53.

Books: Wilkes, Paul; "Robert Coles: Doctor of Crisis", Subtitle: Quietly, modestly, he has observed people in crisis situations and written about them for two decades. While he is now hailed by many as a major social critic and even a saint, he continues to wrestle with his own middle class failures that he feels keep him from accomplishing more. Section 6, March 26, 1978, pp. 14-17, 55-63, 66.

Communication: Berton, Pierre; "The Dionne Years", Subtitle: Their story was an almost mythic saga of the 30's. The quintuplets were adored, exploited and finally abandonned. The extraordinary media campaign that sold them to the American public gave birth to the age of hype. Section 6, April 23, 1978, pp. 12-15, 54-56.

Books: Perelman, S. J.; "How I Learned to Wink and Leer", Subtitle: Perelman takes an affectionate look at the satirical cartoonist Tad, who a half-century ago enriched our language and launched our author on his comedic way. Section 6, April 23, 1978, pp. 16, 80-83.

Books: Atlas, James; "The Theroux Family Arsenal", Subtitle: All happy families are not alike: "The Great Railway Bazaar" made Paul Theroux famous, but he is only the most prominent

	member of a prolific clan of writers. Section 6, April 30, 1978, pp. 22-24, 49, 52-54, 58-64.
Music:	Gould, Glenn; "In Praise of Maestro Stokowski", Subtitle: A genius of the keyboard remembers the crusty yet endearing genius of the podium who — unwittingly — turned him into a stage-door Johnny. Section 6, May 14, 1978, pp. 17-19, 82-94, 106-108.
Books:	Braudy, Susan; "Paper Auction: What Price a 'Hot' Book?", Section 6, May 21, 1978, pp. 18-19, 91-95, 106-109.
Film:	Lindsey, Robert; "The New New Wave of Film Makers", Subtitle: A young group of writer-directors has moved into positions of power in Hollywood. All friends, they trade ideas, help one another get jobs, and even share in profits from one another's films. Section 6, May 28, 1978, pp. 11-15, 33-36.
Books:	Sagan, Carl; "Growing Up With Science Fiction", Subtitle: "Science fiction has led me to science," says Cornell University astronomer Sagan, who writes about the impact of sci-fi on his life and on our society. Section 6, May 28, 1978, pp. 24, 28-31.
Theatre:	Prideaux, Tom; "Tailor-Made Hit of the 30's", Subtitle: "Pins and Needles," put on by the ILGWU, first tickled the consciousness of audiences in 1937. Now the musical takes on a new generation. Section 6, June 4, 1978, pp. 30-31, 34-36.
Books:	Durrell, Lawrence; "With Durrell in Egypt", Subtitle: Lawrence Durrell goes back in an

attempt "to trap that elusive wraith, the spirit of the place, that haunted me while I was there and then continued to haunt my writings after I left". Section 6, June 11, 1978, pp. 42-64.

Music: Horowitz, Joseph; "The Sound of Russian Music in the West", Subtitle: The exodus of the Soviet's great musicians continues. In America, their creative freedom is assured — but their artistic triumphs are mixed with emotional trauma. Section 6, June 11, 1978, pp. 34-38, 106-107.

Music: Giddins, Gary; "It's Dizzy Again", Subtitle: Much to his surprise, Dizzy Gillespie — who has been called the greatest trumpet virtuoso in or out of jazz — finds himself at 60 spearheading a bop revival. Section 6, June 25, 1978, pp. 30-32, 46-48, 56-57, 60.

Photography:
Film: Kneeland, Douglas E.; "Drive-In Time", Subtitle: The fanciful though faded monuments of a car-crazy country still lure millions of Americans to movies out in the open air. Section 6, June 25, 1978, pp. 16-17.

Books: Travers, P. L.; "I Never Wrote for Children", Subtitle: The author of "Mary Poppins" reveals that she was writing for herself, not an audience and suggests that the "child literature" field is a creation of publishers and booksellers. Section 6, July 2, 1978, pp. 16-19, 30.

Books: Fleming, Anne Taylor; "The Private World of Truman Capote", Subtitle: For more than half his life, Truman Capote has been in the headlines — as a literary darling, as a notorious chronicler of the fables of the very rich, and most recently as a self-confessed alcoholic. Here he talks openly of his demons and desires. Section 6, July 9, 1978, pp. 22-25.

Advertising: Shepard, Richard F.; "Coming Attractions: Yesterday's Movie Bills", Subtitle: Posters have been luring people to films for more than 80 years, but their appeal usually ended once the show was over. Today, they are attracting another kind of audience — and bringing high prices. Section 6, July 9, 1978, pp. 14-16.

Theatre: Eder, Richard; "My First Season on the Aisle", Subtitle: After one year on the job, the drama critic of The New York Times discusses the difficulties and delights of his position, considers his power and reflects on the state of the theater. Section 6, July 16, 1978, pp. 17, 20-22, 24, 46-47.

Books: Fleming, Anne Taylor; "Truman Capote's World/ Part 2: The Descent from the Heights", Subtitle: After the success of "In Cold Blood," Capote began to write about his glittering circle, in a book he hoped would be his masterpiece. But "Answered Prayers" created a personal crisis. Section 6, July 16, 1978, pp. 12-15, 44.

Photography: Kramer, Hilton; "The New American Photography", Subtitle: An exhibition opening at the Museum of Modern Art on July 28 is an ambitious attempt to provide a coherent account of contemporary photograpy in the United States. The show is bound to wield considerable influence — and to astonish, even offend, a public now avid for photographs. Section 6, July 23, 1978, pp. 8-13, 24-28.

Rhetoric:	Safire, William; "Y'know What I'm Saying?", Subtitle: Our resident word watcher presents his annual report on the latest crop of vogue words and fad phrases that have been culled from the biggies, the glitterati and the punks. Section 6, July 23, 1978, pp. 22-23.
Film:	Donovan, Carrie; "Wiz Biz", Subtitle: When 12 of America's top fashion talents team up to create 1,200 costumes for a $22 million movie, that's spectacular show biz. Section 6, August 6, 1978, pp. 48-51.
Theatre:	Ferretti, Fred; "Vaudeville Strikes Back", Section 6, August 6, 1978, pp. 24-26.
Film:	Janes, Leo; "That Hollywood Touch", Subtitle: Herb Ross is emerging as a predominate member of Hollywood's director oligarchy, with few peers as a successful film maker. He radiates more human warmth on the screen than any director since Frank Capra. Section 6, November 12, 1978, pp. 16-18, 78-80, 86-87.
Rhetoric:	Friedan, Betty; "The E. R. A. — Does It Play in Peoria?", Section 6, November 19, 1978, pp. 38-39, 130-139.
Books:	Green, Martin; "Carry On, Wodehouse", Subtitle: Though the sun has finally set on Blandings Castle and Bertie Wooster, the popularity of their creator's serious silliness is undiminished. Section 6, November 19, 1978, pp. 64-65, 69-71, 78.
Rhetoric:	Safire, William; "Political Word Match", Subtitle: Our intrepid lexicographer observes

	political phrasemaking in the 70's — at this point in time. Section 6, November 19, 1978, pp. 84, 90-96.
Music:	Winn, Marie; "Zubin Comes to Town", Subtitle: The glamorous Indian conductor from Los Angeles inaugurates a promising new era for the New York Philharmonic orchestra. Section 6, November 19, 1978, pp. 35-37, 116-129.
Books:	Burgin, Richard; "Isaac Bashevis Singer Talks ... About Everything", Section 6, November 26, 1978, pp. 24-26, 32, 36-38, 42-48.
Newspaper:	White, Theodore H.; "Why the Jailing of Farber 'Terrifies Me'", Subtitle: The reporter's right to protect his sources protects the rights of the public, too. Section 6, November 26, 1978, pp. 70-78, 82-84.
Books:	Burgin, Richard; "Isaac Bashevis Singer's Universe", Subtitle: The master storyteller unfolds his own passionate, original version of (natural and supernatural) life. Section 6, December 3, 1978, pp. 38-40, 44-46, 50-52.
Books:	Maynard, Joyce; "Coming of Age With Judy Blume", Subtitle: To the dismay of their parents, millions of preteen-agers are devouring this author's explicit books for children. Section 6, December 3, 1978, pp. 80-86, 90-94.
Books:	Atlas, James; "John Updike Breaks Out of Suburbia", Subtitle: For 20 years, the novelist has translated his life into a masterful chronicle of middle-class anxiety and infidelity. Now he has broadened his vision in a remarkable new

	book set in Africa. Section 6, December 10, 1978, pp. 60-64, 68-76.
Newspaper:	Herbers, John; "Small-Town America: A Portrait", Subtitle: Returning to Brownsville, Tenn., for a class reunion, a journalist discovers the source of the rise in conservatism of the late 1970's. Section 6, December 10, 1978, pp. 186-192.
Film:	Hoge, Warren; "Bette Midler Goes Hollywood", Section 6, December 10, 1978, pp. 52-53, 92-96, 100-108.
Photography:	Seiberling, Dorothy; "Egyptomania, 1850's Style", Section 6, December 10, 1978, pp. 55-57.
Music:	Rubin, Stephen E.; "How Scotto Got to the Top", Subtitle: Soprano Renata Scotto is the Met's reigning diva. It took talent, a "terrible" temper and a personal transformation for her to get there. Section 6, December 24, 1978, pp. 14, 42-43.

Year 1979

Music:	Randall, Tony; "Verdi Would Have Loved Him", Subtitle: Sherrill Milnes is "King of Italian Baritones" in opera today — while remaining very much the Illinois farm boy. Opera expert Randall explains what makes his friend Sherrill rule. Section 6, January 2, 1979, pp. 24-28, 68-69.

Years 1971-1980 — 229

Music:	Collier, James Lincoln; "Jazz in the Jarrett Mode", Subtitle: In creating his hypnotic piano improvisations, Keith Jarrett pursues the 60's ideal of letting it all hang out — and the 70's ideal of making it big. Section 6, January 7, 1979, pp. 17, 35, 38-40.
Music:	Epstein, Helen; "The Man With the Golden Flute", Subtitle: James Galway is a twinkly, hard-sell artist with a fast-growing cult. Already critics are saying "Better than Rampal". Section 6, January 28, 1979, pp. 22, 26, 48-49.
Film:	Gussow, Mel; "The Rising Star of Meryl Streep", Subtitle: An uncommon actress with an uncommon name has blazed forth recently — and rapidly. Broadway and Hollywood cognoscenti have given Meryl Streep choice roles for several years. Now a wide audience is beginning to see why her emotional depth and versatility have earned her comparisons with Olivier. Section 6, February 4, 1979, p. 22.
Books:	Bryan, C. D. B.; "Under the Auchincloss Shell", Subtitle: Wall Street lawyer Louis Auchincloss has written a series of acclaimed novels about WASP enclaves from Newport to New York. Now he tells of how that world shaped him. Section 6, February 11, 1979, pp. 35-37, 61-66.
Television: Dance:	Kornbluth, Jesse; "Merchandising Disco for the Masses", Subtitle: From a network of scattered dance halls, disco has become an industry estimated to generate $4 billion annually, making it as big as network television. Section 6, February 18, 1979, p. 18.

Books:	Gelb, Barbara; "Catching Joseph Heller", Subtitle: On the eve of the appearance of his new novel, the author copes with the anxieties of fame, fortune and the creative process. Section 6, March 4, 1979, p. 14.
Television:	Wershba, Joseph; "Murrow vs. McCarthy: See It Now", Section 6, March 4, 1979, p. 31.
Photography:	Davidson, Bruce; "A Photographer's Life: Selected Frames", Section 6, March 11, 1979, pp. 30-34, 38-46, 48-50, 54.
Theatre:	Thompson, Thomas; "A Dynamo Named Gordon Davidson", Section 6, March 11, 1979, pp. 17-18, 95-100.
Television:	Pryce-Jones, David; "TV Tale of Two Windsors", Subtitle: In England, a recent television series has sparked a hot debate over the 1936 Abdication Crisis and provoked new questions about the famous lovers. Section 6, March 18, 1979, pp. 36-40, 108-111.
Music:	Guralnick, Peter; "The Million Dollar Quartet", Section 6, March 25, 1979, pp. 28-30, 41-45.
Theatre:	Pepper, Curtis Bill; "Talking With Olivier", Subtitle: Our greatest actor, in an unusually frank three-day interview, discusses action, why he left Vivien Leigh and his will to survive. Section 6, March 25, 1979, pp. 18-20, 56-64, 78.
Newspaper:	Baker, Russell; "How to Read Your Newspaper", Section 6, April 8, 1979, p. 12.

Years 1971-1980 — 231

Music: Goodwin, Michael; "They're Still Singing the Blues", Subtitle: Three legendary musicians who will give a rare New York concert this week are virtually our last vital links to the old country blues. Section 6, April 8, 1979, pp. 38-40.

Newspaper: Kleinfield, N. R.; "The Great Press Chain", Subtitle: It owns 78 newspapers now, but the Gannett Company would like to publish an even 100. Section 6, April 8, 1979, pp. 41-44, 48-52, 59-63.

Rhetoric: Stone, I. F.; "I. F. Stone Breaks Socrates Story", Subtitle: An old muckraker sheds fresh light on the 2,500 year-old mystery and reveals some Athenian political realities that Plato did his best to hide. Section 6, April 8, 1979, pp. 22-23, 26, 34-37, 66-68.

Books: Kastner, Joseph; "The Battle of the Bird Books", Subtitle: Publishers are competing fiercely for the booming bird-watching market, and the stakes are high as Roger Tory Peterson revises his famous field guide to the birds. Section 6, April 15, 1979, pp. 16-20, 24-26, 46-48.

Film: Gittelson, Natalie; "The Maturing of Woody Allen", Subtitle: "Until we find a resolution for our terrors, we're going to have an expedient culture." Is this Woody Allen speaking? Yes — the new Woody Allen. His latest film reveals an uncommonly serious artist at work. Section 6, April 22, 1979, pp. 30-32, 102-107.

Film: Cook, Jess; "Jon Voight: The Uneasy Winner", Section 6, April 29, 1979, p. 96.

Theatre: Kornbluth, Jesse; "The Department Store as Theatre", Section 6, April 29, 1979, p. 30.

Theatre: Gussow, Mel; "A Long Life in the Theatre", Subtitle: In his 55-year career, Harold Clurman has directed — with passion — more than 40 plays, and written some of the finest dramatic criticism of our age. Section 6, May 6, 1979, p. 31.

Television: Stein, Harry; "How '60 Minutes' Makes News", Subtitle: Regarded almost universally as the classiest network show on the air, the CBS program inspires awe — as well as controversy involving its distinctive confrontational style. Section 6, May 6, 1979, p. 28.

Film: Culhane, John; "The Muppets In Movieland", Section 6, June 10, 1979, p. 52.

Books: Singular, Stephen; "The Sound and Fury Over Fiction", Subtitle: John Gardner rails against fellow novelists — who have struck back. Now Gardner's on the attack against "commercialism and immorality in modern fiction". Section 6, July 8, 1979, pp. 12-15, 34-39.

Advertising: Baker, Russell; "Walking Ads", Section 6, July 22, 1979, p. 12.

Theatre: Mason, Clifford; "A New Black Theatre", Subtitle: Only black musicals now flourish on Broadway. But Joseph Papp intends to make his new black classical company the best in the world. Section 6, July 22, 1979, p. 28.

Film: Croyden, Margaret; "Getting in Touch With Gurdjieff", Subtitle: This little known mystic

Years 1971-1980 — 233

from Caucasus was a prime-mover of today's self-awareness movement. Now a Peter Brook film will introduce Americans to his "search for the miraculous". Section 6, July 29, 1979, p. 26.

Film: Coppola, Eleanor; "Diary of a Director's Wife", Subtitle: Throughout the making of "Apocalypse Now," director Francis Ford Coppola was dogged by a relentless succession of crises. And for his troubled wife, Eleanor, the filmed provoked a personal apocalypse. Section 6, August 5, 1979, p. 30.

Music: Zuckerman, Eugenia; "Rhapsodizing Over Instruments", Section 6, August 12, 1979, pp. 15-23.

Television: Smith, Desmond; "Television Enters the 80's", Section 6, August 19, 1979, p. 16.

Books: Buckley, Tom; "The Literary Conspiracies of Richard Condon", Section 6, September 2, 1979, pp. 17, 30, 35, 44-45.

Books: Atlas, James; "Life With Mailer", Section 6, September 9, 1979, pp. 52-55, 86-98, 102-107.

Television: Buckley, Tom; "Priming for Prime Time", Section 6, September 9, 1979, p. 56.

Photography: Moore, Gaylen; "Lotte Jacobi: Born With a Photographer's Eye", Section 6, September 16, 1979, pp. 42-44, 69-81.

Theatre: Henahan, Donald; "A Tough New Role for Beverly", Section 6, September 23, 1979, pp. 24-26, 31-32, 76-77, 102, 107.

Books:	Podhoretz, Norman; "How the North Was Won", Subtitle: A scourge of the literary-intellectual establishment examines the influence of some "good ol' boys" who moved north in the 1960's and comes to the opinion that they have a lot to answer for. Section 6, September 30, 1979, pp. 30, 50-64.
Theatre:	O'Malley, Suzanne; "Can the Method Survive the Madness?", Section 6, October 7, 1979, p. 33.
Music:	Rubin, Stephen E.; "Issac Stern: The Power and the Glory", Subtitle: Stern describes himself as a fiddler. But he also fiddles most effectively with power in the music world, where he is an adroit mover and shaker. Section 6, October 14, 1979, pp. 40-41, 62, 66-68, 72-74.
Advertising:	Stanfill, Francesca; "The Marketing of Gloria Vanderbilt", Section 6, October 14, 1979, pp. 28-31, 124-127, 130-131, 137.
Books:	Kornbluth, Jesse; "The Cheever Chronicle", Subtitle: John Cheever, famous for his many elegant and urbane New Yorker stories, has passed through two decades of personal turbulence. At 67, having won the Pulitzer Prize, he is rediscovering "the surprising abundance of life". Section 6, October 21, 1979, pp. 26-28, 102-105.
Television:	Buckley, Tom; "Game Shows — TV's Glittering Gold Mine", Section 6, November 18, 1979, p. 50.
Advertising:	Penney, Alexandra; "Seduction by Packaging", Section 6, November 18, 1979, pp. 166, 193.

Newspaper:	Zion, Sidney; "High Court vs. the Press", Section 6, November 18, 1979, pp. 76, 138, 140-151.

Year 1980

Film:	Schulberg, Budd; "The Inside Story of 'Waterfront'", Section 6, January 6, 1980, p. 28.
Music:	Trustman, Deborah; "Peter Serkin: Playing in a New Key", Section 6, January 13, 1980, pp. 22-27, 61-62, 74.
Books:	Atlas, James; "New Voices in American Poetry", Section 6, February 3, 1980, p. 16.
Film:	Kornbluth, Jesse; "Play It Alone, Brickman", Section 6, February 24, 1980, p. 28.
Television:	Smith, Desmond; "The Wide World of Roone Arledge", Section 6, February 24, 1980, p. 36.
Television:	Baker, Russell; "Popping Up on '60 Minutes'", Section 6, March 2, 1980, p. 16.
Photography:	Edwards, Owen; "He Changed the Face of Photography", Section 6, March 2, 1980, pp. 32-35, 74.
Books:	Gittelson, Natalie; "The Packaging of Judith Krantz", Section 6, March 2, 1980, p. 22.
Music:	Blandford, Linda; "The Strains of a String Quartet", Section 6, March 23, 1980, pp. 44-58.

Radio: Roberts, Chalmers M.; "New Image for Voice of America", Section 6, April 13, 1980, p. 107.

Books: Schwartz, Tony; "The Worlds of Gay Talese", Section 6, April 20, 1980, p. 34.

Film: Schulberg, Budd; "What Makes Hollywood Run Now?", Section 6, April 27, 1980, p. 52.

Photography: Edwards, Owen; "Her Eye is on the City", Subtitle: Shying away from fame, photographer Helen Levitt unobtrusively captures the ironic grace of New York life — and praise from the critics. Section 6, May 4, 1980, pp. 50-56.

Film: Selznick, Daniel; "An Old Pro on the Go Again", Section 6, May 4, 1980, p. 48.

Music: Plaskin, Glenn; "The Secret Career of Horowitz", Subtitle: This highly publicized pianist has kept his life as a teacher quiet. For the first time, his former students tell what they learned and how the relationship affected them. Section 6, May 11, 1980, pp. 90-92, 96-100.

Film: Wilson, William; "Riding the Crest of the Horror Craze", Section 6, May 11, 1980, p. 42.

Film: Schickel, Richard; "A Conjurer of Catastrophes and Castles", Section 6, May 18, 1980, p. 44.

Film: Schickel, Richard; "Far Beyond Reality", Section 6, May 18, 1980, p. 40.

Books: Raines, Howell and Susan Woodley; "Let Us Now Revisit Famous Folk", Section 6, May 25, 1980, p. 31.

Film:	Theroux, Phyllis; "Outgrowing Margaret O'Brien", Section 6, June 1, 1980, p. 60.
Rhetoric:	Safire, William; "On Language", Subtitle: The Word's The Thing. Section 6, June 8, 1980, p. 40.
Music:	Swartley, Ariel; "Ladies Sing the Blues", Section 6, June 29, 1980, pp. 22-23, 35-39, 50.
Theatre:	Gelb, Barbara; "Richard Burton: The Troubled Road Back to 'Camelot'", Section 6, July 6, 1980, p. 12.
Books:	Greenspan, Emily; "Work Begins at 35", Section 6, July 6, 1980, p. 21.
Books:	Franks, Lucinda; "The Emergence of Joyce Carol Oates", Subtitle: For years she kept a careful distance from the world, weaving her tales of violence with exquisite detail. Now this prize-winning writer has entered upon a new stage, with a new outlook and a new Gothic novel of major proportions. Section 6, July 27, 1980, p. 22.
Communication:	Baker, Russell; "The Media Convention", Section 6, August 3, 1980, p. 14.
Photography:	Stanfill, Francesca; "A Vision of Style", Section 6, September 14, 1980, p. 69.
Film:	Harmetz, Aljean; "What Price Glory At Columbia?", Subtitle: Since the ouster of studio president David Begelman in 1978, some of Hollywood's most powerful men have struggled for control of Columbia Pictures. The winner was the one who most enjoyed the fray —

producer Ray Stark. Section 6, September 21, 1980, p. 38.

Press: Power, Philip H.; "Third World vs. The Media", Section 6, September 21, 1980, p. 116.

Music: Trustman, Deborah; "Ozawa's B. S. O. — the Sound and the Fury", Subtitle: At age 100, the Boston Symphony, along with its conductor, grapples with the major changes facing all orchestras. Section 6, October 12, 1980, pp. 88-100.

Theatre: Jablonski, Edward; "The Making of 'Porgy and Bess'", Section 6, October 19, 1980, pp. 88-104.

Photography: Theroux, Paul; and Loke, Margaret; "The Past Recaptured", Section 6, October 19, 1980, p. 32.

Press: Weisman, Steven R.; "The Power of the Press Secretary", Section 6, October 26, 1980, pp. 32-40, 74-92.

Theatre:
Television: Stone, Elizabeth; "Gilda Radner: Goodbye Roseanne, Hello, Broadway", Section 6, November 9, 1980, p. 42.

Film: Davis, Sally Ogle; "Wishing Upon A Falling Star at Disney", Section 6, November 16, 1980, p. 144.

Books: Garis, Leslie; "Sagan: Encore Tristesse", Section 6, November 16, 1980, p. 64.

Magazine: Schoen, Elin; "Going to Press While Doing Time", Section 6, November 16, 1980, pp. 154-160.

Advertising:	Stanfill, Barbara; "Packaging: Much Ado About Christmas", Section 6, November 16, 1980, pp. 170, 185.
Press:	Coe, Robert; "Saga of Sam Shepherd", Section 6, November 23, 1980, p. 56.
Music:	Rubinstein, Leslie; "Oriental Musicians Come of Age", Section 6, November 23, 1980, pp. 30, 78-86, 90-92.
Photography:	_____; "Pictures at Exhibitions", Section 6, November 23, 1980, pp. 62-63.
Film:	Gussow, Mel; "The Seberg Tragedy", Section 6, November 30, 1980, p. 50.
Books:	Shreve, Anita; "The American Short Story: An Untold Tale", Section 6, November 30, 1980, pp. 136-144.
Film:	Moore, Gaylen; "On the Cutting Edge of Film Editing", Section 6, December 14, 1980, p. 129.
Books:	Atlas, James; "A Poetic Triumph", Section 6, December 21, 1980, pp. 32-40.
Television:	Schwartz, Tony; "An Intimate Talk With William Paley", Subtitle: At 79 the CBS chairman looks frankly at his career, his ambitions for the corporation that he built and his renewed appreciation of family and friendship. Section 6, December 28, 1980, p. 14.

Year 1981

Rhetoric: Safire, William; "On Language", Subtitle: Pops and Sons. Section 6, January 4, 1981, pp. 8-10.

Film: Davis, Sally Ogle; "The Struggle of Women Directors", Subtitle: More Women Directors than ever before are Knocking on Hollywood Film Studio Doors, but Few are being Granted a Chance to Succeed — or Fail — with a "Man-sized" Budget. Section 6, January 11, 1981, pp. 34-37, 63, 72-76, 84.

Rhetoric: Safire, William; "On Language", Subtitle: Hit the Ground Running. Section 6, January 11, 1981, pp. 9-11.

Rhetoric: Safire, William; "On Language", Subtitle: Getting Down. Section 6, January 18, 1981, pp. 6, 8.

Books: Trustman, Deborah; "France's First Woman 'Immortal'", Subtitle: The Election of the Writer and Poet Marguerite Yourcenar to the Hitherto All-Male French Academy is Casting the Reticent Maine Resident in Unaccustomed Spotlight. Section 6, January 18, 1981, pp. 18-25, 42-44.

Film: Morgenstern, Joseph; "Sunshine Boy at 85", Subtitle: The Last Surviving Star of Hollywood's Round Table of Legendary Comedians. George Burns is Enjoying Even Greater Success Now than When He and Gracie Allen were in their Heyday. Section 6, January 25, 1981, pp. 26-29.

Rhetoric:	Safire, William; "On Language", Subtitle: Cheap Shots. Section 6, January 25, 1981, p. 9.
Rhetoric:	Safire, William; "On Language", Subtitle: Let the Reader Beware. Section 6, February 1, 1981, p. 10.
Theatre:	Schoen, Elin; "Presenting McCann & Nugent", Subtitle: After Five Years and a String of Hits, Broadway Producers Liz McCann and Nelle Nugent Now Know what it Feels Like to be Stars Themselves. Section 6, February 1, 1981, pp. 33-38, 42-44.
Rhetoric:	Safire, William; "On Language", Subtitle: Working Like Banshees. Section 6, February 8, 1981, p. 11.
Music:	Schonberg, Harold C.; "A Lifetime of Listening", Subtitle: At the Age of 12, Harold Schonberg Decided He would get Paid for what He Loved — Listening to Music. In this Memoir, He Writes about his Career, and his Ideas on the Arts of Music, Performance and Criticism. Section 6, February 8, 1981, pp. 38, 42-46.
Books:	Atlas, James; "The Private Hemingway", Subtitle: From His Unpublished Letters, 1918-1961. Section 6, February 15, 1981, pp. 23-32, 64-71, 83-87, 91.
Television:	Bass, Martin Clark; "Television's Day in Court", Subtitle: The Supreme Court Recently Allowed Trials to be Televised Even over a Defendant's Objection. Will Electronic Coverage Change the Nature of Trials — and of Justice — in the

	United States?. Section 6, February 15, 1981, pp. 36-38, 40-54.
Rhetoric:	Safire, William; "On Language", Subtitle: Beyond Compare. Section 6, February 15, 1981, p. 11.
Rhetoric:	Safire, William; "On Language", Subtitle: Haigravations. Section 6, February 22, 1981, pp. 9-10.
Film:	Buckley, Tom; "The Forman Formula", Subtitle: The Movies of Expatriate Czech Director Milos Forman Show a Unique Understanding of America. Now This Understanding is Being Put to the Test by a Historical Pastiche, "Ragtime". Section 6, March 1, 1981, pp. 28-31, 42-44, 50-53.
Rhetoric:	Safire, William; "On Language", Subtitle: Language Lib. Section 6, March 1, 1981, p. 9.
Photography:	Dower, John W.; "Japan's Photographic Legacy", Section 6, March 8, 1981, pp. 44-54.
Rhetoric:	Safire, William; "On Language", Subtitle: Reaganese. Section 6, March 8, 1981, p. 11.
Television:	Baker, Russell; "Sunday Observer", Subtitle: Riches of the Tube. Section 6, March 15, 1981, p. 17.
Television:	Ledger, Marshall; "The Ascent of Adrian Malone", Subtitle: The Producer has Broadened the Dimensions of "Educational" Television through the Innovative Use of "Created Documentaries". The Results have been such Multipart Series as "The Ascent of Man" and

"Cosmos". Section 6, March 15, 1981, pp. 26, 30-38, 78.

Rhetoric: Safire, William; "On Language", Subtitle: Taking It Neat. Section 6, March 15, 1981, pp. 8-10.

Rhetoric: Safire, William; "On Language", Subtitle: Do You Speak Aspic?. Section 6, March 22, 1981, p. 16.

Film:
Television: Squire, Susan; "The Road to Extradom", Subtitle: Anonymous, Ignored or Looked Down Upon by their own Industry, Treated "Like Cattle" — Extras are Essential to Movies and TV, and Some Earn $150,000 a Year. Section 6, March 22, 1981, pp. 84-94.

Film: Cohen, Barney; "Burt Reynolds: Going Beyond Macho", Section 6, March 29, 1981, pp. 18, 52-57.

Rhetoric: Safire, William; "On Language", Subtitle: Safety Nets. Section 6, March 29, 1981, p. 9.

Rhetoric: Safire, William; "On Language", Subtitle: Standing Corrected. Section 6, April 5, 1981, p. 16.

Rhetoric: Safire, William; "On Language", Subtitle: On "Early On" and on and on. Section 6, April 12, 1981, p. 16.

Rhetoric: Safire, William; "On Language", Subtitle: Crafty Crafting. Section 6, April 19, 1981, p. 9.

Film:
Television: Winfrey, Carey; "A Nice Guy Finishes First", Subtitle: Alan Alda has Succeeded Without Losing his Gentleness and Wit — Qualities which Show Up in his Acting. But Behind the Relaxed Alda Air, there is a Restless Drive and a Generous Creative Gift. In Alda's New Film, which he Wrote, he Stars and — for the First Time — Directs. Section 6, April 19, 1981, pp. 33, 36-46.

Rhetoric: Safire, William; "On Language", Subtitle: Queing for the Net. Section 6, April 26, 1981, p. 16.

Rhetoric: Safire, William; "On Language", Subtitle: Behind the Stick. Section 6, May 3, 1981, p. 16.

Music: Trestman, Deborah; "Opera From the Heart of Texas", Section 6, May 3, 1981, p. 108.

Theatre: Croyden, Margaret; "The Box Office Boom", Section 6, May 10, 1981, p. 27.

Rhetoric: Safire, William; "On Language", Subtitle: Just Bopping Along. Section 6, May 10, 1981, p. 9.

Rhetoric: Safire, William; "On Language", Subtitle: No Boo-Boo. Section 6, May 17, 1981, p. 14.

Rhetoric: Safire, William; "On Language", Subtitle: Cut a Deal. Section 6, May 24, 1981, p. 9.

Public
Relations: Gelb, Leslie H.; "How Haig Is Recasting His Image", Section 6, May 31, 1981, p. 23.

Rhetoric:	Safire, William; "On Language", Subtitle: Life's Little Victories. Section 6, May 31, 1981, p. 9.
Press:	Abrams, Floyd; "The Pentagon Papers A Decade Later", Section 6, June 7, 1981, p. 22.
Rhetoric:	Safire, William; "On Language", Subtitle: Speakerspeak. Section 6, June 7, 1981, p. 10.
Music:	Topping, Audrey; "A Chinese Garden Grows at the Met", Section 6, June 7, 1981, p. 38.
Rhetoric:	Safire, William; "On Language", Subtitle: Psyche Delly. Section 6, June 14, 1981, p. 16.
Rhetoric:	Safire, William; "On Language", Subtitle: Caste Party. Section 6, June 21, 1981, p. 10.
Music:	Zion, Sidney; "Outlasting Rock", Section 6, June 21, 1981, p. 16.
Press:	Jaynes, Gregory; "A Farewell to Africa", Section 6, June 28, 1981, p. 23.
Rhetoric:	Safire, William; "On Language", Subtitle: Out of Left Field. Section 6, June 28, 1981, p. 7.
Books:	Voznesensky, Andrei; "A Russian Poet's Homage to Pasternak", Section 6, June 28, 1981, p. 26.
Rhetoric:	Safire, William; "On Language", Subtitle: Carte Before the Horse. Section 6, July 5, 1981, p. 6.
Film:	Stabiner, Karen; "How to Succeed in Hollywood Without Really Filming", Section 6, July 5, 1981, p. 22.

Film:	Culhane, John; "Jack Lemmon: Behind the Smile", Section 6, July 12, 1981, p. 26.
Rhetoric:	Quinn, Jim; "On Language", Subtitle: Watchdogs of the Word. Section 6, July 12, 1981, p. 7.
Rhetoric:	Cooke, Alistair; "On Language", Subtitle: Presidential Prose. Section 6, July 19, 1981, p. 6.
Rhetoric:	Bolinger, Dwight; "On Language", Subtitle: Voice Imprints. Section 6, July 26, 1981, p. 7.
Rhetoric:	McFadden, Cyra; "On Language", Subtitle: In Defense of Gender. Section 6, August 2, 1981, p. 9.
Rhetoric:	Cantwen, Mary; "On Language", Subtitle: Parlor Parlance. Section 6, August 9, 1981, p. 6.
Books:	Raban, Jonathan; "River Log: Travels of a Modern Huck", Section 6, August 16, 1981, p. 22.
Rhetoric:	Safire, William; "On Language", Subtitle: Boll Weevils Whom Gypsy Moths. Section 6, August 16, 1981, p. 9.
Music:	Scherman, Tony; "Rock'n Retail: Styx on Tour", Section 6, August 16, 1981, p. 32.
Books:	Nabokov, Vladimir; "Nabokov on Dostoyevsky", Section 6, August 23, 1981, p. 35.

Rhetoric:	Safire, William; "On Language", Subtitle: The Bloopie Awards. Section 6, August 23, 1981, p. 8.
Film:	Garis, Leslie; "Translating Fowles Into Film", Section 6, August 30, 1981, p. 24.
Rhetoric:	Safire, William; "On Language", Subtitle: Cocktail Talk. Section 6, August 30, 1981, p. 10.
Rhetoric:	Safire, William; "On Language", Subtitle: Task Force. Section 6, September 6, 1981, p. 6.
Books:	Bernstein, Paul; "Making of a Literary Shogun", Section 6, September 13, 1981, p. 46.
Advertising: Public Relations:	Blumenthal, Sidney; "Marketing the President", Section 6, September 13, 1981, p. 42.
Rhetoric:	Safire, William; "On Language", Subtitle: See You Later, Allegator. Section 6, September 13, 1981, p. 16.
Television:	Schwartz, Tony; "The TV Pornography Boom", Section 6, September 13, 1981, p. 44.
Music:	Holland, Bernard; "Anthony Bliss: Culture and Commerce at the Met", Section 6, September 20, 1981, p. 40.
Rhetoric:	Safire, William; "On Language", Subtitle: Fashionese for Fall. Section 6, September 20, 1981, p. 16.

Press:	Cytowic, Richard E.; "The Long Ordeal of James Brady", Section 6, September 27, 1981, p. 27.
Rhetoric:	Safire, William; "On Language", Subtitle: Greezer Power. Section 6, September 27, 1981, p. 11.
Rhetoric:	Safire, William; "On Language", Subtitle: Winged Words. Section 6, October 4, 1981, p. 10.
Film:	Darnton, Nina; "Poland's Man of Films", Subtitle: (Anrlej Wajda). Section 6, October 11, 1981, p. 113.
Rhetoric:	Safire, William; "On Language", Subtitle: Mr. Justice. Section 6, October 11, 1981, p. 16.
Rhetoric:	Safire, William; "On Language", Subtitle: The Beauty Part. Section 6, October 11, 1981, p. 16.
Music:	Goldberg, Joe; "To Be Young and a Concert Pianist", Subtitle: (Boris Bloch). Section 6, October 18, 1981, p. 82.
Photography:	Markel, Helen; "The Bettman Behind the Archives", Section 6, October 18, 1981, p. 118.
Music:	Coe, Robert; "Philip Glass Breaks Through", Section 6, October 25, 1981, p. 68.
Press:	Gross, Jane; "A Woman Reporter in Yankee Country", Section 6, October 25, 1981, p. 32.
Rhetoric:	Safire, William; "On Language", Subtitle: Homogenized Etymology. Section 6, October 25, 1981, p. 16.

Rhetoric:	Safire, William; "On Language", Subtitle: The Great Out There. Section 6, November 1, 1981, p. 10.
Rhetoric:	Safire, William; "On Language", Subtitle: Schlepper and Bungie. Section 6, November 8, 1981, p. 16.
Communication:	Burgess, Anthony; "Creating a Language for Primitive Man", Section 6, November 15, 1981, p. 102.
Music:	Dunning, Jennifer; "Exchanging the Bow for the Baton", Subtitle: (Pinchas Zukerman). Section 6, November 15, 1981, p. 82.
Books:	Goodman, Susan; "The Legend of the Golden Hare", Subtitle: Masquerade, A Fable Written and Illustrated by Englishman Kit Williams. Section 6, November 15, 1981, p. 64.
Rhetoric:	Safire, William; "On Language", Subtitle: Zapper Again. Section 6, November 15, 1981, p. 16.
Communication:	Quindlen, Anna; "Women's Networks Come of Age", Section 6, November 22, 1981, p. 82.
Rhetoric:	Safire, William; "On Language", Subtitle: Heavy Weather. Section 6, November 22, 1981, p. 18.
Music:	Schonberg, Harold C.; "Acoustics: Still Playing It By Ear", Section 6, November 22, 1981, p. 142.

Rhetoric:	Safire, William; "On Language", Subtitle: Shall We Enhance?. Section 6, November 29, 1981, p. 16.
Music:	Trimble, Lester; "The Unsung American Composer", Section 6, November 29, 1981, p. 74.
Rhetoric:	Safire, William; "On Language", Subtitle: Splitting Hairs. Section 6, December 6, 1981, p. 22.
Rhetoric:	Safire, William; "On Language", Subtitle: Woodshed Blues. Section 6, December 13, 1981, p. 16.
Books:	Cohen, Morton N.; "A Christmas with Lewis Carroll", Section 6, December 20, 1981, p. 24.
Rhetoric:	Safire, William; "On Language", Subtitle: Window Shopping. Section 6, December 20, 1981, p. 10.
Books:	Schwartz, Tony; "Tom Wolfe: The Great Gadfly", Section 6, December 20, 1981, p. 46.
Books:	Martin, Russell; "Writers of the Purple Sage", Section 6, December 27, 1981, p. 18.
Rhetoric:	Safire, William; "On Language", Subtitle: Sleazy Does It. Section 6, December 27, 1981, p. 7.

Year 1982

Rhetoric:	Safire, William; "On Language", Subtitle: Double-A Rating. Section 6, January 3, 1982, p. 6.
Rhetoric:	Safire, William; "On Language", Subtitle: Vehement Objection. Section 6, January 10, 1982, p. 10.
Film:	Cohen, Barney; "Steve Tesich Turns Memories Into Movies", Section 6, January 17, 1982, p. 42.
Rhetoric:	Safire, William; "On Language", Subtitle: From Podunk to the Boonies. Section 6, January 17, 1982, p. 8.
Music:	Schonberg, Harold C.; "A Brave Opera's Black Voices", Section 6, January 17, 1982, p. 28.
Rhetoric:	Safire, William; "On Language", Subtitle: Beefing Up Phrases. Section 6, January 24, 1982, p. 9.
Music:	Holland, Bernard; "Highbrow Music to Hum", Section 6, January 31, 1982, p. 24.
Rhetoric:	Safire, William; "On Language", Subtitle: We Wuz Robbed. Section 6, January 31, 1982, p. 13.
Books:	Mauny, Elizabeth de; "The Winter Years of Nadezhda Mandelsturm", Section 6, February 7, 1982, p. 44.

Rhetoric:	Safire, William; "On Language", Subtitle: Good Courtesanship. Section 6, February 7, 1982, p. 13.
Rhetoric:	Safire, William; "On Language", Subtitle: An Ad Is Born. Section 6, February 14, 1982, p. 6.
Magazine:	_____; "The Atlantic: In Search of a Role", Section 6, February 14, 1982, p. 20.
Books:	Gelb, Barbara; "Being Jerzy Kosinski", Section 6, February 21, 1982, p. 42.
Rhetoric:	Safire, William; "On Language", Subtitle: High Diver. Section 6, February 21, 1982, p. 14.
Theatre:	Lawson, Stuart; "Harvesting Musicals at Goodspeed", Section 6, February 28, 1982, p. 30.
Rhetoric:	Safire, William; "On Language", Subtitle: Traffic Talk. Section 6, February 28, 1982, p. 9.
Rhetoric:	Safire, William; "On Language", Subtitle: Frank and Fruitful Exchange. Section 6, March 7, 1982, p. 9.
Photography:	Bordewich, Fergus M.; "India's Embellished Images", Section 6, March 14, 1982, p. 46.
Music:	Burnsford, Linda; "The New Philadelphia Sound", Section 6, March 14, 1982, p. 26.
Rhetoric:	Safire, William; "On Language", Subtitle: The Leak Age. Section 6, March 14, 1982, p. 14.

Rhetoric:	Safire, William; "On Language", Subtitle: Accent on the Caribbean. Section 6, March 21, 1982, p. 13.
Film:	
Television:	Harmetz, Aljean; "Hollywood's Video Gamble", Section 6, March 28, 1982, p. 40.
Rhetoric:	Safire, William; "On Language", Subtitle: The Present Absent. Section 6, March 28, 1982, p. 10.
Books:	Garis, Leslie; "Rebecca West", Section 6, April 4, 1982, p. 25.
Rhetoric:	Safire, William; "On Language", Subtitle: Publish or Perish. Section 6, April 4, 1982, p. 18.
Film:	Stevens, William K.; "New Life After 'The Last Picture Show'", Section 6, April 4, 1982, p. 43.
Rhetoric:	Safire, William; "On Language", Subtitle: The Meaning of Depression. Section 6, April 11, 1982, p. 9.
Rhetoric:	Safire, William; "On Language", Subtitle: Sluff It All Off. Section 6, April 18, 1982, p. 12.
Television:	Denison, D. C.; "Video Art's Guru", Section 6, April 25, 1982, p. 54.
Rhetoric:	Safire, William; "On Language", Subtitle: More Important(ly). Section 6, April 25, 1982, p. 14.
Rhetoric:	Safire, William; "On Language", Subtitle: Dead Cat on a Line. Section 6, May 2, 1982, p. 14.

Advertising:	Stabiner, Karen; "Tapping the Homosexual Market", Section 6, May 2, 1982, p. 40.
Press:	Herbers, John; "The President and the Press Corps", Section 6, May 9, 1982, p. 45.
Rhetoric:	Safire, William; "On Language", Subtitle: Snake Check. Section 6, May 9, 1982, p. 12.
Film:	Wren, Christopher S.; "On Location with Marco Polo", Section 6, May 9, 1982, p. 63.
Books:	Dillard, Annie; "The Joys of Reading", Section 6, May 16, 1982, p. 47.
Rhetoric:	Safire, William; "On Language", Subtitle: Let Freedom Love. Section 6, May 16, 1982, p. 20.
Books:	Atlas, James; "Derek Walcott: Poet of Two Worlds", Section 6, May 23, 1982, p. 32.
Rhetoric:	Safire, William; "On Language", Subtitle: Burnout. Section 6, May 23, 1982, p. 10.
Theatre:	Lohr, Steve; "The New Face of Kabuki", Section 6, May 30, 1982, p. 12.
Rhetoric:	Safire, William; "On Language", Subtitle: Red Hot "Freeze". Section 6, May 30, 1982, p. 7.
Film:	Lombardi, John; "Lumet: The City Is His Sound Stage", Section 6, June 6, 1982, p. 26.
Rhetoric:	Safire, William; "On Language", Subtitle: My Fellow Americans. Section 6, June 6, 1982, p. 16.

Rhetoric:	Safire, William; "On Language", Subtitle: Middle Initials. Section 6, June 13, 1982, p. 14.
Books:	Thomas, D. M.; "On Literary Celebrity", Section 6, June 13, 1982, p. 24.
Rhetoric:	Safire, William; "On Language", Subtitle: Sherpa Run-up. Section 6, June 20, 1982, p. 8.
Rhetoric:	Safire, William; "On Language", Subtitle: Miss Word of 1982. Section 6, June 27, 1982, p. 9.
Rhetoric:	Safire, William; "On Language", Subtitle: Words at War. Section 6, July 4, 1982, p. 6.
Music:	Stock, Robert W.; "Bands on the March", Section 6, July 4, 1982, p. 12.
Rhetoric:	Safire, William; "On Language", Subtitle: Exit Haigspeak. Section 6, July 11, 1982, p. 8.
Rhetoric:	Mankiewicz, Frank; "On Language", Subtitle: Hands On. Section 6, July 18, 1982, p. 8.
Rhetoric:	Butters, Ronald R.; "On Language", Subtitle: How to Order Eggs. Section 6, July 25, 1982, p. 6.
Books:	Hazelton, Lesley; "Doris Lessing on Feminism, Communism, and 'Space Fiction'", Section 6, July 25, 1982, p. 20.
Music:	Blandford, Linda; "Jonathan Miller Meets Mozart in St. Louis", Section 6, August 1, 1982, p. 22.

Rhetoric:	Steinmetz, Sol; "On Language", Subtitle: The Desexing of English. Section 6, August 1, 1982, p. 6.
Rhetoric:	Weng, Will; "On Language", Subtitle: Crossword Pitfalls. Section 6, August 8, 1982, p. 8.
Rhetoric:	Rosenthal, Jack; "On Language", Subtitle: The Murcan Way. Section 6, August 15, 1982, p. 10.
Rhetoric:	Safire, William; "On Language", Subtitle: Sunny Side Up. Section 6, August 22, 1982, p. 6.
Rhetoric:	Safire, William; "On Language", Subtitle: The Vanishing Haircut. Section 6, August 29, 1982, p. 6.
Rhetoric:	Safire, William; "On Language", Subtitle: Flip-Flop. Section 6, September 5, 1982, p. 8.
Books:	Baker, Russell; "Memoir of a Small-Town Boyhood", Section 6, September 12, 1982, p. 64.
Music:	Graffman, Naomi; "Leon Fleisher's Long Journey Back to the Keyboard", Section 6, September 12, 1982, p. 54.
Rhetoric:	Safire, William; "On Language", Subtitle: The Bloopie Awards. Section 6, September 12, 1982, p. 14.
Newspaper:	Robertson, Nan; "Toxic Shock", Section 6, September 19, 1982, p. 30.

Music:	Rockwell, John; "Why Isn't The Philharmonic Better?", Section 6, September 19, 1982, p. 46.
Rhetoric:	Safire, William; "On Language", Subtitle: Bizbuzz: Interfacing the Nation. Section 6, September 19, 1982, p. 10.
Rhetoric:	Safire, William; "On Language", Subtitle: Countdown to Damage Control. Section 6, September 26, 1982, p. 12.
Books:	Potok, Chaim; "The Bible's Inspired Art", Section 6, October 3, 1982, p. 58.
Rhetoric:	Safire, William; "On Language", Subtitle: The Awful Tooth. Section 6, October 3, 1982, p. 10.
Oratory:	Briggs, Kenneth A.; "The Pope: The World Is His Pulpit", Section 6, October 10, 1982, p. 24.
Rhetoric:	Safire, William; "On Language", Subtitle: Vogue Word Watch. Section 6, October 10, 1982, p. 14.
Rhetoric:	Safire, William; "On Language", Subtitle: A Bottle of Ketchup. Section 6, October 17, 1982, p. 16.
Rhetoric:	Safire, William; "On Language", Subtitle: Of Wimps and Men. Section 6, October 24, 1982, p. 16.
Rhetoric:	Safire, William; "On Language", Subtitle: Terrific Honorific. Section 6, October 31, 1982, p. 12.
Rhetoric:	Safire, William; "On Language", Subtitle: That Icy Tingle. Section 6, November 7, 1982, p. 16.

Rhetoric:	Safire, William; "On Language", Subtitle: Bull Market in Words. Section 6, November 14, 1982, p. 24.
Film:	Serveny, Gitta; "A Life With Gandhi", Section 6, November 14, 1982, p. 70.
Film:	Culhane, John; "Pakula's Approach", Section 6, November 21, 1982, p. 64.
Music:	Rockwell, John; "A Perfectionist on the Podium", Section 6, November 21, 1982, p. 68.
Rhetoric:	Safire, William; "On Language", Subtitle: An Egoistic Diktat in Fortuity. Section 6, November 21, 1982, p. 16.
Music:	Henahan, Donald; "The Conductor As Endangered Species", Section 6, November 28, 1982, p. 58.
Rhetoric:	Safire, William; "On Language", Subtitle: Farewell, My Lovely. Section 6, November 28, 1982, p. 16.
Rhetoric:	Safire, William; "On Language", Subtitle: Leggy. Section 6, December 5, 1982, p. 24.
Rhetoric:	Safire, William; "On Language", Subtitle: Win One for the Dipper. Section 6, December 12, 1982, p. 13.
Rhetoric:	Safire, William; "On Language", Subtitle: Vox of Pop Sixpack. Section 6, December 19, 1982, p. 18.

Rhetoric:	Safire, William; "On Language", Subtitle: Watch What You Say. Section 6, December 26, 1982, p. 6.
Theatre:	White, Timothy; "Theatre's First Couple", Subtitle: (Jessica Tandy and Hume Cronyn). Section 6, December 26, 1982, p. 20.

Year 1983

Music:	Buckley, William F.; "Queen of All Instruments", Section 6, January 2, 1983, p. 18.
Rhetoric:	Safire, William; "On Language", Subtitle: Bag Lady. Section 6, January 2, 1983, p. 6.
Books:	Hadley, Arthur T.; "Celebrating Robert Burns", Section 6, January 9, 1983, p. 34.
Rhetoric:	Safire, William; "On Language", Subtitle: Cap the Entitlement. Section 6, January 9, 1983, p. 9.
Rhetoric:	Safire, William; "On Language", Subtitle: On the Trail of Duke's Mixture. Section 6, January 16, 1983, p. 6.
Rhetoric:	Safire, William; "On Language", Subtitle: My Reception, Your Shivaree. Section 6, January 23, 1983, p. 8.
Music:	Reich, Walter; "The Well Tempered Tenor", Subtitle: (Placido Domingo). Section 6, January 30, 1983, p. 28.

Rhetoric:	Safire, William; "On Language", Subtitle: Ay, There's The Rub. Section 6, January 30, 1983, p. 8.
Rhetoric:	Safire, William; "On Language", Subtitle: Blowing My Whistle. Section 6, February 6, 1983, p. 9.
Music:	Shewey, Don; "The Performing Artistry of Laurie Anderson", Section 6, February 6, 1983, p. 26.
Rhetoric:	Safire, William; "On Language", Subtitle: Rose Were a Rose Were a Rose. Section 6, February 13, 1983, p. 16.
Rhetoric:	Safire, William; "On Language", Subtitle: Chickening In. Section 6, February 20, 1983, p. 9.
Books:	Friedan, Betty; "Twenty Years after The Feminine Mystique", Section 6, February 27, 1983, p. 34.
Rhetoric:	Safire, William; "On Language", Subtitle: Right Stuff in the Belly Pulpit. Section 6, February 27, 1983, p. 19.
Rhetoric:	Safire, William; "On Language", Subtitle: The Squeal Rule. Section 6, March 6, 1983, p. 12.
Books:	Clines, Francis X.; "Poet of the Bogs", Subtitle: (Seamus Henry). Section 6, March 13, 1983, p. 42.
Rhetoric:	Safire, William; "On Language", Subtitle: Raising Cain. Section 6, March 13, 1983, p. 16.

Years 1981-1988 — 261

Books: Photography:	Curtis, Charlotte; "Norman Parkinson", Section 6, March 20, 1983, p. 40.
Music:	Rockwell, John; "Leos Janacek: The Vindication of a Composer", Section 6, March 20, 1983, p. 47.
Rhetoric:	Safire, William; "On Language", Subtitle: Wattle I Do?. Section 6, March 20, 1983, p. 14.
Rhetoric:	Safire, William; "On Language", Subtitle: The Phrase Dick Brigade. Section 6, March 27, 1983, p. 20.
Books:	Gage, Nicholas; "My Mother Eleni", Section 6, April 3, 1983, p. 20.
Rhetoric:	Safire, William; "On Language", Subtitle: Pray, Why Pre?. Section 6, April 3, 1983, p. 12.
Books:	Ottenberg, Eve; "The Rich Visions of Cynthia Ozick", Section 6, April 10, 1983, p. 46.
Rhetoric:	Safire, William; "On Language", Subtitle: Kemp Follower. Section 6, April 10, 1983, p. 14.
Photography:	Gutman, Judith Maria; "Lewis Hine's Last Legacy", Section 6, April 17, 1983, p. 50.
Rhetoric:	Safire, William; "On Language", Subtitle: Tell It to the Marine. Section 6, April 17, 1983, p. 12.
Rhetoric:	Safire, William; "On Language", Subtitle: X Marks the Verb. Section 6, April 24, 1983, p. 12.

Music:	Schonberg, Harold C.; "Low-Key Celebration for a Master", Subtitle: (Brahms). Section 6, April 24, 1983, p. 81.
Theatre:	Gussow, Mel; "Women Playwrights: New Voices in the Theatre", Section 6, May 1, 1983, p. 22.
Rhetoric:	Safire, William; "On Language", Subtitle: The Bloopie Awards. Section 6, May 1, 1983, p. 10.
Television: Music:	Levine, Ed; "TV Rocks With Music", Section 6, May 8, 1983, p. 42.
Rhetoric:	Safire, William; "On Language", Subtitle: Pseudo Salestalk. Section 6, May 8, 1983, p. 10.
Film:	Selznick, Irene Mayer; "My Days in Hollywood", Section 6, May 8, 1983, p. 36.
Rhetoric:	Safire, William; "On Language", Subtitle: Arguendo. Section 6, May 15, 1983, p. 21.
Music:	Holland, Bernard; "In Praise of Early Music", Section 6, May 22, 1983, p. 64.
Rhetoric:	Safire, William; "On Language", Subtitle: Curb the Halting. Section 6, May 22, 1983, p. 12.
Music:	Page, Tim; "The New Romance with Tonality", Subtitle: (David Dan Tredici). Section 6, May 29, 1983, p. 22.
Rhetoric:	Safire, William; "On Language", Subtitle: Feeling Expansive. Section 6, May 29, 1983, p. 8.

Rhetoric:	Safire, William; "On Language", Subtitle: Butterfly Words. Section 6, June 5, 1983, p. 18.
Film: Television:	Lindsey, Robert; "HBO Moves In on Hollywood", Section 6, June 12, 1983, p. 30.
Rhetoric:	Safire, William; "On Language", Subtitle: Boulevard of Broken Words. Section 6, June 12, 1983, p. 20.
Books:	Yagoda, Ben; "Being Serious Funny", Section 6, June 12, 1983, p. 42.
Broadcasting:	Kaufman, Irving R.; "Reassessing the Fairness Doctrine", Section 6, June 19, 1983, p. 16.
Rhetoric:	Safire, William; "On Language", Subtitle: Dangling Man. Section 6, June 19, 1983, p. 8.
Film:	Kakutani, Michiko; "Ingmar Bergman: Summing Up a Life in Film", Section 6, June 26, 1983, p. 24.
Rhetoric:	Safire, William; "On Language", Subtitle: Caught Red-Handed. Section 6, June 26, 1983, p. 8.
Rhetoric:	Safire, William; "On Language", Subtitle: Full Figuring. Section 6, July 3, 1983, p. 6.
Books:	MacShane, Frank; "The Fantasy World of Itale Calvine", Section 6, July 10, 1983, p. 22.
Rhetoric:	Safire, William; "On Language", Subtitle: Under Covert. Section 6, July 10, 1983, p. 6.

Theatre:	Lombardi, John; "Playwrights on the Horizon", Section 6, July 17, 1983, p. 22.
Rhetoric:	Safire, William; "On Language", Subtitle: He That Filches From Me .... Section 6, July 17, 1983, p. 6.
Rhetoric:	Safire, William; "On Language", Subtitle: Play Down the Alibi. Section 6, July 24, 1983, p. 6.
Rhetoric:	Safire, William; "On Language", Subtitle: Abort the Correction. Section 6, July 31, 1983, p. 8.
Music:	Stock, Robert W.; "Pied Piper of the Clarinet", Section 6, July 31, 1983, p. 26.
Rhetoric:	Safire, William; "On Language", Subtitle: Not Knowing From Beans. Section 6, August 7, 1983, p. 6.
Rhetoric:	Safire, William; "On Language", Subtitle: Clause Wits. Section 6, August 14, 1983, p. 8.
Rhetoric:	Butters, Ronald R.; "On Language", Subtitle: Can I Ax You About That Arruh?. Section 6, August 21, 1983, p. 11.
Rhetoric:	Rosenthal, Jack; "On Language", Subtitle: The Words of Summer. Section 6, August 28, 1983, p. 16.
Rhetoric:	Wade, Betsy; "On Language", Subtitle: Memory Banks. Section 6, September 4, 1983, p. 8.
Rhetoric:	Burchfield, Robert; "On Language", Subtitle: The OWLS of the O.E.D.. Section 6, September 11, 1983, p. 32.

Books:	Weinraub, Bernard; "The Artistry of Ruth Prawer Jhabvala", Section 6, September 11, 1983, p. 64.
Books:	Berry, Jason; "A Voice Out of Africa", Subtitle: (Wolf Soyinka). Section 6, September 18, 1983, p. 92.
Rhetoric:	Conniff, Richard; "On Language", Subtitle: The Case for Malediction. Section 6, September 18, 1983, p. 16.
Music:	Howard, Bernard; "A Century of Offstage Life at the Metropolitan Opera", Section 6, September 18, 1983, p. 52.
Censorship:	Abrams, Floyd; "The New Effort to Control Information", Section 6, September 25, 1983, p. 22.
Music:	Huffmann, Paul; "An American in Vienna", Subtitle: (Lorin Maazel). Section 6, September 25, 1983, p. 40.
Rhetoric:	Safire, William; "On Language", Subtitle: Who Ticketed You?. Section 6, September 25, 1983, p. 12.
Theatre:	Dunning, Jennifer; "The New American Actor", Section 6, October 2, 1983, p. 34.
Photography:	Mitgang, Herbert; "Testament to a Lost People", Section 6, October 2, 1983, p. 40.
Rhetoric:	Safire, William; "On Language", Subtitle: Knowing Your Fiddlesticks. Section 6, October 2, 1983, p. 26.

Rhetoric:	Safire, William; "On Language", Subtitle: Welcome to Splitsville. Section 6, October 9, 1983, p. 12.
Rhetoric:	Safire, William; "On Language", Subtitle: Dust Heaps of History. Section 6, October 16, 1983, p. 14.
Books:	Freedman, Samuel G.; "Bearing Witness, The Life and Work of Elie Wiesel", Section 6, October 23, 1983, p. 32.
Film:	Lombardi, John; "Redford's Film Lab in the Rockies", Section 6, October 23, 1983, p. 48.
Rhetoric:	Safire, William; "On Language", Subtitle: The Build-Down Buildup. Section 6, October 23, 1983, p. 16.
Rhetoric:	Safire, William; "On Language", Subtitle: Internecine Incivility. Section 6, October 30, 1983, p. 12.
Rhetoric:	Safire, William; "On Language", Subtitle: Scoreless on the Year. Section 6, November 6, 1983, p. 20.
Rhetoric:	Safire, William; "On Language", Subtitle: A Czar is Not a Tsar. Section 6, November 13, 1983, p. 24.
Books:	Gleick, James; "Stephen Jay Gould, Breaking Tradition with Darwin", Section 6, November 20, 1983, p. 48.

Rhetoric:	Safire, William; "On Language", Subtitle: Cantonlike. Section 6, November 20, 1983, p. 20.
Rhetoric:	Safire, William; "On Language", Subtitle: My Dear Computer. Section 6, November 27, 1983, p. 16.
Film:	Goldsmith, Barbara; "Danger on the Film Set", Section 6, December 4, 1983, p. 122.
Rhetoric:	Safire, William; "On Language", Subtitle: When They Say That, Resilk. Section 6, December 4, 1983, p. 20.
Film:	Gold, Herbert; "Houston Films a Cult Classic", Section 6, December 11, 1983, p. 60.
Rhetoric:	Safire, William; "On Language", Subtitle: Apostrophe Catastrophe. Section 6, December 11, 1983, p. 14.
Rhetoric:	Safire, William; "On Language", Subtitle: Euph Will Be Served. Section 6, December 18, 1983, p. 13.
Books:	Canaday, John; "Treasures of Illumination", Section 6, December 25, 1983, p. 16.
Rhetoric:	Safire, William; "On Language", Subtitle: Stein or Steen?. Section 6, December 25, 1983, p. 6.

Year 1984

Theatre: Gussow, Mel; "The Real Tom Stoppard", Section 6, January 1, 1984, p. 18.

Rhetoric: Safire, William; "On Language", Subtitle: The Walls Have Ears. Section 6, January 1, 1984, p. 6.

Books: Bradley, David; "Novelist Alice Walker: Telling the Black Woman's Story", Section 6, January 8, 1984, p. 24.

Rhetoric: Safire, William; "On Language", Subtitle: The Skinny on Skinny. Section 6, January 8, 1984, p. 16.

Rhetoric: Safire, William; "On Language", Subtitle: Dominating the Momentum. Section 6, January 15, 1984, p. 6.

Rhetoric: Safire, William; "On Language", Subtitle: Tapetalk. Section 6, January 22, 1984, p. 12.

Press: Censorship: Garbus, Martin; "New Challenge to Press Freedom", Section 6, January 29, 1984, p. 34.

Rhetoric: Safire, William; "On Language", Subtitle: Thinking Big. Section 6, January 29, 1984, p. 6.

Press: Middleton, Drew; "Barring Reporters from the Battlefield", Section 6, February 5, 1984, p. 36.

Rhetoric: Safire, William; "On Language", Subtitle: The Woid on -Oid. Section 6, February 5, 1984, p. 12.

Rhetoric:	Safire, William; "On Language", Subtitle: Zapmanship. Section 6, February 12, 1984, p. 9.
Rhetoric:	Safire, William; "On Language", Subtitle: The Beltway Bandits. Section 6, February 19, 1984, p. 16.
Rhetoric:	Safire, William; "On Language", Subtitle: Never Call Retreat. Section 6, February 26, 1984, p. 8.
Rhetoric:	Safire, William; "On Language", Subtitle: Yawners and Sleepers. Section 6, March 4, 1984, p. 14.
Music:	Blandford, Linda; "Purist at the Piano", Subtitle: (Alfred Brendel). Section 6, March 11, 1984, p. 103.
Rhetoric:	Safire, William; "On Language", Subtitle: Punch Line English. Section 6, March 11, 1984, p. 28.
Theatre:	Gussow, Mel; "Dustin Hoffman's 'Salesman'", Section 6, March 18, 1984, p. 36.
Rhetoric:	Safire, William; "On Language", Subtitle: Front-Loading. Section 6, March 18, 1984, p. 18.
Photography:	Harris, Alex; "Gertrude Blom's MAYA", Section 6, March 25, 1984, p. 43.
Rhetoric:	Safire, William; "On Language", Subtitle: Away With You, Nosy Parker. Section 6, March 25, 1984, p. 18.

Music:	Freedman, Samuel G.; "The Words and Music of Stephen Sondheim", Section 6, April 1, 1984, p. 22.
Rhetoric:	Safire, William; "On Language", Subtitle: Who's a Patsy?. Section 6, April 1, 1984, p. 10.
Film:	Harmetz, Aljean; "Coming to Terms With Success", Subtitle: (James Brooks). Section 6, April 8, 1984, p. 47.
Rhetoric:	Safire, William; "On Language", Subtitle: Cardinal Is My Middle Name. Section 6, April 8, 1984, p. 12.
Books:	Bruckner, D. J. R.; "A Candid Talk with Saul Bellow", Section 6, April 15, 1984, p. 52.
Rhetoric:	Safire, William; "On Language", Subtitle: Straightening "Straits". Section 6, April 15, 1984, p. 18.
Books:	Garis, Leslie; "Simeon's Last Case", Section 6, April 22, 1984, p. 20.
Rhetoric:	Safire, William; "On Language", Subtitle: A Monologue on Dialogue. Section 6, April 22, 1984, p. 8.
Photography:	_____; "Flowers Through a Painterly Lens", Subtitle: (Dennis Stock). Section 6, April 22, 1984, p. 33.
Rhetoric:	Safire, William; "On Language", Subtitle: The Sleaze Factor. Section 6, April 29, 1984, p. 22.
Theatre:	_____; "Arthur Kopit: A Life on Broadway", Section 6, April 29, 1984, p. 88.

Books:	Harris, Mark; "Andrew Greely, Novelist, Journalist, Sociologist, Priest", Section 6, May 6, 1984, p. 34.
Rhetoric:	Safire, William; "On Language", Subtitle: The Spirit Is Mean. Section 6, May 6, 1984, p. 20.
Censorship:	Bernstein, Richard; "Opening the Books on Censorship", Section 6, May 13, 1984, p. 28.
Photography:	Bosworth, Patricia; "Diane Arbus: Her Vision, Life, and Death", Section 6, May 13, 1984, p. 42.
Rhetoric:	Safire, William; "On Language", Subtitle: Eurolingo. Section 6, May 13, 1984, p. 14.
Public Relations:	Clines, Francis X.; "James Baker: Calling Reagan's Re-election", Section 6, May 20, 1984, p. 52.
Music:	Page, Tim; "An American Conductor Succeeds at Home", Subtitle: (Leonard Slatkin). Section 6, May 20, 1984, p. 96.
Rhetoric:	Safire, William; "On Language", Subtitle: That Says It All. Section 6, May 20, 1984, p. 16.
Theatre:	Gelb, Barbara; "The Creative Mind, Mike Nichols: The Director's Art", Section 6, May 27, 1984, p. 20.
Rhetoric:	Safire, William; "On Language", Subtitle: Beware the Basher. Section 6, May 27, 1984, p. 8.

Rhetoric:	Safire, William; "On Language", Subtitle: Taint So. Section 6, June 3, 1984, p. 14.
Books:	Dowd, Maureen; "A Writing Odyssey Through India Past and Present", Section 6, June 10, 1984, p. 50.
Rhetoric:	Safire, William; "On Language", Subtitle: Pale Lilac Speaks. Section 6, June 10, 1984, p. 14.
Music:	Pareles, Jon; "Jazz Swings Back to Tradition", Section 6, June 17, 1984, p. 22.
Rhetoric:	Safire, William; "On Language", Subtitle: My Name Ain't Mac, Buddy. Section 6, June 17, 1984, p. 6.
Rhetoric:	Safire, William; "On Language", Subtitle: Sharp Elbows. Section 6, June 24, 1984, p. 9.
Books:	Weber, Bruce; "Raymond Carver, A Chronicler of Blue Collar Despair", Section 6, June 24, 1984, p. 36.
Rhetoric:	Henahan, Donald; "On Language", Subtitle: The Words of Music. Section 6, July 1, 1984, p. 6.
Press:	Joyce, Fay S.; "Notes on the Campaign Trail", Section 6, July 8, 1984, p. 28.
Rhetoric:	Mohr, Charles; "On Language", Subtitle: Warspeak. Section 6, July 8, 1984, p. 8.
Music:	Holland, Bernard; "Capturing Broadway on Record", Section 6, July 15, 1984, p. 30.
Rhetoric:	Rosenthal, Jack; "On Language", Subtitle: Filler Fad. Section 6, July 15, 1984, p. 10.

Rhetoric:	Reinhold, Robert; "On Language", Subtitle: How to Talk 'Texian'. Section 6, July 22, 1984, p. 8.
Rhetoric:	Tannen, Deborah; "On Language", Subtitle: Saying What One Means. Section 6, July 29, 1984, p. 6.
Rhetoric:	Safire, William; "On Language", Subtitle: Goodbye Sex, Hello Gender. Section 6, August 5, 1984, p. 8.
Press:	Miller, Judith; "A Mideast Odyssey", Section 6, August 12, 1984, p. 36.
Rhetoric:	Safire, William; "On Language", Subtitle: Value Versus Principle. Section 6, August 12, 1984, p. 8.
Public Relations:	Suskind, Ron; "The Power of Political Consultants", Section 6, August 12, 1984, p. 32.
Rhetoric:	Safire, William; "Ringing Rhetoric, The Return of Politican Oratory", Section 6, August 19, 1984, p. 22.
Rhetoric:	Smith, Sherwin D.; "On Language", Subtitle: Burger Me No Burgers. Section 6, August 19, 1984, p. 14.
Books:	Croyden, Margaret; "The Sudden Fame of William Kennedy", Section 6, August 26, 1984, p. 33.
Rhetoric:	Safire, William; "On Language", Subtitle: Puffing Up Deflation. Section 6, August 26, 1984, p. 10.

Rhetoric:	Safire, William; "On Language", Subtitle: The Wicked Which and the Comma. Section 6, September 2, 1984, p. 8.
Music:	Shaffer, Peter; "Paying Homage to Mozart", Section 6, September 2, 1984, p. 22.
Film:	Cohen, Barney; "Where B Means Brutal", Section 6, September 9, 1984, p. 150.
Music:	Copeland, Aaron; and Perlis, Vivian; "Looking Back With Aaron Copeland", Section 6, September 9, 1984, p. 82.
Books:	Gussow, Mel; "Antonia Fraser: The Lady Is a Writer", Section 6, September 9, 1984, p. 60.
Rhetoric:	Safire, William; "On Language", Subtitle: Secret Plan. Section 6, September 9, 1984, p. 24.
Public Relations:	Rosen, Jane; "The P. L. O.'s Influential Voice at the U. N.", Section 6, September 16, 1984, p. 58.
Rhetoric:	Safire, William; "On Language", Subtitle: Hide That Agenda. Section 6, September 16, 1984, p. 18.
Rhetoric:	Safire, William; "On Language", Subtitle: Mousse Call. Section 6, September 23, 1984, p. 10.
Film:	Kerr, Walter; "In Praise of Silence in Film", Section 6, September 30, 1984, p. 42.

Rhetoric:	Safire, William; "On Language", Subtitle: Aboard the Zoo Plane. Section 6, September 30, 1984, p. 12.
Rhetoric:	Safire, William; "On Language", Subtitle: Shoo-In. Section 6, October 7, 1984, p. 18.
Photography:	Clines, Francis X.; "Images", Subtitle: (George Tames). Section 6, October 14, 1984, p. 56.
Rhetoric:	Safire, William; "On Language", Subtitle: My Nomen Is Klatura. Section 6, October 14, 1984, p. 14.
Press:	Weisman, Steven R.; "The President and the Press", Section 6, October 14, 1984, p. 34.
Theatre:	Rich, Frank; "A Musical Theater Breakthrough", Section 6, October 21, 1984, p. 52.
Rhetoric:	Safire, William; "On Language", Subtitle: Forgive Me, But.... Section 6, October 21, 1984, p. 14.
Books:	Bruckner, D. J. R.; "With Art and Craftsmanship, Books Regain Former Glory", Section 6, October 28, 1984, p. 37.
Rhetoric:	Safire, William; "On Language", Subtitle: Banner Words. Section 6, October 28, 1984, p. 12.
Photography:	Ritchin, Fred; "Photography's New Bag of Tricks", Section 6, November 4, 1984, p. 42.

Rhetoric:	Safire, William; "On Language", Subtitle: Debating Words. Section 6, November 4, 1984, p. 16.
Books:	Clines, Francis X.; "Allen Ginsberg: Intimations of Mortality", Section 6, November 11, 1984, p. 68.
Rhetoric:	Safire, William; "On Language", Subtitle: Terminate the Neutralize. Section 6, November 11, 1984, p. 20.
Rhetoric:	Safire, William; "On Language", Subtitle: Shape Up or Ship Out. Section 6, November 18, 1984, p. 22.
Music:	Waleson, Heidi; "Beaux Arts Trio, an Enduring Sound", Section 6, November 18, 1984, p. 76.
Music:	Huffman, Paul; "Ghena Dimitrova: A Diva Discovered", Section 6, November 25, 1984, p. 75.
Rhetoric:	Safire, William; "On Language", Subtitle: Lavish It On. Section 6, November 25, 1984, p. 12.
Rhetoric:	Safire, William; "On Language", Subtitle: Let a Simile Be Your Umbrella. Section 6, December 2, 1984, p. 16.
Music:	Duka, John; "Sting: A Rock Star Transcends the Form", Section 6, December 9, 1984, p. 67.
Rhetoric:	Safire, William; "On Language", Subtitle: The Linear Cambe. Section 6, December 9, 1984, p. 18.

Books:	Lehman, David; "The Creative Mind, John Ashberry: The Pleasures of Poetry", Section 6, December 16, 1984, p. 62.
Rhetoric:	Safire, William; "On Language", Subtitle: Free World, So-Called. Section 6, December 16, 1984, p. 18.
Television:	Ephron, Nora; "Living With My VCR", Section 6, December 23, 1984, p. 16.
Rhetoric:	Safire, William; "On Language", Subtitle: The Gotcha! Gang Strikes. Section 6, December 23, 1984, p. 7.
Rhetoric:	Safire, William; "On Language", Subtitle: Drudgery It Ain't. Section 6, December 30, 1984, p. 6.
Books:	Tagoda, Ben; "Elmore Leonard's Rogues Gallery", Section 6, December 30, 1984, p. 20.

Year 1985

Rhetoric:	Safire, William; "On Language", Subtitle: The Post-Holiday Strip. Section 6, January 6, 1985, p. 6.
Rhetoric:	Miller, Jim Wayne; "On Language", Subtitle: Beaucoons of Words. Section 6, January 13, 1985, p. 9.
Rhetoric:	Safire, William; "On Language", Subtitle: The Odd Decouple. Section 6, January 20, 1985, p. 11.

Rhetoric:	Safire, William; "On Language", Subtitle: Beware the Junk-Bond Bust-Up. Section 6, January 27, 1985, p. 10.
Music:	Blandford, Linda; "The Public At Last Finds Benita Valente", Section 6, February 3, 1985, p. 32.
Rhetoric:	Safire, William; "On Language", Subtitle: The Boffin Speaks. Section 6, February 3, 1985, p. 11.
Rhetoric:	Safire, William; "On Language", Subtitle: Vigilante. Section 6, February 10, 1985, p. 9.
Rhetoric:	Safire, William; "On Language", Subtitle: What Lie Implies. Section 6, February 17, 1985, p. 16.
Rhetoric:	Safire, William; "On Language", Subtitle: Acronym Sought. Section 6, February 24, 1985, p. 9.
Film:	Vincour, John; "Clint Eastwood, Seriously", Section 6, February 24, 1985, p. 16.
Books:	Greene, Graham; "The Tenth Man: A Rediscovery", Section 6, March 3, 1985, p. 38.
Rhetoric:	Safire, William; "On Language", Subtitle: Medium-Rare Book Lingo. Section 6, March 3, 1985, p. 20.
Books:	Vincour, John; "The Soul-Searching Continues for Graham Greene", Section 6, March 3, 1985, p. 36.

Music:	Crutchfield, Will; "A Very Special Tosca", Section 6, March 10, 1985, p. 34.
Rhetoric:	Safire, William; "On Language", Subtitle: The Case of the President's Case. Section 6, March 10, 1985, p. 18.
Photography:	Luke, Margaret; "Collecting's Big Thrill Is the Chase", Subtitle: (Sam Wagstaff). Section 6, March 17, 1985, p. 40.
Rhetoric:	Safire, William; "On Language", Subtitle: All Engines Full Retronym. Section 6, March 17, 1985, p. 18.
Rhetoric:	Safire, William; "On Language", Subtitle: New Name for "Star Wars". Section 6, March 24, 1985, p. 14.
Film: Theatre: Music:	Freedman, Samuel G.; "The War and The Arts", Section 6, March 31, 1985, p. 50.
Rhetoric:	Safire, William; "On Language", Subtitle: Drunk Again. Section 6, March 31, 1985, p. 10.
Film:	Culhane, John; "Louis Malle: An Outsider's Odyssey", Section 6, April 7, 1985, p. 28.
Books:	Kleinfield, N. R.; "A Golden Touch for Best Sellers", Section 6, April 7, 1985, p. 32.
Rhetoric:	Safire, William; "On Language", Subtitle: Say Uncle — and Make My Day. Section 6, April 7, 1985, p. 10.

Books:	Aksyonov, Vassily; "An Exile in Literary America", Section 6, April 14, 1985, p. 52.
Rhetoric:	Safire, William; "On Language", Subtitle: Is a Problem. Section 6, April 14, 1985, p. 14.
Photography:	Farber, Harold; "A Centennial Celebration of the Adirondacks", Section 6, April 21, 1985, p. 52.
Theatre:	Freedman, Samuel G.; "The Gritty Eloquence of David Mamet", Section 6, April 21, 1985, p. 32.
Rhetoric:	Safire, William; "On Language", Subtitle: Public Diplomacy. Section 6, April 21, 1985, p. 14.
Rhetoric:	Safire, William; "On Language", Subtitle: You Not Tarzan, Me Not Jane. Section 6, April 28, 1985, p. 20.
Music:	Emerson, Ken; "The Creative Mind, David Byrne: Thinking Man's Rock Star", Section 6, May 5, 1985, p. 54.
Rhetoric:	Safire, William; "On Language", Subtitle: Come As You Are. Section 6, May 5, 1985, p. 17.
Rhetoric:	Safire, William; "On Language", Subtitle: Brooke Shields vs. McCallis Et Al. Section 6, May 12, 1985, p. 14.
Books:	Carlisle, Olga; "A Talk With Milan Kuwdera", Section 6, May 19, 1985, p. 72.
Music:	Freedman, Samuel G.; "The Glory of Carnegie Hall", Section 6, May 19, 1985, p. 44.

Rhetoric:	Safire, William; "On Language", Subtitle: There, There. Section 6, May 19, 1985, p. 20.
Rhetoric:	Safire, William; "On Language", Subtitle: Hypersexism and the Feds. Section 6, May 26, 1985, p. 10.
Theatre:	_____; "The Craft of the Playwright", Subtitle: A Conversation between Neil Simon and David Rabe. Section 6, May 26, 1985, p. 36.
Theatre:	Freedman, Samuel G.; "Last of the Red-Hot Producers", Section 6, June 2, 1985, p. 53.
Rhetoric:	Safire, William; "On Language", Subtitle: Whose Oxymoron Is Gored?. Section 6, June 2, 1985, p. 16.
Rhetoric:	Safire, William; "On Language", Subtitle: A Toast to White Bread. Section 6, June 9, 1985, p. 18.
Music:	Baraka, Amiri; "Miles Davis", Section 6, June 16, 1985, p. 24.
Rhetoric:	Eskenazi, Gerald; "On Language", Subtitle: Wordgame Champs. Section 6, June 16, 1985, p. 12.
Theatre:	Kakutani, Michiko; "The Public and Private Joe Papp", Section 6, June 23, 1985, p. 14.
Rhetoric:	Newman, Edwin; "On Language", Subtitle: Baybuh, Baybuh. Section 6, June 23, 1985, p. 8.
Rhetoric:	Rosenthal, Jack; "On Language", Subtitle: From Art to Zap. Section 6, June 30, 1985, p. 7.

Rhetoric:	Gin, Ernest; "On Language", Subtitle: Hamburgers and Amerikaners. Section 6, July 7, 1985, p. 6.
Public Relations:	Sanger, David E.; "The Changing Image of I.B.M.", Section 6, July 7, 1985, p. 12.
Rhetoric:	Hall, Donald; "On Language", Subtitle: A Fear of Metaphors. Section 6, July 14, 1985, p. 6.
Film:	Leaming, Barbara; "Orson Welles: The Unfulfilled Promise", Section 6, July 14, 1985, p. 12.
Music:	Page, Tim; "The Music of Ellen Zwilich", Section 6, July 14, 1985, p. 26.
Rhetoric:	Safire, William; "On Language", Subtitle: Emphasis on Stress. Section 6, July 21, 1985, p. 9.
Music:	Shewey, Don; "On The Go With David Griffin", Section 6, July 21, 1985, p. 28.
Rhetoric:	Safire, William; "On Language", Subtitle: The Derogator. Section 6, July 28, 1985, p. 12.
Rhetoric:	Safire, William; "On Language", Subtitle: Inartful Dodger. Section 6, August 4, 1985, p. 8.
Rhetoric:	Safire, William; "On Language", Subtitle: Unwed Words. Section 6, August 11, 1985, p. 9.
Books:	Griffin, Peter; and Hemingway, Ernest; "The Young Hemingway: Three Unpublished

	Stories", Section 6, August 18, 1985, pp. 14, 16, 19, 21.
Rhetoric:	Safire, William; "On Language", Subtitle: Words of the Right. Section 6, August 18, 1985, p. 8.
Books:	Kaufman, Michael T.; "Polish Echoes — And Ironies", Section 6, August 25, 1985, p. 26.
Photography:	Maddow, Ben; "W. Eugene Smith: Through A Lens Darkly", Section 6, August 25, 1985, p. 30.
Rhetoric:	Safire, William; "On Language", Subtitle: Wines Without Caps. Section 6, August 25, 1985, p. 8.
Rhetoric:	Safire, William; "On Language", Subtitle: Codswallop, Poppycock, and Horse Feathers. Section 6, September 1, 1985, p. 8.
Books:	James, Carolyn; "The Michener Phenomenon", Section 6, September 8, 1985, p. 44.
Rhetoric:	Safire, William; "On Language", Subtitle: DARE is Here!. Section 6, September 8, 1985, p. 20.
Theatre: Film: Television:	Kleiman, Dena; "The Malkovich Magnetism", Section 6, September 15, 1985, p. 52.
Rhetoric:	Safire, William; "On Language", Subtitle: Arcane Brown Bag. Section 6, September 15, 1985, p. 18.

Music:	Crutchfield, Will; "James Levine: New Era at the Met", Section 6, September 22, 1985, p. 22.
Press:	Lelyveld, Joseph; "South Africa: Dream or Reality", Section 6, September 22, 1985, p. 40.
Rhetoric:	Safire, William; "On Language", Subtitle: Back to Tool. Section 6, September 22, 1985, p. 14.
Press:	Abrams, Floyd; "Why We Should Change the Libel Law", Section 6, September 29, 1985, p. 34.
Theatre:	Gussow, Mel; "David Hare: Playwright as Provocateur", Section 6, September 29, 1985, p. 42.
Rhetoric:	Safire, William; "On Language", Subtitle: Playing in Pretoria. Section 6, September 29, 1985, p. 8.
Rhetoric:	Safire, William; "On Language", Subtitle: Invasion of the Verbs. Section 6, October 6, 1985, p. 12.
Rhetoric:	Safire, William; "On Language", Subtitle: Prexy Isn't Sexy Anymore. Section 6, October 13, 1985, p. 16.
Books:	Doctorow, E. L.; "The Artist as a Young Boy", Section 6, October 20, 1985, p. 27.
Rhetoric:	Safire, William; "On Language", Subtitle: Name Your Poison. Section 6, October 20, 1985, p. 14.

Books:	Weber, Bruce; "The Myth Maker", Subtitle: The Creative Mind of E. L. Doctorow. Section 6, October 20, 1985, p. 24.
Rhetoric:	Safire, William; "On Language", Subtitle: Caviar, General?. Section 6, October 27, 1985, p. 14.
Rhetoric:	Safire, William; "On Language", Subtitle: Forewards March. Section 6, November 3, 1985, p. 12.
Communication:	Clymer, Adam; "Polling America", Section 6, November 10, 1985, p. 37.
Rhetoric:	Safire, William; "On Language", Subtitle: The Self-Clasping Squeeze. Section 6, November 10, 1985, p. 16.
Music:	Holland, Bernard; "A Very Special Soprano", Subtitle: (Kathleen Battle). Section 6, November 17, 1985, p. 59.
Rhetoric:	Safire, William; "On Language", Subtitle: Summitspeak. Section 6, November 17, 1985, p. 16.
Theatre:	Schneider, Alan; "Waiting For Beckett", Section 6, November 17, 1985, p. 47.
Rhetoric:	Safire, William; "On Language", Subtitle: Our Pluralistic World. Section 6, November 24, 1985, p. 22.
Broadcasting:	Geist, William E.; "Merchandising Dr. Ruth", Section 6, December 1, 1985, p. 58.

Rhetoric:	Safire, William; "On Language", Subtitle: Only Foolin'. Section 6, December 1, 1985, p. 16.
Film:	Hoffman, Eva; "After the New Wave, Tavernier", Section 6, December 8, 1985, p. 96.
Theatre:	Nightingale, Benedict; "Michael Flynn, The Entertaining Intellect", Section 6, December 8, 1985, p. 67.
Rhetoric:	Safire, William; "On Language", Subtitle: Zing 'em With Zugzwang. Section 6, December 8, 1985, p. 16.
Music:	Godwin, Gail; "A Novelist Sings A Different Tune", Section 6, December 15, 1985, p. 59.
Film:	Maslin, Janet; "The Pollack Touch", Section 6, December 15, 1985, p. 54.
Rhetoric:	Safire, William; "On Language", Subtitle: Dishing the Full Plate. Section 6, December 15, 1985, p. 12.
Rhetoric:	Safire, William; "On Language", Subtitle: Name That Dog. Section 6, December 22, 1985, p. 8.
Film:	Harmetz, Aljean; "The Man Re-animating Disney", Section 6, December 29, 1985, p. 12.
Rhetoric:	Safire, William; "On Language", Subtitle: When Does "Close" Count?. Section 6, December 29, 1985, p. 6.

Year 1986

Rhetoric: Safire, William; "On Language", Subtitle: Of Yobbos and Gits. Section 6, January 5, 1986, p. 6.

Books: Heller, Joseph; "Joseph Heller: The Road Back", Section 6, January 12, 1986, p. 30.

Rhetoric: Safire, William; "On Language", Subtitle: Piggyback Slam-Dunking. Section 6, January 12, 1986, p. 8.

Photography: Goldberg, Vicki; "An Eye for Ageless Beauty", Subtitle: (Laura Gilpin). Section 6, January 19, 1986, p. 34.

Film: James, Caryn; "Auteur! Auteur! ", Subtitle: The Creative Mind of Woody Allen. Section 6, January 19, 1986, p. 18.

Rhetoric: Safire, William; "On Language", Subtitle: Sack Pig's Aperodic Non-Life-Style. Section 6, January 19, 1986, p. 12.

Television: Goodwin, Michael; "TV Sports Money Machine Falters", Section 6, January 26, 1986, p. 26.

Rhetoric: Safire, William; "On Language", Subtitle: Secs Appeal. Section 6, January 26, 1986, p. 6.

Rhetoric: Safire, William; "On Language", Subtitle: Buzz Off, Interceptor. Section 6, February 2, 1986, p. 10.

Theatre: Campbell, Colin; "The Tyranny of the Yale Critics", Section 6, February 9, 1986, p. 20.

Film:	Freedman, Samuel G.; "From the Heart of Texas", Subtitle: (Horton Foote). Section 6, February 9, 1986, p. 30.
Rhetoric:	Safire, William; "On Language", Subtitle: Watch My Style. Section 6, February 9, 1986, p. 12.
Rhetoric:	Safire, William; "On Language", Subtitle: Moon of My Delight. Section 6, February 16, 1986, p. 10.
Rhetoric:	Safire, William; "On Language", Subtitle: Gypping the Pharisaic Tribe. Section 6, February 23, 1986, p. 12.
Music:	Waleson, Heidi; "The Rise of a Young Conductor", Subtitle: (Gerald Schwarz). Section 6, February 23, 1986, p. 38.
Newspaper:	Berkow, Ira; "A Writer Called Red Smith", Section 6, March 2, 1986, p. 40.
Rhetoric:	Safire, William; "On Language", Subtitle: Of "The" I Sing. Section 6, March 2, 1986, p. 14.
Telephone:	Epstein, Nadine; "Et Voila! Le Minitec!", Subtitle: (Video-Phone). Section 6, March 9, 1986, p. 46.
Rhetoric:	Safire, William; "On Language", Subtitle: The Caplet Solution. Section 6, March 9, 1986, p. 8.
Television:	Salmans, Sandra; "Tinker's Prime Time at ABC", Section 6, March 9, 1986, p. 24.

Books:	Grizzuti, Barbara; "American Catholic in Rome", Section 6, March 16, 1986, p. 57.
Books:	Le Carre, John; "Pym Takes Cover", Section 6, March 16, 1986, p. 42.
Books:	Lelyveld, Joseph; "Le Carre's Toughest Case", Section 6, March 16, 1986, p. 40.
Rhetoric:	Safire, William; "On Language", Subtitle: Kotcha!. Section 6, March 16, 1986, p. 24.
Rhetoric:	Safire, William; "On Language", Subtitle: The '86 Rhetorical Watch. Section 6, March 23, 1986, p. 8.
Television:	Horowitz, Joy; "The Madcap Behind Moonlighting", Subtitle: (Glenn Caron). Section 6, March 30, 1986, p. 24.
Rhetoric:	Safire, William; "On Language", Subtitle: Delicious Delicto. Section 6, March 30, 1986, p. 8.
Rhetoric:	Safire, William; "On Language", Subtitle: Canute's Bum Rap. Section 6, April 6, 1986, p. 8.
Film:	Ward, Alex; "David Rayfel's Script Magic", Section 6, April 6, 1986, p. 24.
Newspaper:	McDonnell, Patrick; "Krazy Kat", Subtitle: Highbrow Burlesque. Section 6, April 13, 1986, p. 44.
Rhetoric:	Safire, William; "On Language", Subtitle: But It Would Be Wrong. Section 6, April 13, 1986, p. 16.

Rhetoric:	Safire, William; "On Language", Subtitle: Free Falling Onto a Sandbag. Section 6, April 20, 1986, p. 12.
Rhetoric:	Safire, William; "On Language", Subtitle: The Time Has Come. Section 6, April 27, 1986, p. 14.
Music:	Goldberg, Joe; "Andre Previn, Back in L.A.", Section 6, May 4, 1986, p. 38.
Rhetoric:	Safire, William; "On Language", Subtitle: Surgical Strike. Section 6, May 4, 1986, p. 12.
Rhetoric:	Safire, William; "On Language", Subtitle: Discussing Discussants. Section 6, May 11, 1986, p. 10.
Rhetoric:	Safire, William; "On Language", Subtitle: Recuse My Dust. Section 6, May 18, 1986, p. 18.
Books:	Howard, Maureen; "Can Writing Be Taught in Iowa?", Section 6, May 25, 1986, p. 34.
Rhetoric:	Safire, William; "On Language", Subtitle: Dry My Bier. Section 6, May 25, 1986, p. 8.
Music:	Bernhardt, Clyde E. B.; and Harris, Sheldon; "The Memoirs of a Jazzman", Section 6, June 1, 1986, p. 28.
Rhetoric:	Safire, William; "On Language", Subtitle: Class Cleavage. Section 6, June 1, 1986, p. 12.
Books:	Amichai, Yehuda; "An Amichai Sampler", Section 6, June 8, 1986, p. 42.

Books:	Auter, Robert; "Israel's Master Poet", Subtitle: (Yehuda Amichai). Section 6, June 8, 1986, p. 40.
Film:	Horowitz, Joy; "From Slapstick to Yuppie Fantasy", Subtitle: (Ivan Reitman). Section 6, June 15, 1986, p. 30.
Rhetoric:	Safire, William; "On Language", Subtitle: Subjoin the Fun. Section 6, June 15, 1986, p. 8.
Rhetoric:	Safire, William; "On Language", Subtitle: Invasion of the Arbs. Section 6, June 22, 1986, p. 6.
Music:	Holden, Stephen; "Cabaret's Bright Young Star", Subtitle: (Michael Feinstein). Section 6, June 29, 1986, p. 20.
Rhetoric:	Safire, William; "On Language", Subtitle: What Is An "American"?. Section 6, June 29, 1986, p. 6.
Rhetoric:	Safire, William; "On Language", Subtitle: Redundadundadundant. Section 6, July 6, 1986, p. 6.
Film:	Rosenbaum, Ron; "Acting: The Creative Mind of Jack Nicholson", Section 6, July 13, 1986, p. 12.
Rhetoric:	Safire, William; "On Language", Subtitle: Arrogance of Power. Section 6, July 13, 1986, p. 6.

Rhetoric:	Dionne, E. J.; "On Language", Subtitle: Latin Dead? Veni, Vidi, Vici. Section 6, July 20, 1986, p. 8.
Rhetoric:	Considine, Tim; "On Language", Subtitle: Starting From Scratch. Section 6, July 27, 1986, p. 6.
Television:	Jones, Alex S.; "The Anchors", Subtitle: Who They Art, What They Do, The Tests They Face. Section 6, July 27, 1986, p. 12.
Rhetoric:	Schmemann, Serge; "On Language", Subtitle: The Fading Tovarish. Section 6, August 3, 1986, p. 8.
Rhetoric:	Rosenthal, Jack; "On Language", Subtitle: Gender Benders. Section 6, August 10, 1986, p. 8.
Rhetoric:	Bernstein, Richard; "On Language", Subtitle: Gallic Gall. Section 6, August 17, 1986, p. 8.
Television:	Lindsey, Robert; "From 'Hill Street' to 'L. A. Law'", Section 6, August 24, 1986, p. 30.
Rhetoric:	Safire, William; "On Language", Subtitle: With All Deliberate Vulgarity. Section 6, August 24, 1986, p. 8.
Rhetoric:	Lindsey, Robert; "On Language", Subtitle: Calling Dr. Spin. Section 6, August 31, 1986, p. 8.
Music:	Rockwell, John; "Berstein Triumphant", Section 6, August 31, 1986, p. 14.

Rhetoric:	Safire, William; "On Language", Subtitle: Don't Touch That Dial. Section 6, September 7, 1986, p. 14.
Music:	Pareles, Jon; "The Return of Cyndi Lauper", Section 6, September 14, 1986, p. 72.
Rhetoric:	Safire, William; "On Language", Subtitle: That Secret Desire. Section 6, September 14, 1986, p. 30.
Music:	Crutchfield, Will; "Vocal Burnout at the Opera", Section 6, September 21, 1986, p. 51.
Rhetoric:	Safire, William; "On Language", Subtitle: Don't Make Me Blush. Section 6, September 21, 1986, p. 20.
Press:	Taubman, Phillip; "The Perils of Reporting From Moscow", Section 6, September 21, 1986, p. 59.
Film:	Dowd, Maureen; "Testing Himself", Subtitle: (Paul Newman). Section 6, September 28, 1986, p. 16.
Rhetoric:	Safire, William; "On Language", Subtitle: Hail to the C. E. O.. Section 6, September 28, 1986, p. 8.
Music:	Hoffman, Eva; "Julliard: A Renewed Quartet", Section 6, October 5, 1986, p. 28.
Rhetoric:	Safire, William; "On Language", Subtitle: Set-Up, Trumped-Up, But Not Framed-Up. Section 6, October 5, 1986, p. 8.

Books:	Symons, Julian; "The Queen of Crime: P. P. James", Section 6, October 5, 1986, p. 48.
Books:	McCullough, David; "Aviator Authors", Section 6, October 12, 1986, p. 50.
Rhetoric:	Safire, William; "On Language", Subtitle: Running to Daylight. Section 6, October 12, 1986, p. 8.
Film:	Capa, Cornell; "A Compassionate Camera", Section 6, October 19, 1986, p. 50.
Rhetoric:	Safire, William; "On Language", Subtitle: In a New York Minute. Section 6, October 19, 1986, p. 12.
Books:	James, Henry; "Hugh Merrow", Section 6, October 26, 1986, p. 55.
Books:	Ozick, Cynthia; "A Master's Mind", Subtitle: (Henry James). Section 6, October 26, 1986, p. 52.
Rhetoric:	Safire, William; "On Language", Subtitle: Disinformation Prep Schol. Section 6, October 26, 1986, p. 10.
Music:	McGuigan, Cathleen; "The Avant-Garde Courts Corporations", Subtitle: The Brooklyn Academy of Music Raises Millions. Section 6, November 2, 1986, p. 34.
Public Relations:	Roberts, Steven V.; "Politicking Goes High-Tech", Section 6, November 2, 1986, p. 38.

Rhetoric:	Safire, William; "On Language", Subtitle: The Erroneous Eagle and the Cross-Eyed Bear. Section 6, November 2, 1986, p. 10.
Books:	Kleinfield, N. R.; "The Supermarket of Books", Subtitle: (Waldenbooks). Section 6, November 9, 1986, p. 44.
Public Relations:	Patton, Phil; "The Selling of Michael Jordan", Section 6, November 9, 1986, p. 48.
Rhetoric:	Safire, William; "On Language", Subtitle: Meet My Whatsit. Section 6, November 9, 1986, p. 10.
Books:	Levine, Richard M.; "Murder, They Write", Section 6, November 16, 1986, p. 90.
Film:	Oney, Steve; "A Character Actor Reaches Stardom", Subtitle: (Harry Dean Stanton). Section 6, November 16, 1986, p. 52.
Rhetoric:	Safire, William; "On Language", Subtitle: Brother, Can You Spare a Question?. Section 6, November 16, 1986, p. 22.
Rhetoric:	Safire, William; "On Language", Subtitle: Hits and Errors. Section 6, November 23, 1986, p. 18.
Rhetoric:	Safire, William; "On Language", Subtitle: Operation Not-So-Staunch. Section 6, November 30, 1986, p. 14.
Music:	Sloven, Jane; "Samuel Ramey: A Voice Like a Lion's Roar", Section 6, November 30, 1986, p. 50.

Books:	Bradley, David; "On Rereading 'Native Son'", Section 6, December 7, 1986, p. 68.
Rhetoric:	Safire, William; "On Language", Subtitle: Gifts for Glossolalines. Section 6, December 7, 1986, p. 20.
Music:	Blandford, Linda; "Championing the New Music", Section 6, December 14, 1986, p. 74.
Advertising:	Kleiner, Art; "Master of the Sentimenal Sell", Subtitle: (Hal Riley). Section 6, December 14, 1986, p. 52.
Rhetoric:	Safire, William; "On Language", Subtitle: When "No Plans" Means "Get Ready". Section 6, December 14, 1986, p. 14.
Television:	Yagoda, Ben; "Not-So-Instant Replay", Section 6, December 14, 1986, p. 65.
Film:	Croyden, Margaret; "A Drama of Age and Exile", Subtitle: (Yuri Lyubimov). Section 6, December 21, 1986, p. 34.
Rhetoric:	Safire, William; "On Language", Subtitle: Who Shot John?. Section 6, December 21, 1986, p. 6.
Television: Press:	Boyer, Peter J.; "CBS News in Search of Itself", Section 6, December 28, 1986, p. 14.
Public Relations:	Greenfield, Jeff; "A Master's in Manipulation", Section 6, December 28, 1986, p. 33.
Rhetoric:	Safire, William; "On Language", Subtitle: By the Beautiful Sea. Section 6, December 28, 1986, p. 8.

Year 1987

Rhetoric:	Safire, William; "On Language", Subtitle: Nine Yards to Imbroglio. Section 6, January 4, 1987, p. 8.
Television:	Baker, Russell; "A Writer's TV Block", Section 6, January 11, 1987, p. 12.
Rhetoric:	Safire, William; "On Language", Subtitle: Let Us Distance Ourselves. Section 6, January 11, 1987, p. 9.
Theatre:	Gussow, Mel; "Clarke Work", Subtitle: In Martha Clarke's Art, Drama and Dance are Unified .... Section 6, January 18, 1987, p. 31.
Rhetoric:	Safire, William; "On Language", Subtitle: Locust Valley Lockjaw. Section 6, January 18, 1987, p. 8.
Television:	Moran, Malcolm; "Will Instant Replay Trip the Ref?", Section 6, January 25, 1987, p. 24.
Rhetoric:	Safire, William; "On Language", Subtitle: Finding's Losing. Section 6, January 25, 1987, p. 10.
Rhetoric:	Safire, William; "On Language", Subtitle: Oh, Fudge. Section 6, February 1, 1987, p. 8.
Press:	Burns, John F.; "A Reporter's Odyssey In Unseen China", Section 6, February 8, 1987, p. 29.

Books:	Garis, Leslie; "Didion & Donne: The Rewards of Literary Marriages", Section 6, February 8, 1987, p. 18.
Rhetoric:	Safire, William; "On Language", Subtitle: The Gotcha! Gang Strikes Again. Section 6, February 8, 1987, p. 10.
Rhetoric:	Safire, William; "On Language", Subtitle: Mr. Boaaprop. Section 6, February 15, 1987, p. 8.
Propaganda:	_____; "Postage-Size Propaganda", Section 6, February 15, 1987, p. 38.
Rhetoric:	Safire, William; "On Language", Subtitle: When I Make A Mistake. Section 6, February 22, 1987, p. 10.
Music:	Botsford, Keith; "The Pollini Sound", Section 6, March 1, 1987, p. 30.
Rhetoric:	Safire, William; "On Language", Subtitle: Poetic Allusion Watch. Section 6, March 1, 1987, p. 12.
Photography:	_____; "Photojournalism's Colorful Era", Section 6, March 1, 1987, p. 32.
Rhetoric:	Safire, William; "On Language", Subtitle: Couch Potatoes and Lounge Lizards. Section 6, March 8, 1987, p. 10.
Film:	_____; "Somebody to Talk About", Subtitle: The Performance Artist Spalding Gray may hit it Big with his Epic-monogue Feature Film. Section 6, March 8, 1987, p. 40.

Years 1981-1988 — 299

Theatre:	Freedman, Samuel G.; "A Voice from the Street", Subtitle: August Wilson's Plays Portray the Sound and Feel of Black Poverty. Section 6, March 15, 1987, p. 36.
Telephone:	Lax, Eric; "Ma Bell's Revenge", Section 6, March 15, 1987, p. 12.
Rhetoric:	Safire, William; "On Language", Subtitle: Miss Feasance of 1987. Section 6, March 15, 1987, p. 6.
Photography:	_____; "In Search of America, Photos by Jake Sternfield", Section 6, March 15, 1987, p. 32.
Film:	Jarowitz, Tama; "Adventures in Tinseltown", Section 6, March 22, 1987, p. 32.
Books:	Jones, Malcolm; "Moralist of the South", Subtitle: Walker Percy's Novels .... Section 6, March 22, 1987, p. 42.
Rhetoric:	Starr, Douglas; "On Language", Subtitle: Paying the Devil. Section 6, March 22, 1987, p. 6.
Books:	Kakutani, Michiko; "Our Woman of Letters", Subtitle: (Mary McCarthy). Section 6, March 29, 1987, p. 60.
Rhetoric:	Safire, William; "On Language", Subtitle: Bravo Zulu!. Section 6, March 29, 1987, p. 18.
Press: Books:	Kaufman, Irving R.; "The Creative Process and Libel", Section 6, April 5, 1987, p. 28.

Rhetoric:	Safire, William; "On Language", Subtitle: The Gruntled Employee. Section 6, April 5, 1987, p. 12.
Television:	Fabrikant, Geraldine; "Not Ready for Prime Time", Section 6, April 12, 1987, p. 30.
Rhetoric:	Safire, William; "On Language", Subtitle: Useful Idiots of the West. Section 6, April 12, 1987, p. 8.
Music:	Woodward, Richard B.; "Four Jazzmen, One Great Voice", Section 6, April 12, 1987, p. 46.
Rhetoric:	Safire, William; "On Language", Subtitle: Teed Off Over Teed Up. Section 6, April 19, 1987, p. 10.
Rhetoric:	Safire, William; "On Language", Subtitle: The Paw's That Refresh. Section 6, April 26, 1987, p. 10.
Books:	Davidson, Sara; "On Tour With Rock Hudson", Section 6, May 3, 1987, p. 54.
Rhetoric:	Safire, William; "On Language", Subtitle: Vamping Till Ready. Section 6, May 3, 1987, p. 14.
Photography:	Cole, Charlie; "Our Spy on High", Subtitle: (Portfolio). Section 6, May 10, 1987, p. 30.
Rhetoric:	Safire, William; "On Language", Subtitle: The Modifiers of Mother. Section 6, May 10, 1987, p. 10.
Rhetoric:	Safire, William; "On Language", Subtitle: Love That Dare. Section 6, May 17, 1987, p. 10.

Rhetoric:	Safire, William; "On Language", Subtitle: Weather Report: Yucky. Section 6, May 24, 1987, p. 8.
Press:	Freedman, Samuel G.; "Murder Hits Home", Subtitle: A Reporter Returns to His Hometown ... and Becomes United in Grief. Section 6, May 31, 1987, p. 20.
Rhetoric:	Safire, William; "On Language", Subtitle: Jimny Cricket Sings Again. Section 6, May 31, 1987, p. 10.
Rhetoric:	Tauber, Peter; "Notes on a Brief Campaign", Subtitle: A Speech Writer's Inside View of Gary Hart's Campaign. Section 6, May 31, 1987, p. 48.
Rhetoric:	Safire, William; "On Language", Subtitle: Going Gentle on My Mind. Section 6, June 7, 1987, p. 6.
Film:	Dupont, Joan; "France's Leading Man", Subtitle: (Gerard Depardieu). Section 6, June 14, 1987, p. 38.
Rhetoric:	Safire, William; "On Language", Subtitle: The Earth Makes Its Move. Section 6, June 14, 1987, p. 12.
Music:	Goldensohn, Marty; "Midlife Music", Section 6, June 21, 1987, p. 48.
Music:	Palma, Anthony De; "Ruben Blades: Up From Salsa", Section 6, June 21, 1987, p. 24.

Rhetoric:	Safire, William; "On Language", Subtitle: Fawn Hall's Shredding, Ek-setera. Section 6, June 21, 1987, p. 8.
Rhetoric:	Safire, William; "On Language", Subtitle: Effective Immediately. Section 6, June 28, 1987, p. 6.
Books:	Lawrence, Rae; "Pop Fiction for Smart Girls", Section 6, July 5, 1987, p. 20.
Rhetoric:	Safire, William; "On Language", Subtitle: Gimmie A Breakpoint. Section 6, July 5, 1987, p. 8.
Photography:	Goldberg, Vicki; "The Unflinching Eye", Subtitle: (Mary Ellen Mark). Section 6, July 12, 1987, p. 12.
Rhetoric:	Weisman, Steven R.; "On Language", Subtitle: Doing the Neeful. Section 6, July 12, 1987, p. 6.
Advertising:	Baker, Russell; "The Joys of Adland", Section 6, July 19, 1987, p. 16.
Rhetoric:	Miller, Bryan; "On Language", Subtitle: Chewing on Words. Section 6, July 19, 1987, p. 10.
Rhetoric:	Considine, Tim; "On Language", Subtitle: Hi, Spy!. Section 6, July 26, 1987, p. 18.
Books: Film:	Graham, Sheilah; "The Room Where Scott Died", Subtitle: (Sheilah Graham/F. Scott Fitzgerald). Section 6, July 26, 1987, p. 20.

Rhetoric:	Powers, Alan W.; "On Language", Subtitle: Head Over Googol. Section 6, August 2, 1987, p. 10.
Rhetoric:	Rosenthal, Jack; "On Language", Subtitle: The Ring of Truth. Section 6, August 2, 1987, p. 12.
Film:	Mieher, Stuart; "Spike Lee's Gotta Have It", Section 6, August 9, 1987, p. 26.
Music:	Rockwell, John; "Music Every Which Way", Section 6, August 16, 1987, p. 32.
Rhetoric:	Safire, William; "On Language", Subtitle: Glossary of a Scandal. Section 6, August 16, 1987, p. 12.
Press:	Safire, William; "Lincoln Meets the Press", Section 6, August 23, 1987, p. 26.
Rhetoric:	_____; "On Language", Subtitle: A Word From Our Sponsor. Section 6, August 23, 1987, p. 12.
Books:	Horowitz, Joy; "Mysteries From a Novelist Nun", Subtitle: (Sister Carol Ann O'Marie). Section 6, August 30, 1987, p. 34.
Rhetoric:	Safire, William; "On Language", Subtitle: State of Ploy. Section 6, August 30, 1987, p. 16.
Rhetoric:	Safire, William; "On Language", Subtitle: Hermen Eutic's Original Intent. Section 6, September 6, 1987, p. 10.
Rhetoric:	Safire, William; "On Language", Subtitle: The Incongruous "We". Section 6, September 13, 1987, p. 10.

Film:	Pepper, Curtis Bill; "Still Mastroianni", Section 6, September 20, 1987, p. 46.
Books:	Ruhlman, Michael; "A Writer at His Best", Subtitle: (Reynolds Price). Section 6, September 20, 1987, p. 60.
Rhetoric:	Safire, William; "On Language", Subtitle: Long Time No See. Section 6, September 20, 1987, p. 34.
Rhetoric:	Safire, William; "On Language", Subtitle: No Heavy Lifting. Section 6, September 27, 1987, p. 12.
Music:	_____; "John Cougar Mellencamp: Rebel With A Cause", Section 6, September 27, 1987, p. 40.
Music:	Croyden, Margaret; "Peter Brook Creates a Nine-Hour Epic", Section 6, October 4, 1987, p. 36.
Rhetoric:	Safire, William; "On Language", Subtitle: The Penumbra of Desuetude. Section 6, October 4, 1987, p. 16.
Photography:	_____; "Frozen in Time", Subtitle: Long Lost Photographs of Roald Amundsen's Historic Expedition to the South Pole. Section 6, October 4, 1987, p. 46.
Theatre:	Rich, Frank; and Aronson, Lisa; "He Made the Stage Come Alive", Subtitle: (Boris Aronson). Section 6, October 11, 1987, p. 52.

Rhetoric:	Safire, William; "On Language", Subtitle: Murder Board at the Skunk Works. Section 6, October 11, 1987, p. 18.
Photography:	Wolkenberg, Frank; "Out of Darkness", Section 6, October 11, 1987, p. 62.
Rhetoric:	Safire, William; "On Language", Subtitle: Piece of Work. Section 6, October 18, 1987, p. 14.
Film:	Weber, Bruce; "Cher's Next Act", Section 6, October 18, 1987, p. 42.
Rhetoric:	Safire, William; "On Language", Subtitle: I'll Stand Alone. Section 6, October 25, 1987, p. 12.
Television:	Shah, Diane K.; "Starting Over", Subtitle: TV's Grant Tinker. Section 6, October 25, 1987, p. 26.
Magazine:	Atlas, James; "A Magazine Junkie", Section 6, November 1, 1987, p. 22.
Theatre:	Loke, Margarett; "Butch: Dance of Darkness", Section 6, November 1, 1987, p. 40.
Rhetoric:	Safire, William; "On Language", Subtitle: Goons and Ginks and Company Finks. Section 6, November 1, 1987, p. 18.
Advertising:	Kleiner, Art; "Bare Knuckles on Madison Avenue", Subtitle: The Sale of the Ted Bates Agency .... Section 6, November 8, 1987, p. 34.
Press:	Priac, Frank J.; "A Reporter's Reporter", Section 6, November 8, 1987, p. 96.

Rhetoric:	Safire, William; "On Language", Subtitle: What Happened to the Market?. Section 6, November 8, 1987, p. 18.
Books:	Auchincloss, Louis; "Recognizing Gaddis", Section 6, November 15, 1987, p. 36.
Rhetoric:	Safire, William; "On Language", Subtitle: Too Clever by Three Quarters. Section 6, November 15, 1987, p. 18.
Photography:	Ackerly, John; "Fire in Tibet", Subtitle: (Photographs). Section 6, November 22, 1987, p. 36.
Theatre:	Freedman, Samuel G.; "Leaving His Imprint on Broadway", Subtitle: (Lloyd Richards). Section 6, November 22, 1987, p. 38.
Music:	Graffman, Naomi; "On the Road to Biloxi", Subtitle: (Eugene Istomin). Section 6, November 22, 1987, p. 72.
Rhetoric:	Safire, William; "On Language", Subtitle: Character Issue. Section 6, November 22, 1987, p. 18.
Rhetoric:	Jennings, Gary; "On Language", Subtitle: Old and Novel. Section 6, November 29, 1987, p. 16.
Books:	Marzorati, Gerald; "Living and Writing the Peasant Life", Subtitle: (John Berger). Section 6, November 29, 1987, p. 38.
Advertising:	Zuckerman, Edward; "How Now to Sell a Cow?", Section 6, November 29, 1987, p. 68.

Film:	Boyd, William; "Cockney Charisma", Subtitle: Bob Hoskins, Britain's Unlikely Leading Man. Section 6, December 6, 1987, p. 52.
Books:	Colbert, Elizabeth; "Literary Feminism Comes of Age", Section 6, December 6, 1987, p. 110.
Rhetoric:	Safire, William; "On Language", Subtitle: Running the Traps. Section 6, December 6, 1987, p. 30.
Rhetoric:	Safire, William; "On Language", Subtitle: Know Ye By These Presents. Section 6, December 13, 1987, p. 14.
Theatre:	Rockwell, John; "Andrew Lloyd Weber: Superstar", Section 6, December 20, 1987, p. 28.
Rhetoric:	Safire, William; "On Language", Subtitle: I Am Appalled. Section 6, December 20, 1987, p. 20.
Rhetoric:	Safire, William; "On Language", Subtitle: Smiles of a Summer Night. Section 6, December 27, 1987, p. 8.

Year 1988

Books:	Atlas, James; "Chicago's Grumpy Gurus", Subtitle: Best-selling Professor Allan Bloom and the Chicago Intellectuals. Section 6, January 3, 1988, p. 12.
Rhetoric:	Safire, William; "On Language", Subtitle: Nyet Problem on Snow Jobs. Section 6, January 3, 1988, p. 6.

Rhetoric:	Safire, William; "On Language", Subtitle: Damm That Tinker. Section 6, January 10, 1988, p. 12.
Rhetoric:	Safire, William; "On Language", Subtitle: Beware the W-Word. Section 6, January 17, 1988, p. 12.
Theatre: Music:	Sacks, David; "She's the Top", Subtitle: With "Anything Goes" Patti LuPone is again the Belle of Musical Theater. Section 6, January 24, 1988, p. 22.
Rhetoric:	Safire, William; "On Language", Subtitle: Ruling the Jet Set. Section 6, January 24, 1988, p. 12.
Books: Theatre:	Morris, Sylvia Jokes; "In Search of Clare Booth Luce", Section 6, January 31, 1988, p. 22.
Rhetoric:	Safire, William; "On Language", Subtitle: Grovel, Grovel, Grovel. Section 6, January 31, 1988, p. 8.
Books:	Whitmore, George; "Bearing Witness", Subtitle: Having Written about the Devastating Effects of AIDS on Others, The Author now Describes the Impact of the Disease upon Himself. Section 6, January 31, 1988, p. 14.
Film:	Harmetz, Aljean; "Who Makes Disney Run?", Section 6, February 7, 1988, p. 28.

Rhetoric:	Safire, William; "On Language", Subtitle: The Juddering Justice Shtick. Section 6, February 7, 1988, p. 12.
Television:	Volk, Patricia; "Let's Make A Deal", Subtitle: Big Bucks Enticed NBC to Stay in New York. Section 6, February 7, 1988, p. 32.
Rhetoric:	Safire, William; "On Language", Subtitle: Falling In Love Wtih Luv. Section 6, February 14, 1988, p. 16.
Rhetoric:	Safire, William; "On Language", Subtitle: The Player's The Thing. Section 6, February 21, 1988, p. 14.
Rhetoric:	Safire, William; "On Language", Subtitle: You Pays Your Money. Section 6, February 28, 1988, p. 16.
Rhetoric:	Safire, William; "On Language", Subtitle: Here I Sit, No Warts at All. Section 6, March 6, 1988, p. 18.
Press:	Taubman, Phillip; "The K. G. B. and Me", Section 6, March 6, 1988, p. 40.
Theatre:	Gerard, Jeremy; "David Hwang: Riding on the Hyphen", Subtitle: A Chinese-American Playwright's Journey into Mainstream American Theater. Section 6, March 13, 1988, p. 44.
Photography:	Luke, Margaret; "'Facts Within Frames', Gary Winogrand's Last Work", Section 6, March 13, 1988, p. 40.

Rhetoric:	Safire, William; "On Language", Subtitle: Phantom of the Phrases. Section 6, March 13, 1988, p. 16.
Television:	Leiser, Ernest; "The Little Network That Could", Subtitle: Started on the Cheap, CNN is now a Major Player.... Section 6, March 20, 1988, p. 30.
Rhetoric:	Safire, William; "On Language", Subtitle: Weenies of the World, Unite!. Section 6, March 20, 1988, p. 12.
Film:	Kaplan, James; "Jonathan Demme's Offbeat America", Section 6, March 27, 1988, p. 48.
Rhetoric:	Safire, William; "On Language", Subtitle: Fewer Bursts, Less Bursting. Section 6, March 27, 1988, p. 22.
Rhetoric:	Safire, William; "On Language", Subtitle: Slinging Muddle. Section 6, April 3, 1988, p. 10.
Books:	Weber, Bruce; "Richard Ford's Uncommon Characters", Section 6, April 10, 1988, p. 50.
Television:	Frank, Rueven; "1948 Live... From Philadelphia... It's the National Conventions", Section 6, April 17, 1988, p. 36.
Film:	Morgenstern, Joe; "The Great Collaborator", Subtitle: Jean-Claude Carriere: The Screenwriter of Choice for the World's Finest Directors. Section 6, April 17, 1988, p. 28.

Rhetoric:	Safire, William; "On Language", Subtitle: Who Will Indict the Indicters?. Section 6, April 17, 1988, p. 10.
Music:	Rockwell, John; "Settling the Score", Subtitle: How does a Conductor Approach a Masterwork?. Section 6, April 24, 1988, p. 54.
Rhetoric:	Safire, William; "On Language", Subtitle: Rack Up That City on a Hill. Section 6, April 24, 1988, p. 18.
Books:	Anderson, Patrick; "King of the Techno-Thriller", Subtitle: (Tom Clancy). Section 6, May 1, 1988, p. 54.
Theatre:	Quintero, Jose; "Carlotta and the Master", Subtitle: Eugene O'Neill's Widow. Section 6, May 1, 1988, p. 56.
Rhetoric:	Safire, William; "On Language", Subtitle: The Bloopie Awards. Section 6, May 1, 1988, p. 26.
Rhetoric:	Safire, William; "On Language", Subtitle: Dry's New High. Section 6, May 8, 1988, p. 14.
Books:	Rothstein, Mervyn; "Homegrown Fiction", Subtitle: Bobbie Ann Mason Blends Springsteen and Nabukou. Section 6, May 15, 1988, p. 50.
Rhetoric:	Safire, William; "On Language", Subtitle: Pushing the Envelope. Section 6, May 15, 1988, p. 20.
Rhetoric:	Safire, William; "On Language", Subtitle: Beware of Greeks Wearing Lifts. Section 6, May 22, 1988, p. 8.

Books:	Dana, Robert; "Poetic Injustice", Subtitle: The Story of Two American Poets Living and Writing in a Country in which Poetry Counts for Little. Section 6, May 29, 1988, p. 22.
Rhetoric:	Safire, William; "On Language", Subtitle: Day Care, Child Care, Word Care. Section 6, May 29, 1988, p. 8.
Books:	Atlas, James; "On Campus: The Battle of the Books", Subtitle: Are the Classics Racist and Sexist?. Section 6, June 5, 1988, p. 24.
Rhetoric:	Safire, William; "On Language", Subtitle: Kissing and Telling About Kiss-and-Tell. Section 6, June 5, 1988, p. 16.
Rhetoric:	Safire, William; "On Language", Subtitle: No Shades of Gray. Section 6, June 12, 1988, p. 12.
Rhetoric:	Safire, William; "On Language", Subtitle: Inside Baseball. Section 6, June 19, 1988, p. 10.
Newspaper:	Dolan, Mary Ann; "When Feminism Failed", Subtitle: An Editor of a Major Newspaper, the Author made sure to Back other Women. But They Embraced the Worst of Male Ways. Section 6, June 26, 1988, p. 20.
Rhetoric:	Safire, William; "On Language", Subtitle: Smiles of a Moscow Night. Section 6, June 26, 1988, p. 8.
Music:	White, Timothy; "Back from the Bottom", Subtitle: Beach Boy Brian Wilson. Section 6, June 26, 1988, p. 24.

Rhetoric:	Safire, William; "On Language", Subtitle: The Smartest Word. Section 6, July 3, 1988, p. 4.
Press:	Simon, Paul; "What I Learned: Reflections on My Run". Section 6, July 3, 1988, p. 18.
Music:	Pareles, Jon; "Heavy Metal, Weighty Words", Subtitle: The Band Metallica Brings a Grim Sense of Purpose to the Raucous Patry of Teenage Rock. Section 6, July 10, 1988, p. 26.
Rhetoric:	Safire, William; "On Language", Subtitle: On Tezisy Street. Section 6, July 10, 1988, p. 8.
Rhetoric:	Safire, William; "On Language", Subtitle: Coiner's Corner. Section 6, July 17, 1988, p. 8.
Film:	Lindsey, Robert; "Francis Ford Coppola: Promises to Keep", Section 6, July 24, 1988, p. 22.
Rhetoric:	Safire, William; "On Language", Subtitle: Poetic Allusion Watch. Section 6, July 24, 1988, p. 8.
Rhetoric:	Safire, William; "On Language", Subtitle: Possessing Dukakis. Section 6, July 31, 1988, p. 8.
Rhetoric:	Safire, William; "On Language", Subtitle: You Say Potato.... Section 6, August 7, 1988, p. 10.
Television:	Blonsky, Marshall; "Ted Koppel's Edge", Section 6, August 14, 1988, p. 14.
Radio:	Keillor, Garrison; "Everything's Up-to-Date in South Roxy", Subtitle: An Urban Fable from

	the Chronicler of Lake Wobegon. Section 6, August 14, 1988, p. 18.
Rhetoric:	Yagoda, Ben; "On Language", Subtitle: Tense Talk. Section 6, August 14, 1988, p. 8.
Film:	Heron, Kim; "Telling Stories With Light", Subtitle: The British Cinematographer Chris Menges Turns his Eye to Directing. Section 6, August 21, 1988, p. 32.
Rhetoric:	Reinhold, Robert; "On Language", Subtitle: Let the Credits Roll. Section 6, August 21, 1988, p. 18.
Books:	Selzer, Richard; "The Pen and the Scalpel", Subtitle: A Doctor Walks in and out of a Dozen Short Stories a Day .... Section 6, August 21, 1988, p. 30.
Press:	Atlas, James; "The Case of Paul de Man", Subtitle: In his Youth was the Eminent Critic a Pro-Nazi Journalist or an Immature Opportunist?. Section 6, August 28, 1988, p. 36.
Rhetoric:	Rosenthal, Jack; "On Language", Subtitle: Misheard, Misread, Misspoken. Section 6, August 28, 1988, p. 18.
Rhetoric:	Safire, William; "Read My Lips", Section 6, September 4, 1988, p. 22.
Books:	Plante, David; "In the Heart of Literary London", Subtitle: A Day with Margaret Drabble, Novelist, and Michael Holroyd, Biographer. Section 6, September 11, 1988, p. 42.

Rhetoric:	Safire, William; "On Language", Subtitle: Rot at the Top. Section 6, September 11, 1988, p. 24.
Music:	Boyer, Peter J.; "Sony and CBS Records: What a Romance!", Section 6, September 18, 1988, p. 34.
Rhetoric:	Safire, William; "On Language", Subtitle: Drop That Card. Section 6, September 18, 1988, p. 20.
Books:	Bernstein, Richard; "Howard's Way", Subtitle: A Master Translator Takes on the Challenge of his Career — Marcel Proust. Section 6, September 25, 1988, p. 40.
Television:	Priac, Frank J.; "Freeze! You're on TV", Subtitle: How "America's Most Wanted" has led to the Arrest of 22 Fugitives. Section 6, September 25, 1988, p. 56.
Rhetoric:	Safire, William; "On Language", Subtitle: Eat your Peas. Section 6, September 25, 1988, p. 20.
Books:	_____; "In Other Words", Subtitle: Proust — The Original and Three Translations. Section 6, September 25, 1988, p. 42.
Music:	Butsford, Keith; "Maverick Violinist", Subtitle: (Givon Kremer). Section 6, October 2, 1988, p. 50.
Rhetoric:	Safire, William; "On Language", Subtitle: Mother's Work. Section 6, October 2, 1988, p. 16.

Photography:	_____; "The Wit and Wisdom of Elliott Erwitt", Subtitle: A Photographer's Album. Section 6, October 2, 1988, p. 45.
Rhetoric:	Safire, William; "On Language", Subtitle: Debatemanship. Section 6, October 9, 1988, p. 12.
Photography:	Woodward, Richard B.; "It's Art, but Is It Photography?", Subtitle: A New Generation of Artists with Cameras is Gaining Acclaim by Blurring the Distinction. Section 6, October 9, 1988, p. 28.
Rhetoric:	Safire, William; "On Language", Subtitle: Gaffe Me Your Tired. Section 6, October 16, 1988, p. 20.
Rhetoric:	Safire, William; "On Language", Subtitle: Sit on My Laptop. Section 6, October 23, 1988, p. 18.
Rhetoric:	Safire, William; "On Language", Subtitle: Like Ugly on an Ape. Section 6, October 30, 1988, p. 20.
Television:	Schine, Cathleen; "From Lassie to Pee-Wee", Section 6, October 30, 1988, p. 38.
Books:	Atlas, James; "Speaking Ill of the Dead", Section 6, November 6, 1988, p. 40.
Film:	Norman, Michael; "Dennis Quaid Can't Sit Still", Section 6, November 6, 1988, p. 48.
Rhetoric:	Safire, William; "On Language", Subtitle: Hit My Hot Button. Section 6, November 6, 1988, p. 22.

Rhetoric:	Safire, William; "On Language", Subtitle: Sound Bite, Define Yourself. Section 6, November 13, 1988, p. 24.
Television:	Ward, Alex; "TV's Tormented Master", Section 6, November 13, 1988, p. 38.
Rhetoric:	Safire, William; "On Language", Subtitle: People of Color. Section 6, November 20, 1988, p. 18.
Books:	Weber, Bruce; "Andre DuBus's Hard-Luck Stories", Section 6, November 20, 1988, p. 48.
Film:	White, Timothy; "The Rumpled Anarchy of Bill Murray", Section 6, November 20, 1988, p. 38.
Newspaper:	Hempel, Amy; "Laugh Line", Subtitle: Working the Wacky Side — Two Women Shine as Cartoonists. Section 6, November 27, 1988, p. 44.
Rhetoric:	Safire, William; "On Language", Subtitle: The Feeling Is Mutual. Section 6, November 27, 1988, p. 20.
Film:	Colling, Glenn; "Up to New Tricks", Subtitle: Penn and Tellers are Taking their Black Magic to the Screen. Section 6, December 4, 1988, p. 82.
Rhetoric:	Safire, William; "On Language", Subtitle: Gifts of Gab for 1981. Section 6, December 4, 1988, p. 26.

318 — *Mass Media: Marconi to MTV*

Rhetoric:	Bernstein, Richard; "On Language", Subtitle: Youthspeak. Section 6, December 11, 1988, p. 22.
Television:	Shah, Diane K.; "The Good Fortune of Pat Sajak", Subtitle: TV's Genial Game-show Host goes up against Carson. Section 6, December 11, 1988, p. 42.
Film:	Lindsey, Robert; "The Dangerous Leap of Stephen Frears", Subtitle: A Small-Budget English Director Goes Hollywood. Section 6, December 18, 1988, p. 40.
Rhetoric:	Staples, Brent; "On Language", Subtitle: High on the Five. Section 6, December 18, 1988, p. 18.
Film:	Bryson, Bill; "Cleese Up Close", Subtitle: Seriously, This Writer, Actor, and Director is the Funniest Man in Britain. Section 6, December 25, 1988, p. 14.
Rhetoric:	Safire, William; "On Language", Subtitle: The Unhappy Campers. Section 6, December 25, 1988, p. 8.
Music:	Schwarzbaum, Lisa; "American Diva, Italian Style", Section 6, December 25, 1988, p. 20.
Photography:	Wegman, William; "On Dasher, On Dancer, On Fay", Subtitle: Photographs by William Wegman. Section 6, December 25, 1988, p. 18.

Headings By Page

Advertising 6, 16, 35, 38, 45, 51, 52, 53, 56, 59, 69, 77, 82, 84, 88, 103, 110, 137, 149, 150, 166, 169, 179, 185, 189, 190, 208, 211, 218, 225, 232, 234, 239, 247, 254, 296, 302, 305, 306

Books 11, 17, 18, 21, 27, 28, 29, 36, 38, 39, 94, 96, 99, 106, 116, 117, 121, 130, 131, 138, 139, 151, 154, 156, 158, 159, 160, 163, 164, 168, 170, 178, 182, 183, 185, 191, 198, 199, 204, 205, 206, 207, 211, 214, 215, 219, 220, 221, 222, 223, 224, 225, 226, 227, 229, 230, 231, 232, 233, 234, 235, 236, 237, 238, 239, 240, 241, 245, 246, 247, 249, 250, 251, 252, 253, 254, 255, 256, 257, 259, 260, 261, 263, 265, 266, 267, 268, 270, 271, 272, 273, 274, 275, 276, 277, 278, 279, 280, 282, 283, 284, 285, 287, 289, 290, 291, 294, 295, 296, 298, 299, 300, 302, 303, 304, 306, 307, 308, 310, 311, 312, 314, 315, 316, 317

Broadcasting 18, 20, 121, 123, 124, 133, 217, 263, 285

Censorship 31, 36, 37, 61, 64, 66, 67, 85, 86, 91, 166, 197, 216, 265, 268, 271

Communication 40, 49, 51, 52, 58, 61, 62, 64, 65, 66, 67, 70, 85, 98, 99, 102, 103, 113, 137, 141, 168, 169, 176, 178, 184, 185, 186, 188, 198, 202, 205, 210, 214, 222, 237, 249, 285

Dance 229

Film 5, 11, 15, 17, 19, 20, 21, 22, 23, 24, 25, 26, 27, 28, 29, 31, 32, 33, 34, 35, 36, 37, 38, 39, 41, 42, 43, 44, 45, 46, 47, 48, 49, 50, 51, 52, 54, 55, 56, 57, 59, 60, 62, 63, 64, 65, 66, 67, 68, 69, 70, 71, 72, 73, 74, 75, 76, 77, 78, 79, 80, 81, 82, 83, 84, 85, 86, 87, 88, 89, 90, 91, 92, 93, 94, 95, 96, 97, 98, 99, 100, 101, 102, 103, 104, 105, 106, 107, 108, 109, 110, 111, 112, 113, 115, 116, 117, 118, 121, 122, 123, 124, 125, 126, 127, 128, 129, 130, 132, 133, 134, 135, 136, 137, 138, 139, 141, 142, 143, 144, 145, 146, 147,

148, 149, 150, 152, 153, 155, 158, 159, 160, 161, 162, 163, 164, 165, 166, 167, 168, 170, 171, 172, 173, 174, 175, 176, 177, 180, 181, 182, 183, 184, 185, 186, 187, 188, 189, 190, 192, 193, 194, 195, 196, 197, 198, 199, 201, 202, 203, 204, 205, 206, 207, 208, 209, 210, 211, 212, 213, 214, 215, 216, 217, 218, 220, 221, 223, 224, 226, 228, 229, 231, 232, 233, 235, 236, 237, 238, 239, 240, 242, 243, 244, 245, 246, 247, 248, 251, 253, 254, 258, 262, 263, 266, 267, 270, 274, 278, 279, 282, 283, 286, 287, 288, 289, 291, 293, 294, 295, 296, 298, 299, 301, 303, 304, 305, 307, 308, 310, 313, 314, 316, 317, 318

Literature 162

Magazine 10, 24, 27, 28, 29, 33, 34, 42, 70, 98, 136, 157, 168, 181, 195, 202, 205, 238, 252, 305

Music 20, 51, 64, 65, 71, 116, 117, 118, 120, 138, 140, 141, 146, 150, 151, 152, 153, 161, 162, 173, 184, 188, 193, 217, 219, 220, 221, 222, 223, 224, 227, 228, 229, 230, 231, 233, 234, 235, 236, 237, 238, 239, 241, 244, 245, 246, 247, 248, 249, 250, 251, 252, 255, 256, 257, 258, 259, 260, 261, 262, 264, 265, 269, 270, 271, 272, 274, 276, 278, 279, 280, 281, 282, 284, 285, 286, 288, 290, 291, 292, 293, 294, 295, 296, 298, 300, 301, 303, 304, 306, 308, 311, 312, 313, 315, 318

Newspaper 1, 2, 3, 4, 5, 6, 11, 12, 14, 17, 18, 19, 21, 22, 24, 26, 27, 30, 34, 37, 38, 39, 44, 45, 46, 47, 49, 50, 53, 54, 60, 61, 63, 66, 68, 85, 92, 93, 104, 106, 107, 108, 113, 116, 117, 119, 125, 127, 131, 145, 148, 159, 160, 162, 163, 164, 171, 172, 180, 187, 190, 191, 192, 194, 195, 196, 197, 199, 200, 201, 204, 205, 206, 209, 210, 216, 218, 220, 227, 228, 230, 231, 235, 256, 288, 289, 312, 317

Oratory 129, 130, 257

Photography 4, 5, 6, 7, 11, 13, 18, 19, 21, 28, 30, 31, 34, 37, 38, 63, 66, 69, 135, 155, 175, 176, 217, 218, 219, 220, 224, 225, 228, 230, 233, 235, 236, 237, 238, 239, 242, 248, 252, 261, 265, 269, 270, 271,

275, 279, 280, 283, 287, 298, 299, 300, 302, 304, 305, 306, 309, 316, 318

Poems 161

Press 32, 37, 44, 57, 58, 61, 62, 65, 66, 67, 69, 70, 71, 73, 74, 80, 81, 84, 87, 93, 96, 101, 102, 104, 119, 120, 121, 144, 165, 168, 169, 195, 201, 202, 203, 206, 216, 238, 239, 245, 248, 254, 268, 272, 273, 275, 284, 293, 296, 297, 299, 301, 303, 305, 309, 313, 314

Propaganda 24, 31, 32, 38, 39, 57, 58, 59, 62, 65, 73, 78, 89, 147, 150, 178, 181, 298

Public Relations 16, 32, 38, 41, 42, 123, 168, 174, 179, 216, 244, 271, 273, 274, 282, 294, 295, 296

Radio 20, 29, 30, 36, 39, 40, 41, 42, 44, 45, 46, 47, 48, 49, 51, 52, 53, 54, 55, 56, 58, 60, 61, 62, 63, 64, 67, 69, 72, 74, 75, 77, 78, 79, 80, 82, 83, 84, 85, 86, 87, 88, 89, 90, 91, 92, 93, 97, 98, 100, 101, 103, 105, 106, 109, 112, 114, 115, 120, 127, 137, 139, 141, 156, 162, 166, 176, 188, 199, 201, 202, 213, 236, 313

Recording 43

Rhetoric 9, 11, 14, 16, 20, 35, 37, 41, 43, 47, 50, 51, 56, 57, 58, 60, 62, 64, 69, 70, 71, 73, 74, 84, 87, 94, 95, 97, 100, 101, 109, 115, 116, 117, 126, 142, 143, 151, 152, 153, 155, 160, 161, 177, 179, 197, 198, 226, 231, 237, 240, 241, 242, 243, 244, 245, 246, 247, 248, 249, 250, 251, 252, 253, 254, 255, 256, 257, 258, 259, 260, 261, 262, 263, 264, 265, 266, 267, 268, 269, 270, 271, 272, 273, 274, 275, 276, 277, 278, 279, 280, 281, 282, 283, 284, 285, 286, 287, 288, 289, 290, 291, 292, 293, 294, 295, 296, 297, 298, 299, 300, 301, 302, 303, 304, 305, 306, 307, 308, 309, 310, 311, 312, 313, 314, 315, 316, 317, 318

Satire 157

Semantics 151, 152, 153

Telegraph 10, 12, 13, 25

Telephone 1, 5, 6, 7, 11, 12, 13, 16, 18, 21, 32, 43, 61, 66, 71, 94, 175, 214, 288, 299

Television 5, 13, 46, 48, 68, 72, 88, 94, 100, 103, 104, 105, 106, 107, 108, 110,

111, 112, 114, 115, 118, 119, 120, 121, 122, 124, 125, 126, 127, 128, 130, 131, 133, 134, 135, 136, 137, 138, 139, 141, 142, 143, 144, 145, 146, 147, 149, 152, 154, 156, 157, 158, 160, 161, 162, 163, 164, 165, 166, 169, 170, 171, 172, 173, 174, 179, 180, 181, 182, 183, 184, 186, 187, 188, 189, 190, 191, 192, 193, 194, 195, 196, 197, 199, 200, 201, 202, 203, 204, 206, 207, 208, 209, 210, 211, 212, 213, 216, 219, 229, 230, 232, 233, 234, 235, 238, 239, 241, 242, 243, 244, 247, 253, 262, 263, 277, 283, 287, 288, 289, 292, 296, 297, 300, 305, 309, 310, 313, 315, 316, 317, 318

Theatre 1, 2, 3, 4, 5, 7, 8, 9, 10, 14, 15, 16, 17, 23, 36, 37, 38, 39, 50, 57, 59, 61, 62, 64, 70, 72, 73, 77, 81, 93, 94, 97, 99, 101, 109, 115, 116, 117, 118, 119, 120, 123, 127, 128, 129, 130, 131, 132, 133, 134, 135, 136, 137, 138, 139, 140, 141, 142, 143, 144, 145, 146, 147, 148, 149, 150, 151, 152, 153, 154, 155, 156, 157, 158, 159, 160, 168, 169, 170, 171, 173, 174, 178, 183, 184, 185, 187, 193, 195, 197, 198, 199, 200, 201, 203, 207, 210, 212, 213, 214, 215, 216, 218, 219, 220, 221, 223, 225, 226, 230, 232, 233, 234, 237, 238, 241, 244, 252, 254, 259, 262, 264, 265, 268, 269, 270, 271, 275, 279, 280, 281, 283, 284, 285, 286, 287, 297, 299, 304, 305, 306, 307, 308, 309, 311

Wireless 2, 4, 6, 7, 11, 12, 13, 14, 15, 16, 18, 19, 22, 23, 25, 26, 34, 40, 46, 52, 55

Authors by Page

Abrams, Floyd 218, 245, 265, 284
Ackerly, John 306
Adams, Mildred 50, 62
Addams, Charles 122
Ade, George 27
Adler, Barbara S. 115
Agel, Jerome B. 186
Ager, Cecilia 149, 163
Aikman, Duncan 50, 66
Aksyonov, Vassily 280
Alpert, Hollis 173, 180, 181, 183
Alvarez, A. 207, 211
Amichai, Yehuda 290
Anderson, Mary 15
Anderson, Patrick 311
Archer, Eugene 171
Asimov, Isaac 170
Askenas, Ruth 84
Astrahan, Anthony 208
Atkinson, Brooks 72, 127, 130
Atlas, James 222, 227, 233, 235, 239, 241, 254, 305, 307, 312, 314, 316
Auchincloss, Louis 306

Auter, Robert 291
Baedecker, Arthur J. 164
Bagdikian, Ben H. 203, 204, 213
Baker, Russell 127, 230, 232, 235, 237, 242, 256, 297, 302
Baldwin, Hanson W. 108
Ball, Joseph M. 89
Banfield, A. W. 55
Bankhead, Tallulah 124
Baraka, Amiri 281
Barber, Red 108
Barclay, Dorothy 106, 108, 114, 120, 124, 154, 164, 166, 169
Barry, Iris 90
Barry, Richard 25
Barthel, Joan 185, 187, 191, 196, 208
Bartholow, Dr. Paul 34
Bass, Martin Clark 241
Baxter, Beverly 93, 99
Beal, Sam 102
Beard, Miriam 42, 44
Beavan, John 148, 158
Behrman, S. N. 184

Bender, James F. 84, 85, 87
Bender, Jane F. 86
Bendiner, Robert 118, 120, 195
Benjamin, Milton R. 214
Bent, Silas 41, 43
Benton, William 89
Berger, Meyer 67, 82, 94, 124
Berger, Oscar 88
Bergman, Lewis 76, 194
Berkow, Ira 288
Bernhardt, Clyde E. B. 290
Bernstein, Paul 247
Bernstein, Richard 271, 292, 315
Berry, Jason 265
Berstein, Richard 318
Berton, Pierre 222
Bevan, Ian 128
Bigelow, Poultney 37
Birchall, Frederick T. 73
Blandford, Linda 235, 255, 269, 278, 296
Blashfield, Edwin H. 29
Blonsky, Marshall 313
Blum, Sam 179, 186, 188, 192
Blumenthal, Ralph 202
Blumenthal, Sidney 247

Bolinger, Dwight 246
Borland, Hal 71
Bordewich, Fergus M. 252
Bosworth, Patricia 271
Botsford, Keith 199, 298
Bourbon, Diana 37
Boutillier, Peggy Le 98
Boyd, William 307
Boyer, Peter J. 296, 315
Bracker, Milton 71, 74, 106, 122, 156
Bradley, David 268, 296
Bradshaw, Jon 217
Brady, Thomas F. 94, 109
Braendle, Fred J. 28
Brantley, Robin 213
Braudy, Susan 193, 201, 223
Brennan, Frederick H. 100
Brenner, Anita 59
Bride, Harold 23
Briggs, John 140
Briggs, Kenneth A. 257
Brock, H. I. 39, 45, 48, 63, 64
Brockway, Jean 55
Brook, H. I. 57, 70, 81
Brown, John L. 94
Brown, Nona B. 161
Brubeck, Dave 151

Bruckner, D. J. R. 270, 275
Brustein, Robert 205, 210
Brut, Harvey 106
Bryan, C. D. B. 229
Bryson, Bill 318
Buck, Louise 191
Buckley, Tom 195, 205, 208, 233, 234, 242
Buckley, William F. Jr. 259
Burchfield, Robert 264
Burger, H. H. 90
Burgess, Anthony 194, 200, 249
Burgin, Richard 227
Burns, James MacGregor 126
Burns, John F. 297
Burnsford, Linda 252
Butsford, Keith 315
Butters, Ronald R. 255, 264
Byas, Hugh 66
Callender, Harold 57
Cameron, James 206
Campbell, Colin 287
Campbell, Kenneth 98
Canaday, John 267
Canby, Vincent 187, 189
Cantwen, Mary 246
Capa, Cornell 294

Carew, Dudley 88
Carey, Alida L. 141
Carlisle, John M. 58
Carlisle, Olga 280
Carmody, Deirdre 217
Carry, Joan 185
Carson, Lettie Gay 159
Carter, Hodding 109
Carthew, Anthony 181
Cater, Douglas 168
Catledge, Turner 69
Cesare, Oscar 40
Chalmer, Stephen 12
Chasins, Abram 151
Chenery, William L. 32
Cherne, Leo 125
Cherne, Leo M. 115
Childs, Marquis W. 123
Churchill, Allen 112
Churchill, Douglas 72
Churchill, Douglas W. 59, 60, 64, 68, 71, 72, 75
Churchill, Lillian 74
Cianfarra, Jane 137
Clark, Delbert 62, 64
Clark, Ernest R. 86
Clark, Evans 42
Clarke, Arthur C. 156

Clarke, Joseph I. C. 16
Cleave, Maureen 184
Clines, Francis X. 260, 271, 275, 276
Clurman, Harold 118, 148, 153, 168, 175
Clymer, Adam 285
Cobb, Jane 77
Coe, Robert 239, 248
Cohan, George M. 61
Cohen, Barney 243, 251, 274
Cohen, Morton N. 250
Colbert, Claudette 165
Colbert, Elizabeth 307
Cole, Charlie 300
Cole, Malvine 121
Collier, Bernard Law 197
Collier, James Lincoln 229
Colling, Glenn 317
Colling, Larry 177
Collins, A. Frederick 5
Collins, James E. 35
Colton, Helen 103
Commanger, Henry Steele 121
Conaway, James 200, 201
Conniff, Richard 265
Considine, Tim 292, 302
Cook, Jess Jr. 231

Cook, Lilyn M. 83
Cooke, Alistair 246
Cooper, Kent 86
Copeland, Aaron 105, 274
Coppola, Eleanor 233
Corbin, John 2, 3, 5
Cortesi, Arnaldo 135
Cotler, Gordon 125, 160, 196
Cottam, Harold Thomas 23
Crankshaw, Edward 179
Craven, Thomas 81
Crawford, Bruce 63
Crisler, Ben 74
Crowther, Bosley 73, 75, 76, 77, 78, 80, 82, 83, 87, 90, 93, 95, 103, 110, 116, 117, 118, 122, 129, 142, 153
Crowther, Robert 87
Croy, Homer 32
Croyden, Margaret 232, 244, 273, 296, 304
Crozier, Eric 118
Crutchfield, Will 279, 284, 293
Culhane, John 194, 195, 205, 210, 213, 232, 246, 258, 279
Cullman, Marguerite W. 109
Cunningham, Frederic Jr. 190

Curtis, Charlotte 261
Cushing, Charles P. 36
Cytowic, Richard E. 248
d'Alessio 88
Daley, Arthur 103
Daley, Robert 201, 206, 207
Dana, Robert 312
Daniell, Raymond 94
Darnton, Nina 248
Davidson, Bill 206, 208, 210, 211
Davidson, Bruce 230
Davidson, Sara 300
Davis, Kenneth S. 116, 143
Davis, Melton S. 181, 197
Davis, Sally Ogle 238, 240
Davison, W. Phillips 100
DeCasseres, Benjamin 35, 36, 37, 38
Denison, D. C. 253
Deitz, Howard 90
Deri, Emery 47
Derier, Caman 142
Desfor, Harold D. 77
Devree, Charlotte 143
Devree, Howard 74
Dillard, Annie 254
Dionne, E. J. Jr. 292

Doctorow, E. L. 284
Dolan, Mary Ann 312
Donovan, Carrie 226
Doty, Roy 105
Douglas, Paul H. 155
Dowd, Maureen 272, 293
Dower, John W. 242
Duffus, R. L. 52, 57, 58, 72, 130
Duka, John 276
Dukes, Paul 37
Dunlap, Orrin E. Jr. 56, 57, 58, 60, 61, 63, 67
Dunning, Jennifer 249, 265
Dupont, Joan 301
Durand, Lionel J. 85
Duranty, Walter 61
Durdin, Peggy 131
Durrell, Lawrence 223
Dyott, G. M. 47
Eames, David 218
Eaton, Walter Prichard 39, 59, 62
Eder, Richard 215, 217, 221, 225
Edson, Lee 188
Edwards, Owen 219, 235, 236
Egan, Leo 129

Elliott, Osborn 218
Ellman, Richard 182
Emerson, Ken 280
Emperle, A. M. 36
Ephron, Nora 277
Epstein, Helen 220, 229
Epstein, Nadine 288
Eskenazi, Gerald 281
Esslin, Martin 183
Ethrige, Marc 91
Evans, Bergen 152
Even, Edward T. 172, 174
Everson, William 173
Everson, William K. 176
Fabrikant, Geraldine 300
Falk, Sam 175
Farber, Harold 280
Fay, Gerald 136
Fayant, Frank 17
Feld, Rose 51
Feldman, Sidney 112
Ferretti, Fred 226
Fisher, Nancy 190
Flatley, Guy 186, 212, 218
Fleming, Anne Taylor 224, 225
Foote, Robert O. 103
Foreman, Carl 172

Forman, Margaret 32
Fox, Frederic 171
Frank, Rueven 310
Frankel, Charles 164
Franklin, Rebecca 109, 133, 151
Franks, Lucinda 237
Free, E. E. 51
Free, Lloyd 92
Freed, Clarence I. 40
Freedman, Samuel G. 266, 270, 279, 280, 281, 288, 299, 301, 306
Freeman, David 202
Freeman, Don 105
Freeman, William C. 35
Friedan, Betty 226, 260
Frieland, Samuel 191
Fuller, Eunice Barnard 65
Funke, Lewis 93, 115, 149, 170
Gage, Nicholas 261
Galbraith, John Kenneth 216
Galliene, Richard Le 37
Gallup, George 103
Gander, L. Marsiand 114
Gans, Herbert J. 194
Garbus, Martin 268

Garis, Leslie 238, 247, 253, 270, 298
Geddes, Norman Bel 97
Geist, William E. 285
Gelb, Arthur 127
Gelb, Barbara 204, 212, 215, 220, 230, 237, 252, 271
Gelb, Leslie H. 244
Gelder, Robert Van 76
Gerard, Jeremy 309
Giddins, Gary 224
Gilbert, Gama 71
Gilroy, Harry 116, 119
Gin, Ernest 282
Giniger, Henry 131
Gittelson, Natalie 231, 235
Gleick, James 266
Glueck, Grace 216
Godwin, Gail 286
Gold, Herbert 208, 267
Goldberg, Joe 248, 290
Goldberg, Vicki 287, 302
Goldensohn, Marty 301
Goldner, Nancy 213
Goldsmith, Barbara 267
Goldway, Samuel 65
Goldwyn, Samuel 87, 96, 102, 107

Golman, Eric F. 169
Golsmith, Margaret O. 39
Goodheart, Arthur L. 150
Goodman, Daniel Carson 25
Goodman, Ezra 177
Goodman, Susan 249
Goodwin, Michael 220, 231, 287
Gould, Glenn 223
Gould, Jack 90, 94, 100, 101, 104, 108, 112, 115, 119, 121, 122, 124, 125, 127, 136, 142, 145, 154, 161, 163, 164, 166, 170
Graffman, Naomi 256, 306
Graham, Al 84
Graham, Sheilah 302
Gramant, Sanchi De 193
Green, Francis Vinton 31
Green, Martin 226
Greene, Graham 278
Greenbaum, Lucy 89
Greenfeld, Josh 199
Greenfield, Jeff 197, 210, 212, 216, 296
Greenspan, Emily 237
Grierson, Walter 24
Griffin, Peter 282
Grizzuti, Barbara 289

Gross, Jane 248
Gruen, John 198
Gumpert, Martin 116
Guralnick, Peter 230
Gussow, Mel 200, 210, 215, 216, 218, 221, 229, 232, 239, 262, 268, 269, 274, 284, 297
Guthrie, Tyrone 132, 137, 141, 146, 156, 160
Gutman, Judith Maria 261
Hadley, Arthur T. 259
Hager, Alice Rogers 57
Halberstam, Michael J. 199
Hale, William Bayard 14
Hall, Donald 282
Hall, Mordaunt 39, 41, 42
Hanley, Parke F. 54
Hano, Arnold 174, 183, 199
Harbord, Major Gen. J. G. 45
Harmetz, Aljean 205, 237, 253, 270, 286, 308
Harrington, John Walker 32, 36
Harrington, Stephanie 203, 205, 209
Harris, Alex 269
Harris, Mark 206, 271
Harrison, Emma 163

Hartley, Rev. Lyman Richard 95
Hawkins, Robert F. 157
Hayes, Helen 157
Hayward, Walter B. 44
Hazelton, Lesley 255
Hechenger, Grace 199
Hechinger, Grace and Fred M. 160
Heffner, Richard D. 152
Heller, Joseph 287
Hellman, Peter 194
Hempel, Amy 317
Henahan, Donald 201, 233, 258, 272
Henderson, W. J. 1
Hennessee, Judith Adler 200
Herbers, John 228, 254
Herling, John 144
Heron, Kim 314
Herrmann, Helen Markel 110
Hershfield, Harry 117
Hewson, E. Wendell 114
Hill, Frank E. 62
Hill, Gladwin 138
Hitchcock, Alfred 109
Hitler, Adolph 78
Holbrook, Stewart 106

Authors By Page — 331

Hodierne, Robert 195
Hoffman, Eva 286, 293
Hoge, Warren 228
Hoggart, Richard 172
Holden, Stephen 291
Holland, Bernard 247, 251, 262, 272, 285
Homan, William H. 185
Honan, William H. 186, 188
Hood, Raymond M. 54
Hopkins, Arthur 83, 94
Horowitz, Joseph 224
Horowitz, Joy 289, 291, 303
Houghton, Norris 140
Howard, Bernard 265
Howard, Maureen 290
Huffman, Paul 265, 276
Hughes, Richard 178
Hume, Brit 202
Hurd, Charles W. B. 61
Huston, Lester A. 64
Hutchens, John K. 78, 79, 80, 81, 82, 83, 84
Irving, Carter 41
Jablonski, Edward 238
Jacobs, Hayes B. 175
James, Carolyn 283
James, Caryn 287
James, Henry 294
Jamison, Barbara Berch 122, 123, 124, 125
Janes, Leo 226
Jarowitz, Tama 299
Javasky, Victor S. 200
Javits, Jacob K. 115
Jaynes, Gregory 245
Jennings, C. Robert 147
Jennings, Gary 306
Jones, Alex S. 292
Jones, Henry Arthur 36
Jones, Malcolm 299
Johnson, Sheila K. 198
Johnston, Tracy 204
Jorden, William J. 196
Jowitt, Deborah 207, 214
Joyce, Fay S. 272
Kaempffert, Waldemar 48, 54, 58, 68, 69
Kakutani, Michiko 263, 281, 299
Kalb, Bernard 110
Kamm, Henry 199
Kantor, Ken 105
Kaplan, James 310
Karp, David 183
Karpt, Ruth 96

Kasindorf, Martin 201, 203, 204
Kastner, Joseph 231
Katz, Alvin 112
Kaufman, George S. 145
Kaufman, Irving R. 263, 299
Kaufman, Michael T. 283
Kavanaugh, James V. 189
Keating, John 168
Keating, Kenneth B. 180
Keats, John 172
Keillor, Garrison 313
Kelly, Fred C. 21
Kemler, Edgar 131
Kempe, Richard 129
Kendall, Elaine 170
Kennedy, Mopsy Strange 202
Kenworthy, E. W. 136
Kerr, Walter 187, 189, 195, 197, 203, 274
Kieran, James 67
Kilmer, Joyce 26, 27, 28, 29
Kirsch, Robert 178
Klauber, Adolph 1, 2, 3, 4, 8, 9
Kleen, Howard 184
Kleiman, Dena 283
Klein, Allen 123
Kleiner, Art 296, 305
Kleinfield, N. R. 231, 279, 295
Kneeland, Douglas E. 224
Knott, Seymour H. 114
Kornbluth, Jesse 229, 232, 234, 235
Kostelanetz, Richard 185, 186
Kramer, Hilton 188, 220, 225
Kristol, Irving 197
Kronenberger, Louis 168
Krutch, Jos. Wood 162, 163
Krutch, Joseph Wood 139, 153
Kurland, Alan E. 188
Lampton, William J. 4
Lang, Daniel 70
Langer, Lawrence 94
Lanier, Robin 209
Lardner, John 133
Lasch, Christopher 181
Latham, Aaron 219
Lathaw, Rarou 198
Laughton, Charles 116
Laurette, Talor 108
Lauterbach, Richard E. 108
Lawrence, Rae 302
Lawson, Stuart 252
Lax, Eric 299
Layman, Edward A. 66

Ledger, Marshall 242
Lefferts, Barney 138, 143
Lehman, David 277
Leiser, Ernest 310
Lejeune, C. A. 72, 74, 77, 96
Lelyveld, Joseph 218, 219, 284, 289
Lengyel, Emil 56, 57
Leonard, John 190, 191, 192
Lerner, Alan Jay 173
LeShan, Eda J. 184
Lester, Elenore 193
Leverett, Norman 121
Levick, M. B. 39
Leviero, Anthony 104
Levine, Ed 262
Levine, M. 188
Levine, Richard M. 211, 295
Levines, Harry 131
Levy, Alan 182, 191, 192, 207
Lewis, Anthony 180, 200
Lewis, Flora 168, 171
Lewis, R. C. 98
Lieberman, Henry R. 102
Lieberson, Goddard 138
Lindsey, Robert 217, 223, 263, 292, 313, 318
Lingemen, Richard R. 190

Lipset, Seymour Martin 176
Lipsyte, Robert M. 173
Litwak, Leo E. 179
Lohr, Steve 254
Loke, Margarett 305
Lombardi, John 254, 264, 266
Long, Tania 80
Losey, Joseph 175
Losser, David 49
Louchheim, Aline B. 116
Low, David 65
Lowery, Helen Bullitt 33, 35, 40
Lowry, Walker 101
Luce, Gay 198
Lukas, J. Anthony 216
Luke, Margaret 279, 309
Lyons, Gene 218
Macgowan, Kenneth 92
Mackenzie, Catherine 60, 75, 80
MacLeish, Archibald 85
MacMahon, Henry 36
MacShane, Frank 263
MacWilliams, Walter E. 52
Maddow, Ben 283
Magenknecht, Edward 160
Maliver, Bruce L. 197

Mallon, Paul 61
Maney, Richard 139, 159
Mankiewicz, Frank 255
Mapes, Harold T. 30
Marashian, O. M. 104
March, Joseph Moncure 78
Maremaa, Thomas 201, 212
Markel, Helen 85, 140, 248
Markel, Lester 107, 169, 181, 186
Markfield, Wallace 184, 215
Markham, S. F. 70
Marowitz, Charles 201, 203, 208
Marshall, Edward 25, 26
Martin, John 120, 127
Martin, Russell 250
Martyn, T. J. C. 52, 54
Marx, Arthur 126
Marzorati, Gerald 306
Maslin, Janet 286
Mason, Clifford 232
Mason, James 95, 97
Masson, Thomas L. 38
Matthews, Brander 35
Mauny, Elizabeth de 251
Mauriac, Claude 151
Maxwell, Robert J. 187

Mayer, Martin 184, 202
Maynard, Joyce 227
McCormick, Anne O'Hare 45, 49, 55, 56
McCullough, David 294
McDermott, John F. 193
McDonnell, Patrick 289
McFadden, Cyra 246
McGuigan, Cathleen 294
McIntyre, William A. 145
McKenna, W. E. 4
McLean, Robert 148
McPherson, James 209
Meehan, Thomas 166, 178, 182, 193, 202, 209, 210
Meiklijohn, Alexander 100
Middleton, Drew 92, 95, 148, 268
Mieher, Stuart 303
Miller, Bryan 302
Miller, Jim Wayne 277
Miller, Judith 273
Millstein, Gilbert 111, 116, 117, 118, 119, 123, 125, 126, 129, 130, 132, 133, 134, 135, 136, 137, 140, 141, 147, 150, 153, 155, 156, 157, 158, 159, 160, 170
Milne, A. A. 92
Minnigerode, F. L. 46

Authors By Page — 335

Minow, Newton N. 172

Mitgang, Herbert 121, 155, 158, 160, 265

Mohr, Charles 272

Monroe, Elizabeth 117

Moore, Gaylen 233, 239

Moran, Malcolm 297

Morehouse, Ward 169

Morgan, Henry 91

Morgan, Ted 204, 211, 213, 216

Morgansen, Thomas G. 83, 84

Morgenstern, Joe 310

Morgenstern, Joseph 240

Morgenthau, Hans S. 164

Morris, James 166

Morris, John 141

Morris, Sylvia Jokes 308

Moses, Robert 107, 110, 149, 172

Mosley, Leonard 177

Mossman, Elliot 220

Murphy, Eugene 190

Murray, William 192

Musgrave, Francis 106

Myers, Robert Cobb 102

Nabokov, Vladimir 246

Nathan, Paul S. 83

Navasky, Victor S. 185

Neville, Richard 216

Nevins, Allan 73, 96, 99, 113

Newman, Edwin 281

Newman, Ernest 117

Newstadt, Rick 207

Nichols, Lewis 50, 51, 56, 63, 90, 97, 98, 99, 144

Nichols, Robert 43

Nightingale, Benedict 286

Norman, Michael 316

Nugent, Frank S. 64, 67, 70, 71, 74, 75, 79, 81, 82, 86, 89, 91, 93, 95, 97

O'Malley, Suzanne 234

Oney, Steve 295

Orwell, George 201

O'Shea, Ruth 104

Ottenberg, Eve 261

Owen, Russell 56

Ozick, Cynthia 294

Packard, Vance 150

Page, Tim 262, 271, 282

Palma, Anthony De 301

Palmer, Colonel Frederick 68

Papageorge, Tod 219

Pareles, Jon 272, 293, 313

Patton, Phil 295

Pearson, Hayin S. 107
Peck, Ira 114
Peck, Seymour 123, 126, 127, 128, 133, 135, 136, 137, 139, 140, 141, 142, 143, 144, 145, 152, 153, 154, 155, 157, 158, 159, 163, 164, 165, 170, 171, 172, 174, 175, 176, 177, 180, 181
Pemberton, Brock 73
Pendennis 10
Penney, Alexandra 234
Penton, Brian 84
Pepis, Betty 110, 121
Pepper, Curtis Bill 230, 304
Perelman, S. J. 222
Phillips, Cabell 78, 101
Phillips, R. Le Clerc 43
Pirandello, Luigi 50
Plante, David 314
Plaskin, Glenn 236
Plemmer, Charlotte and Dennis 146
Plums, Barbara 184
Podhoretz, Norman 234
Pope, Virginia 49, 56
Potok, Chaim 257
Powell, Theodore 104
Power, Philip H. 238

Powers, Alan W. 303
Preston, Stuart 135
Priac, Frank J. 305, 315
Price, Bryon 85
Price, Clair 46, 53, 58, 64, 70
Prideaux, Tom 223
Pritchett, V. S. 154, 221
Proctor, Mary 21
Pryce-Jones, David 230
Pryor, Thomas M. 69, 86, 115, 128, 143, 158, 196
Pyles, Thomas 151
Quindlen, Anna 218, 249
Quinn, Jim 246
Quintero, Jose 311
Raban, Jonathan 246
Raines, Howell and Susan Woodley 236
Randall, Tony 228
Raper, H. R. Theva 169
Rashid, Albert 104
Raskin, A. H. 187
Recording 43
Reeves, Earl 48
Reeves, Richard 216
Reich, Walter 259
Reinert, Al 222
Reinhold, Robert 273, 314

Reinity, Bertram 51
Reisner, Konrad 111
Reynolds, Horace 162
Reynolds, William 125
Reznick, Sidney 87
Rice, Diana 36
Rich, Frank 275, 304
Richardson, Dow 77
Richler, Mordecai 209
Riddeliot, Renfield 40
Riechenthal, Gene 120
Ritchin, Fred 275
Robbins, L. H. 57, 61, 62, 65, 66, 67, 69, 71
Robbins, R. H. 73, 74
Roberts, Chalmers M. 236
Roberts, Steven V. 294
Robertson, Nan 256
Robinson, Florett 80
Rockwell, John 257, 258, 261, 292, 303, 307, 311
Roiphe, Anne 204
Rosen, Jane 274
Rosen, Norma 205
Rosenbaum, Ron 291
Rosenthal, A. M. 109, 115, 203
Rosenthal, Jack 256, 264, 272, 281, 292, 303, 314

Ross, Albion 65
Ross, Betty 49
Ross, Mitchell S. 221
Rothstein, Mervyn 311
Rovere, Richard H. 194
Rubin, Stephen E. 219, 228, 234
Rubinstein, Leslie 239
Rudish, Leslie 112
Ruhlman, Michael 304
Russell, Bertrand 117
Russell, Herbert 67
Rutter, Eldon 52
Sacks, David 308
Safire, William 198, 226, 237, 240, 241, 242, 243, 244, 245, 246, 247, 248, 249, 250, 251, 252, 253, 254, 255, 256, 257, 258, 259, 260, 261, 262, 263, 264, 265, 266, 267, 268, 269, 270, 271, 272, 273, 274, 275, 276, 277, 278, 279, 280, 281, 282, 283, 284, 285, 286, 287, 288, 289, 290, 291, 292, 293, 294, 295, 296, 297, 298, 299, 300, 301, 302, 303, 304, 305, 306, 307, 308, 309, 310, 311, 312, 313, 314, 315, 316, 317, 318
Sagan, Carl 223

Sale, Kirk J. 192
Salisbury, Harrison E. 102, 111, 119, 147
Salmans, Sandra 288
Samuels, Gertrude 97, 118, 121, 138, 146
Sandek, Robert 171
Sanger, David E. 282
Sarnoff, David 139
Sarson, Evelyn 193
Schary, Dore 107, 212
Schecter, Leonard 189
Scheffauer, Herman G. 45
Scheider, P. S. 162
Scherman, Tony 246
Scherffauer, Herman George 43
Schickel, Richard 192, 199, 202, 236
Schine, Cathleen 316
Schlesinger, Arthur Jr. 187, 199
Schmemann, Serge 292
Schmidt, Dana Adams 117
Schneider, Alan 285
Schoen, Elin 238, 241
Schonberg, Harold 152, 221
Schonberg, Harold C. 163, 241, 249, 251, 262

Schulberg, Budd 235, 236
Schultz, Bert 188
Schumach, Murray 96, 101, 128, 137, 154, 168, 174
Schwab, Armand Jr. 166
Schwartz, Daniel 72, 91
Schwartz, Emanuel K. 168
Schwartz, Harry 108, 139
Schwartz, Henry 101
Schwartz, Tony 236, 239, 247, 250
Schwartzman, Paul 215
Schwarzbaum, Lisa 318
Schwarzschild, Leopold 101
Seiberling, Dorothy 219, 228
Seldes, Gilbert 126
Seligson, Marcia 195
Selzer, Richard 314
Selznick, Daniel 236
Selznick, Irene Mayer 262
Serling, Rod 145
Serveny, Gitta 258
Seton, Grace Thompson 38
Shabad, Theodore 176
Shaffer, Peter 274
Shah, Diane K. 305, 318
Shalett, Sidney M. 77
Shanefield, Daniel 189

Shanley, J. P. 144
Shanley, John P. 156
Shaw, Allanson 44
Shearer, Lloyd 89, 95, 96
Sheed, Wilfrid 140, 141
Sheehan, Susan 200
Shelby, Gertrude W. 48
Shenker, Israel 189
Shepard, Richard F. 225
Sher, Dick 177
Sherrill, Robert 197
Sherwood, Robert E. 93
Shewey, Don 260, 282
Shickel, Richard 201
Shifin, Arthur 188
Shreve, Anita 239
Siepmann, Charles A. 144
Simon, John 209
Simon, Paul 313
Simonson, Lee 81
Simpson, Louis 211
Singh, Khushwant 214
Singular, Stephen 232
Siren, Oswald 38
Skinner, Cornelia Otis 155
Skinner, Otis 59
Slenter, Israel 182

Sloven, Jane 295
Smith, Desmond 233, 235
Smith, Godfrey 183, 185
Smith, Henry Louis 31
Smith, Merriam 130
Smith, Osmond 173
Smith, Ralph Lee 190
Smith, Sherwin D. 273
Smith, T. V. 117
Smith, Victor 4
Spearing, James 48
Springer, Axel 190
Squire, Susan 243
Stabiner, Karen 245, 254
Stanfill, Barbara 239
Stanfill, Francesca 234, 237
Stang, Joanne 146, 152, 155, 156, 166
Stanley, Fred 85
Stanley, Fred M. 86
Staples, Brent 318
Starr, Douglas 299
Stein, Harry 232
Steinmetz, Sol 256
Sterba, James P. 195
Stern, Richard 214
Stevens, William K. 253
Stewart, Robert Sussman 185

Stock, Robert W. 255, 264
Stone, Elizabeth 238
Stone, I. F. 220, 231
Stone, Shepard 59
Storey, Walter 53
Storey, Walter Rendell 52, 69
Sullivan, Frank 110
Sulzberger, Arthur Hays 119
Sulzberger, C. L. 121
Suskind, Ron 273
Swados, Harvey 187, 190
Swartley, Ariel 237
Symons, Julian 204, 294
Tagoda, Ben 277
Talese, Gay 146
Talese, Gay J. 132
Talley, Truman H. 37
Tannen, Deborah 273
Tauber, Peter 301
Taubman, H. Howard 64, 65
Taubman, Howard 120, 146, 150, 153
Taubman, Phillip 293, 309
Taylor, Telford 111, 112
Tebbutt, Geoffrey 70
Theroux, Paul 238
Theroux, Phyllis 237
Thomas, D. M. 255

Thompson, Charles Willis 40, 41, 43, 53
Thompson, Herbert C. 46
Thompson, Robert L. 87
Thompson, Thomas 230
Tinckom-Fernandez, W. 42
Toland, John 189
Tolchin, Martin 168
Toledano, Edward 103
Tolischus, Otto D. 62
Topping, Audrey 169, 245
Townsend, James B. 22
Travers, P. L. 224
Trestman, Deborah 244
Trimble, Lester 250
Trumbull, Robert 122
Truscott, Lucian K. IV 221
Trustman, Deborah 235, 238, 240
Turney, Walter S. 11
Tyman, Kenneth 116, 118, 130
Valentine, Elizabeth R. 77
Van Voorst, L. Bruce 190
Velk, Thomas 191
Vincour, John 278
Volk, Patricia 309
Voznesensky, Andrei 245
Wade, Betsy 264

Authors By Page — 341

Waggoner, Walter M. 88
Waleson, Heidi 276, 288
Walker, Stanley 143, 165
Wallace, Carroll 165
Wallace, Mike 157
Walthan, John 183
Walton, Theodocia 36
Ward, Alex 289, 317
Ward, Barbara 120, 142
Waring, Houston 104
Warren, Constance 126
Watkins, Harold 106
Watts, Claude S. 42
Watts, Stephen 116
Wax, Judith 206
Weaver, Paul H. 213
Weber, Bruce 272, 285, 305, 310, 317
Webster, Margaret 113
Wechsberg, Joseph 161
Wegman, William 318
Weightman, John 184
Weil, Henry 86
Weinraub, Bernard 194, 265
Weinstein, Marybeth 138
Weisman, Steven R. 238, 275, 302
Wells, H. G. 46, 47

Weng, Will 256
Wershba, Joseph 230
Weston, Marybeth 160
Wharton, Hazel K. 69
White, Owen P. 41, 42
White, Theodore H. 116, 227
White, Timothy 259, 312, 317
Whiteside, Thomas 106
Whitman, Arthur 176
Whitmore, George 308
Wicker, Tom 179
Wienrauf, Bernard 198
Wilkes, Paul 222
Williamson, S. T. 47
Williamson, Samuel T. 101
Wilson, John S. 161, 162
Wilson, P. W. 41, 42, 50, 60, 63
Wilson, William 236
Wilstach, Frank J. 37
Winfrey, Carey 244
Winn, Marie 227
Wishengrad, Morton 149
Wiskari, Wener 165
Wolfe, Bernard 182, 187
Wolff, Ruth 219
Wolkenberg, Frank 305
Wood, Julius B. 70

Wood, Michael 214
Wood, Thomas 99
Woodward, A. C. 116
Woodward, Richard B. 300, 316
Woolf, S. J. 49, 51, 58, 68, 79, 81, 91, 95, 97, 99
Worsthorne, Pergrine 171
Wren, Christopher S. 254
Yagoda, Ben 263, 296, 314
Yearra, T. R. 35
Young, James C. 44, 54
Zion, Sidney 235, 245
Zuckerman, Edward 306
Zuckerman, Eugenia 233
Zukor, Adolph 66

REF P 90 . F56 1989